H e turned her face up, wanting to kiss the closed eyelids, so nearly translucent with tears, wanting to kiss away her pain, but he wiped her streaked cheek with a callused thumb instead, ꞏ   ꞏ.

She c   **Date Due**   immer
of tears ꞏ   nahue.
How dic

Palisades.
Pure Romance.

FICTION THAT FEATURES CREDIBLE CHARACTERS AND

ENTERTAINING PLOT LINES, WHILE CONTINUING TO UPHOLD

STRONG CHRISTIAN VALUES. FROM HIGH ADVENTURE

TO TENDER STORIES OF THE HEART, EACH PALISADES

ROMANCE IS AN UNDILUTED STORY OF LOVE,

FROM BEGINNING TO END!

A PALISADES HISTORICAL ROMANCE

BETRAYED

LORENA McCOURTNEY

PALISADES

BETRAYED
published by Palisades
a part of the Questar publishing family

© 1996 by Lorena McCourtney
International Standard Book Number: 0-88070-756-9

Cover illustration by George Angelini
Cover designed by David Carlson and Mona Weir-Daly
Edited by Diane Noble

Scripture quotations are from:
The New King James Version (NKJV) © 1984 by Thomas Nelson, Inc.

Printed in the United States of America

For information:
QUESTAR PUBLISHERS, INC.
POST OFFICE BOX 1720
SISTERS, OREGON 97759

96 97 98 99 00 01 02 — 10 9 8 7 6 5 4 3 2 1

To my mother,

*with thanks for her memories of the depression years—
and much, much more.*

Cast all your anxiety on him
because he cares for you.

1 PETER 5:7, NIV

Prologue

Fall 1930
Castle Beach, Oregon

Shea Donahue waited patiently while Molly offered last-minute instructions on the care of six-month-old baby Jessie. It was the first time she had left the baby with someone else for an entire day.

"Molly, dear," Mrs. Siikanen finally said gently, "I raised eight children and three grandchildren. I think I know how it's done."

Molly laughed and apologized as she placed Jessie in Mrs. Siikanen's hands, the same capable hands that also played the organ at church every Sunday. "We'll be back by—?" She glanced at Shea.

"Not until I catch the biggest salmon in the sea," he said with a wink. "Or dark. Whichever comes first."

"Who says you're going to catch the biggest fish?" Molly's spirited toss of head sent flashes of sunlight dancing through the sleek, dark braid that hung almost to her waist.

Shea laughed. Molly could raise a bountiful garden, indignantly shoo away a bear sniffing around the back porch, and expertly wield a hammer as they built their cabin together. And still be the most delicate, sophisticated Sunday school teacher at church the next morning. He didn't doubt that she could also be top fisherman of the day.

"You catch the biggest fish and you'll get that extra bookcase you've been wanting. I catch the biggest fish and you have to make a strawberry pie," he challenged. Molly was a terrific cook, but she hated to make pies, so he always had to finagle to get one.

"It's a deal," she agreed.

Actually, win or lose, she'd get that bookcase. He had already started building it as a gift for her birthday.

They both kissed the baby. Then Shea drove the truck to the dock, where his brother Adam was tossing a trio of bulky gray life preservers into the open wooden boat. People always had trouble believing the two men were brothers. Adam was short and dark, Shea, big and brawny, "as red-haired as a Viking," their mother used to say with amazement. No other known relative had that coloring. Although one did now: baby Jessie's hair held the same flame-colored glints as her father's.

"Do we have everything?" Shea asked. The two men had their own fishing gear, but the boat was borrowed from a friend of Adam's. His brother sloshed a gas can with a reassuringly full sound. "Gas, tool box, bait. Yep, I think we're set."

Shea stowed the lunch under a seat. Beyond the harbor, the calm Pacific gleamed like a blue mirror with lacy frills of surf at the bar where river and sea met. Gulls wheeled and squawked in the morning sunshine. Shea untied the bow and used an oar to shove the boat from the dock.

At the stern, Adam yanked on the crank rope to start the small outboard engine. He stopped to rest after five pulls, then looked up at his brother. "You want to give it a try?"

Shea scooted around Molly to get to the other end of the boat. He never pushed his help on Adam, but he was always there to lend a hand if needed. Adam had recovered from the logging accident, but the scarred limbs would never be as strong as they once were.

Shea gave the crank two powerful pulls, and the little engine sputtered briskly. Adam reclaimed his position and guided the boat around the end of the dock. Today the often bumpy meeting point of river and sea appeared calm, but Shea tossed life preservers to Molly and Adam as a precaution. They did get an unexpected drenching when an oversized wave broke over the boat. Some women would have moaned about a wrecked hairdo. Not Molly. She just wrung salt water out of her braid, laughed, and started bailing.

"Don't I look glamorous?" she asked cheerfully.

"Darlin', you're the most gorgeous person in this boat," Shea agreed grandly, for which she impudently stuck out her tongue at him.

No, Molly was not the glamorous type. Lovely, yes, but much, much more. She was sweet and loving, a wonderful wife and mother. Shea's passion for her deepened a little more each day they were together. Yet there was plenty of love left in his heart for baby Jessie, and still more for Adam. In God's infinite wisdom, Shea realized with fresh appreciation, he had created love so that it just kept expanding and multiplying.

On the open sea, Adam headed the boat toward a good fishing area beyond a trio of jutting rocks known as the Three Sisters. Once there, Molly expertly baited her pole. With her father and brother, she'd been fishing this ocean much longer than Shea had.

Shea settled against the bow of the boat with the life preserver as a backrest and stretched his long legs to let his sea-splashed clothes dry. The boat rocked soothingly, water lapping gently against wood that smelled faintly of old fish. In the distance the coast mountains draped a ragged blue silhouette against the clear sky. Closer, the blunt shapes of the Sisters rose straight from the sea, their ragged tops making safe havens for nesting seabirds. The sea was always rough around the Sisters, treacherous underwater currents and rocks creating whirlpools and wild surges that sprayed crashing white water against the dark cliffs even on this calm day. But from the boat the sound was a muted roar more lulling than menacing.

Shea pulled his cap over his face. A perfect fall day, he thought with pure satisfaction. Some experts were warning that the nation was sinking into a long, disastrous depression, but he was still working. He had a wife he loved, the sweetest baby in the world, an almost-finished cabin in the woods. And now he had a bite on his line!

He leaped to his feet, and after a brief battle hauled in the silver-gray fish, not the biggest salmon in the sea but a respectable twenty or so pounds. Adam and Molly waited expectantly for their turns, Adam occasionally starting the small engine to move the boat farther out after drifting with the currents toward the Sisters.

They kept on fishing even while they ate their venison sandwiches, but by midafternoon Shea's salmon was still the lone catch. By then the usual breeze had risen, but it did no more than ruffle the surface of the sea. It was the pink sunburn glowing on Molly's nose that made Shea say they'd better head in.

"And I won't hold you to the promise of strawberry pie," he added magnanimously to Molly.

She scooped up a handful of seawater and playfully tossed it at him. "Oh, you'll get your pie."

They reeled in their lines and stowed their gear. When Shea looked up again, he was startled to see how close they had drifted to the middle Sister. He could see the wet sheen where waves climbed the steep sides as if reaching hungrily for the top. Adam immediately cranked the engine.

He yanked the rope only three times before glancing at his brother. Shea wasted no time clambering the length of the rocking boat. Closer to the Sisters, the currents swirling around underwater rocks eddied the boat into a slow spin. Something grated ominously on the boat's underside.

"Get your life preserver on," he called over his shoulder to Molly.

He cranked once, twice. No response. A sudden dip of the boat sloshed seawater over the side. They had to get away from there, immediately. Another hard crank. The rope snapped. Shea crashed backward. Even before he shook his head to clear it, Shea could see Adam frantically digging in the tool box for another rope.

"There isn't one in here!"

Shea lurched over to help. There had to be an extra rope. Every boat carried one! The engine was useless without it.

But none was there.

The cliffs rose starkly above them, suddenly so close that Shea could throw an oar and hit the middle Sister. He didn't even remember grabbing for his life preserver, but he found himself tying it on. Molly, eyes wide, silently clutched the middle seat, feet braced against the rough pitching of the boat. The crash of waves exploding against the cliffs rose to an ominous roar.

Shea glanced to the north, just beyond the Sisters, where sunlight reflected off a ruffled, calm surface. To the south, twinkling waves continued the same innocent dance; farther out, the bar between river and sea was still no more than a lacy frill. If they could just get beyond this trap of crashing sea and boiling whirlpools!

Shea motioned Molly toward the bow and stationed himself on the middle seat. Adam knelt by the engine, desperately trying to improvise something workable with the broken crank rope. Shea got a solid grip on the oars and dug in. His muscles were hard and powerful from rough work in the woods, but the sea felt alive, a living entity grabbing at the oars, mocking his strength with its own. Spray from seawater crashing into the rocks drenched them. Shea could taste the salt and feel its icy sting on his back.

The boat suddenly rose. The monster lifted them on its back and tossed them with a shrug of watery shoulders. Shea rowed frantically. A white-hot poker of pain shot through his shoulders and back. The maelstrom of white water pulled them toward the narrow passageway between the rocks.

One oar flailed the air as the sea whipped the boat on its side. The other oar hit an underwater rock. Its impact vibrated through Shea's shoulder and neck. Then the water flung the boat the opposite direction, and he saw only the oar's splintered stub remaining. The boat lurched and tipped. Molly screamed.

"Hold on!" he yelled. "We're going over—"

He hit the water broadside. An underwater tornado whirled and spun and tossed him, held him under until his lungs screamed for air, then scornfully shot him upward like a helpless cork. Briefly he saw Adam's limp form in the life preserver lying face down in the water.

Salt water rushed into his mouth, choking him. He caught a glimpse of Molly bobbing in the water. They paddled desperately toward each other. For a moment their hands touched. Then the sea tore them apart. A wave caught Molly, slamming her against the cliff. She grabbed hold and for a moment hung there, arms outstretched, her gaze locked with his, helplessly clinging to the slick rocky surface.

Frantically he swam toward her again. *Lord, please,* he begged silently, *please, please, please*— Then a mountain of a wave collapsed on him. Shea plunged down, down, into the underwater graveyard of rocks and darkness.

16

One

◆❧◆

Summer 1933
Gideon, Indiana

Ⓘf all the vegetables we've chopped this summer were laid side by side," Charlie Richards muttered, "they'd bridge the Atlantic." She took a malicious whack at a turnip. The cut piece shot across the soup kitchen like a cannonball. "At least then maybe I could get to Paris," she added with a sigh.

Rosalyn Fallon laughed as she lined up a half dozen carrots, preparing to slice through them all at the same time. "Paris! We haven't done *that* many, Charlie. Only enough to build a highway to Cincinnati."

With a sniff, Charlie examined her wine-red fingernails to make sure they hadn't chipped, then grabbed another turnip. "A bridge to anywhere would be better than this." She glanced around the steamy kitchen. "I'm serious, Roz. I want to get out of this depressing place." Suddenly brightening, Charlie sat up straighter on the tall stool, her beautiful face animated. "Paris *is* a good idea. We'll take an ocean liner. Oh, Roz! Let's do it! We'll buy dozens of beautiful gowns. Imagine how you'll dazzle Robbie when we get back!"

"We can't just run off and enjoy ourselves. Not with so much suffering around us. It just wouldn't be right." Rosalyn paused, then smiled at her friend. "Besides, Charlie, I'm just not the dazzling type." Her mirror told her she was pretty, with a slender figure, shiny brown hair, gentle chocolate-colored eyes, and a healthy glow to her skin. But heads didn't turn when she entered a room—not the way they did when Charlie sauntered in.

"We've done our share of helping the poor," Charlie pouted. "You've dragged me down here every day for *weeks.*"

That wasn't entirely true. Charlie frequently begged off for various frivolous reasons. Yet Paris was a tempting idea. Robbie had spent a year in Europe, and the stories he related made France sound fascinating and glamorous.

Charlie went on, not about to give up. "Besides, Roz, you'll be through working here soon anyway. Instead of going back to college—take some time off. Come with me to Paris."

Rosalyn laughed, slowly shaking her head. When her childhood friend set her mind to something, she didn't give it up easily. Rosalyn scooped a pile of chopped vegetables into a bucket, carried the container to the gas stove, and then dumped its contents into a large black kettle.

"Ugh," Charlie murmured as the smell of simmering stew rose from the steaming kettle. "I'm glad I don't have to eat this stuff."

The volunteers in the soup kitchen had to work with whatever supplies were available. Today, Rosalyn had to admit, the stew had a strong aroma of old mutton that was far from appetizing. Nothing like the appealing scents that came out of the kitchen at home, where their long-time cook, Hattie, turned out succulent chicken and hearty roasts. Nor the scents that had once emanated from this very kitchen, where a French chef had reigned. The hotel was closed now, another bankrupt victim of the financial disasters entangling the nation in this summer of 1933, and the once-elegant dining room held only plain wooden tables and benches for the daily gathering of the hungry.

"Seriously," Rosalyn began, looking at Charlie with affection. "What *are* you going to do this fall?"

"Have fun," Charlie declared promptly. She put down her knife and rested her chin in her hands. Under the glare of bare bulbs that hung from the high ceiling her pale golden hair gleamed like Marlene Dietrich's. "Sleep late. See how many parties I can make last until dawn. Talk Daddy into buying me a new car."

Rosalyn didn't know whether to be amused or dismayed at Charlie's list. "Do you ever think about going back to school?"

Charlie wrinkled her nose in distaste. "All that studying and cramming for tests—" She shook her head. "I just don't have time for it."

"But you used to talk about becoming a teacher. It was your passion. You couldn't wait to finish school."

Charlie rolled her blue eyes in a you're-nagging-me-again expression.

Rosalyn didn't want to badger her friend, but she cared. Charlie had drifted aimlessly since their graduation last year. They were not as close as they had been when Charlie lived with the Fallons after her mother's death eight years earlier, but Rosalyn still thought of Charlie as her beloved sister. Even now she knew that they would do anything for each other, just as they had in their childhood days. Like the time when daring Charlie got stranded climbing a towering elm to rescue a yowling cat, and Rosalyn, though dizzily afraid of heights, had scaled the tree to rescue her friend. And the time when Rosalyn wasn't invited to join a popular high school club, and Charlie had scornfully rejected her own invitation.

But Charlie was different now. She had changed more than her name since she'd discarded "old-fashioned" and "boring" Charlotte in favor of Charlie. In the last year, while Rosalyn was away at Wellesley, Charlie had joined a fast crowd. She liked to dance and party and sometimes giggled about how much champagne she'd had to drink.

As if sensing Rosalyn's troubled uneasiness, Charlie smiled and reached over to squeeze her hand. "I know. You're worried because you're a whole month older than I am and think it's your job to mother me. But I'm fine. Honest. One of these days I'll settle down all prim and proper. I promise."

"What *do* you really want out of life?" There was soft affection in Rosalyn's voice as she spoke.

Charlie looked thoughtful, and for the briefest moment Rosalyn thought she'd made her friend think seriously about the future. Then Charlie's eyes widened. "I want to go to Paris! Just as I said a few minutes ago. It's truly my heart's desire, Roz." Then she tilted her chin upward. "Why should we suffer just because others are? And, after all, Fallon-Richards Pharmaceuticals has certainly done its share donating to the needy. It's not as if we haven't tried to do *something*," she added in a virtuous tone.

That was true. The pharmaceutical company in which their fathers were partners had indeed been generous with donations of money and medicines for those in need.

Rosalyn used Charlie's comment to remind her friend of the closeness they'd shared in the past. "Do you remember how we planned to someday run our fathers' company?" She chuckled. "You even wanted to change the name to Fallon-Richards and Daughters Pharmaceuticals." Rosalyn still planned to enter the family business after completing her education, but Charlie had lost interest long ago—in the company, in teaching, in nearly everything she used to hold dear.

Her friend dismissed the reminder with a breezy wave. "Picture us instead," she said dreamily, "standing on the deck of a big ocean liner, our hair streaming in the wind, half a dozen handsome young officers from the ship surrounding us adoringly, smitten with our charms…"

Rosalyn laughed. "I'm not sure Robbie would appreciate that. But it would be lovely to get away. She paused to lift her hair and cool her neck, damp from the summer heat and the steamy kitchen.

"We can go to the office right now and talk to our fathers, and we'll be sailing within a week," Charlie urged.

At almost twenty, Rosalyn and Charlie both considered themselves competent, independent adults. But Rosalyn strongly doubted that their fathers were going to be enthusiastic about an unescorted trip to Paris.

"Daddy won't like it, but I can persuade him," Charlie added with airy confidence.

True, Rosalyn agreed. Since her mother's death, Charlie had been expertly "persuading" her father. She had a powerful cache of weapons, everything from sweet pleadings to pretty pouts and torrents of tears.

Rosalyn didn't know if she could persuade her father, but, tempted as she was by the idea of a trip to Paris, she mentally sighed and rejected it. God had seen fit to grant their families prosperity in these years of economic disaster, but that was no reason to ignore the sad plight of others.

Charlie looked at her and sighed aloud, apparently recognizing that Paris was out. "Let's go to a movie tonight, then."

"Aren't you going out with Paul? Or Warren or George?"

Charlie dismissed her current suitors with a few brisk chops of knife on potato. "Paul lost his job. All Warren talks about is the ghastly prospect of his family's carpet factory going union. George dances as if he had anchors tied to both feet."

"Charlie, I'm sorry, but I told Robbie I'd have dinner with him."

Charlie didn't resent the turndown. "Don't be sorry when you have a date with a guy like Robbie Grenwich!" Her gaze darted over Rosalyn's shoulder. "And speaking of the most handsome, charming man in town—"

A pair of hands closed over Rosalyn's eyes. She rested her chopping knife on the counter. The hands were warm and manly, smooth but not soft.

"Guess who."

The voice was an almost perfect imitation of movie tough-guy James Cagney, but Rosalyn would have recognized him even without Charlie's giveaway clue and the faint scent of familiar after-shave lotion. She pretended to be mystified. "I just have no idea—"

"Does this give you a clue?" A light kiss feathered her cheek.

"Why, yes, of course! It's that good-looking guy who delivers the milk," she teased.

"The milkman!" Robbie yelped in mock dismay. He pulled his hands away from her eyes, and they grinned at each other affectionately.

"What are you doing here?" Rosalyn's voice reflected her delight.

Robbie was a sophisticated twenty-six, with a lanky physique, an air of recklessness, teasing blue eyes, and an irresistible grin. They had met when Rosalyn was home from college over the Christmas holidays. He'd been too far ahead of her in school for them to have been friends earlier, but she had been familiar with his name as the star basketball player who led the local team to a state championship. After high school he'd gone on to college for a couple of years but then decided a global education was more important than textbooks and spent the next year traveling the world from London to Paris to Bombay. After his return home he had entered the family business, Grenwich Enterprises, which

owned two radio stations and a string of prosperous movie theaters. Robbie had been seeing Rosalyn several times a week since
her return from college for the summer. She was still filled with
astonishment and excitement that he was attracted to her.

He was wearing tan trousers in the fashionable, loose-fitting,
cuffed style, with a white shirt and striped tie. His dark brown
hair was rumpled, wind-tossed from driving with the top down
on his new Studebaker roadster. Probably, Rosalyn thought ruefully, going faster than he should have been. He leaned against
the counter with an easy, loose-jointed gracefulness.

"I'm driving in to Indianapolis on business." He gave Charlie
a genial nod and then said to Rosalyn, "How about coming with
me? We'll have dinner there and catch a movie this evening."

"Oh, I'd like that!" Rosalyn glanced at the big clock on the far
kitchen wall. "But I won't be through here for several hours."

"Couldn't you leave early?"

"Go ahead, Roz," Charlie urged. She rolled her expressive
eyes and grabbed a turnip from the waiting pile. "I'll peel and
chop twice as fast to make up for your absence."

Rosalyn doubted that, considering Charlie's usual dilatory
approach to work here. Even so, she was sorely tempted, especially
when Robbie tucked an escaped tendril of hair behind her ear.
His fingertips lingered, and she felt that sweet, shivery tingle that
had become familiar only since she'd known him.

"I'd love to go." She blushed at how revealing those words
were. "But I can't leave. They'd be short-handed without me."

Robbie looked momentarily annoyed, but then he sighed
with a deliberate touch of melodrama. "I suppose I should have
known my dedicated humanitarian couldn't be enticed away
from her duty." He kissed her lightly on the cheek again.

"Pick you up about seven, then?"

She nodded, and he started back the way he had come, never

seeming to do more than saunter casually but covering the distance with surprising speed.

Charlie groaned. She aimed a manicured finger at one of the vegetables awaiting the knife. "Rosalyn Fallon, you have no better sense than that turnip," she declared. "If you're not careful, someone is going to grab him right out from under your nose. Robbie Grenwich is a catch. Don't forget that rumor—" She lifted an eyebrow Rosalyn's direction.

The delicate reference was to a whisper of gossip they'd both heard, that Robbie had been seen with a beautiful woman he had once dated, a woman who was making a name for herself as the first female reporter for the local newspaper.

"He says he isn't seeing anyone else, and I trust him," Rosalyn stated firmly.

Charlie, graceful fingers idly spinning a turnip, gave Rosalyn a knowing glance.

"You're in love with him, aren't you?"

Rosalyn hastily started to deny any such powerful emotion, then, more honestly, with a blush and a smile admitted, "Maybe."

"You should be. He's good-looking, rich, fun, charming, and so sophisticated. And that delicious voice!"

Delicious. Rosalyn laughed at the word, but she had to admit that Robbie's voice coming over the radio indeed sounded "delicious." And even more delicious when it was whispering sweet, tender words in her ear.

Only one thing made her uneasy with her growing feelings for Robbie. That was the absence of God in his life. Robbie always listened patiently when she spoke about God's love and the joy of knowing him, though sometimes he teased her about her childlike faith. He attended church with her, and she thrilled to the power of his voice when he sang the old hymns. He had, she knew, done some rather wild living in the past. He admitted to a weakness for gambling. She knew he liked to drive too fast, and she'd heard rumors of a fiery temper.

But he seemed open to exploring his spiritual side and strongly hinted that he would someday like to know God in the same intimate way that she did. Rosalyn's feelings for him kept rising like a soaring balloon that couldn't be held down.

"So, when are you two getting married?" Charlie inquired.

Rosalyn's sudden rosy glow had nothing to do with the heat of the kitchen.

"We aren't talking about marriage yet!"

"You mean he hasn't asked you to marry him?"

"No."

"Why not?"

"I suppose he just isn't ready for that big step yet."

"Then it's up to you to give him a push in the right direction. I could get any man I wanted to propose," Charlie added with sunny self-confidence.

Such a statement might have sounded foolishly egotistical coming from someone else, but in Charlie's case it was probably accurate. Charlie collected proposals the way some girls collected souvenir dance programs. She was petite, beautiful, and vivacious—a born flirt.

Mistaking Rosalyn's silence for doubt about her abilities, Charlie tossed out a challenge. "Name someone. Anyone. And I'll bet you—oh, these new earrings, that I can get him to propose within two weeks." Charlie tossed her blond head, and the dangling jet and silver earrings danced under her delicate earlobes.

Rosalyn laughed. "No, thanks. I believe you." She also didn't care to be responsible for the broken heart of some unfortunate man when Charlie carelessly dazzled and dumped him.

"I'm also willing to give you the benefit of my experience and expertise to help you snag Robbie," Charlie offered, sounding unexpectedly serious.

"Snag him! You make him sound like a trout swimming in a stream."

Charlie smiled in complacent agreement. "Exactly."

Two

harlie, complaining that the heat in the soup kitchen was giving her a headache, left for home before it was time to serve the meal.

A few minutes later, Rosalyn began ladling stew from the steaming cauldron. She offered people a smile and a little hope as she scooped mutton and vegetables into their waiting bowls. Those who came here, often for their only meal of the day, were not just anonymous faces to her. She liked being involved in their lives. She cared about every detail.

"Hi, Meg." Rosalyn dug into her pocket and handed her a slip of paper with a number on it. Meg's husband was in a tuberculosis ward somewhere out west. She knew the young mother was struggling to care for her twin daughters.

"My neighbor needs to hire someone to do some cleaning for her. I thought you might be interested."

Meg took the phone number gratefully. At her side the little girls, once bubbling with mischievousness, now pushed their bowls along the counter with solemn faces, their laughter and playfulness gone. Rosalyn's heart ached for the changes the hard times had wrought in them.

And there was big, muscular Benny, strong and eager to work. But he was also bewildered and angry because, unable to find more than occasional day labor, he had to bring his pregnant wife to the soup kitchen for food.

Next in line was a dapper little man with a luxuriant mustache. Rosalyn teased him, bringing a pleased smile to his face. Then she inquired about the ill daughter of a stout Irish woman who held out her bowl to be filled. And she offered a friendly greeting to the lone men who were often seen only once as they passed through town, some heading east, some west, all desperate. She worried about Mrs. Reutger, a frail elderly woman, who was not in line. She had lost her widow's pension when her husband's company went bankrupt. Rosalyn made a mental note to check on her if she was absent again tomorrow.

Near the end of the line, she noticed a family she hadn't seen before. There were two small boys and a boy of about twelve. The oldest child looked especially ragged, his dark eyes large with hunger. Rosalyn made certain that his bowl of stew had a good chunk of meat. Later she was dismayed to hear a volunteer down the line regretfully tell the family that the day's supply of milk had already run out.

Children shouldn't have to go without milk!

Rosalyn waited until the last few stragglers had been served and then hurried to a grocery store on a nearby side street. When she returned she set the sack containing two quart bottles of milk on the bench beside the mother.

"Something for the boys," she whispered, not explaining further or waiting for thanks.

Back home, Rosalyn kicked off her shoes and was sipping a glass of iced tea in her mother's cool and airy sitting room when the maid announced a telephone call. Ellen returned with a troubled line between the fine hazel eyes.

"That was your father. He'll be late again tonight."

"Robbie and I can have dinner here with you," Rosalyn said quickly.

"No, no. Hattie can make a sandwich for me. I'll eat dinner with Oliver later. To make certain he does eat."

"Is something wrong?" Rosalyn asked, mildly alarmed.

"He's been working so hard for months now." Ellen returned to the chair at her dainty rosewood desk, where she was addressing invitations for a charity tea. "I hope he'll take some time off. Maybe relax and go hunting this fall."

Rosalyn could remember her father and his friends driving to a lodge out west to hunt and fish, returning with impressive racks of antlers and delicious smoked salmon, but he hadn't done it for some years now. "Will you go along?"

Ellen touched the lace flounce at her throat. "Hunting and fishing at a wilderness lodge in Oregon?" She raised her eyebrows. "Oh, I don't think so, dear."

Rosalyn smiled. Her mother, for all her wonderful and godly attributes, was not exactly a wilderness person. Ellen had moved from her father's loving protection on a comfortable southern plantation to the same security with her husband. She had always known a fine home and genteel life with servants and all the modern conveniences.

After a pause to reconsider, however, Ellen added firmly, "But I'd certainly go if it would encourage Oliver to take a vacation."

Rosalyn, however, actually wanted to see Oregon. She pictured its soaring mountains and lush forests. But guns and hunting? No. And she'd be back in college by fall, of course.

A short time later, Rosalyn was in her bedroom just slipping into her new pumps, when the doorbell signaled Robbie's arrival. The maid let him in, and a murmur of voices drifted up the stairway as he and her mother made comfortable small-talk. She heard him laugh, that open, good-humored laugh that was another of the many things she loved about him.

She stared wide-eyed at her reflection in the mirror, her hazel eyes shining brighter than the gleam of the polished wood of the four-postered bed behind her. There, she'd admitted it. She loved him! The admission both panicked and exhilarated her. She resisted an urge to climb on the bed and bounce to the ceiling with girlish exuberance.

Downstairs, she managed to greet Robbie decorously, and he put his arm around her shoulders as they walked down the wide front steps together. "You look lovely, the best thing I've seen all day." He nuzzled her temple, and she smiled up at him.

They chatted easily over their dinners of pheasant and wild rice. Then they slipped once again into the sleek roadster, and headed to the downtown Star, the most opulent of his family's string of theaters, where a line stretched around the block. Even in this time of economic hardship people still went to the movies frequently. They were an inexpensive escape from everyday problems.

But when Rosalyn saw the name of the movie blazing on the marquee her spirits dropped.

Robbie swung the snappy Studebaker into an alley beside the theater. A sign said "No Parking," but as an executive of Grenwich Enterprises he seemed able to get away with ignoring the order.

Rosalyn hadn't attended the movies as frequently as others her age, although she'd seen quite a few lately with Robbie. But the advertisements for this particular show proudly described it as "bold and sensational," and a review bluntly said it was unfit to be seen.

Robbie seemed to sense her discomfort. He smiled and playfully tapped the tip of her nose with his forefinger. "Look at this line, *ma cherie*. But you get to breeze right in. No waiting."

Rosalyn took a deep breath, hoping he would understand, and started to explain her feelings.

Frowning, Robbie suddenly interrupted her, placing a finger on her lips. "You don't have to tell me," he said. "I should have realized."

But when Robbie screeched the automobile down the alley as if a bolt of lightning were after them, Rosalyn wondered at his sincerity. He said nothing more about the incident, however, and drove them to a different Grenwich theater in a nearby town.

After the movie, his usual good humor returned. They stopped for ice cream and he entertained her with stories about the radio station. He also mentioned a new weekly show for women hosted by the female newspaper reporter that Rosalyn had heard he'd been seen with. Rosalyn felt her cheeks glow with relief; she was glad she hadn't questioned him about it.

At her door Robbie kissed her, holding her a little closer and longer than usual. Then he told her he would be out of town on company business for several days. "I'll miss you," he whispered huskily. Charlie would have wrapped up a proposal on the spot, Rosalyn thought wryly as she went inside.

Ellen was listening to the console radio in the living room, her hands busy with embroidery work. A faint evening breeze from an open window swayed the jet beads on the lamp behind her and flickered shadows over the graceful curve of the grand piano. Rosalyn's father wasn't home yet, and Rosalyn detected a small worry-line on her mother's usually smooth forehead.

"He hasn't called?"

"No."

Rosalyn felt a small ripple of uneasiness. He must know they'd worry at this late hour. It was unlike him to be inconsiderate of another's feelings.

"You haven't tried to telephone him?" Rosalyn asked.

"No. He mentioned a conference, and I didn't want to disturb him."

Rosalyn hesitated only a moment before going to the telephone in the adjoining room that served as both office and library. She had just picked up the receiver of the candlestick phone when she heard the sound of a vehicle in the driveway. Peering through the lace curtains, she saw the long silhouette of her father's four-door Packard. The headlamps flickered off, but the door didn't open.

Quietly, not wanting to alarm her mother, Rosalyn slipped out the side door. She ignored the curved walkway and dashed across the neatly clipped lawn, still damp from the day's watering. Inside the car she could see the dark bulk of her father's slumped figure.

She tapped on the window. "Father?" They shared a warm closeness and it frightened her to see him this way.

His reaction time was slow, as if the air around him had an unnatural thickness. When his head finally turned, it was the tired movement of an old man. She yanked the door open. "Father? Are you all right?"

His hands suddenly gripped the steering wheel, knuckles gleaming like skeletal bones in the dim glow of the streetlights.

"It's all gone, Rozzie," he said, using the name he had called her when she was a little girl. His voice was hoarse and ragged. "We've done everything we could, but it's all gone."

In the living room a few minutes later, Rosalyn listened as her father related the details of the disastrous financial collapse. Ellen sat across from her, composed, but her hazel eyes reflecting the same shock and pain that Rosalyn felt.

It had started with the best of intentions, her father was saying.

Several years ago he and Henry Richards had decided it was time to improve and expand Fallon-Richards Pharmaceuticals. In that era of booming stock market, putting company funds into stocks had seemed a quick and appropriate way to raise the money necessary for expansion. When the stock market crashed in 1929, the entire investment crashed with it.

Fallon-Richards Pharmaceuticals was not ruined; the loss simply canceled any hopes for expansion. But as the nation plunged into depression, the pharmaceutical company also found itself in deep financial difficulty, and because of those earlier losses there were no financial reserves to fall back on. Over time, Oliver and Henry had been forced to mortgage or borrow on everything they owned to keep the company going. Now the company was bankrupt, and the creditors were swarming. They would take everything.

"We probably should have closed the company doors months ago, instead of digging ourselves deeper into our financial hole," Oliver said with a despairing shake of his head. "But we hoped we'd pull out. We didn't have the heart to turn out everyone who worked for us." He put his head in his hands. "Now they're all out of work despite our efforts...and so am I." His voice sank to little more than a whisper, and he wiped a hand across his eyes as if trying to clear a blurry vision. "I'm sorry, so very sorry..."

"I don't need to return to college," Rosalyn said. And so he would know she hadn't lost faith in him she swiftly added, "I can go back later."

The eyes her father lifted to her were deep wells of desolation. He didn't argue. He simply said, "Thank you, Rosalyn," with a sad dignity that emphasized the desperation of their situation. If there were any way he could make it possible, she knew he would have insisted she go.

"I'll get a job, too," Rosalyn added.

"I'm so very sorry," her father repeated with an unfamiliar, uncharacteristic helplessness. "Because of my bad judgment, now both of you must suffer."

"You mustn't blame yourself!" Rosalyn exclaimed. "It's happening everywhere."

"We still have the Lord and each other," Ellen added quietly. "We'll manage."

There was one more bright spot in this dark sea of loss. The house was heavily mortgaged, but Oliver was reasonably certain he could save it. The servants would have to be dismissed and household expenses trimmed to the quick, but they would still have their home.

They joined hands, then, praying not only for strength and courage for themselves, but also for the Lord's compassion on all those workers whose lives would be irrevocably altered by the closing of the company. Afterward they cried and smiled and hugged each other, and Rosalyn went up to her bedroom with the comforting conviction that, no matter what the hardships, they were safe in God's loving hands.

Yet in the morning, as the three of them sat in the breakfast room eating Hattie's scrambled eggs and fluffy biscuits, the unpleasant details of the crisis loomed large and immediate.

Rosalyn was more concerned about elderly Hattie and their long-time gardener and handyman, Geoffrey, than she was about herself. What would become of them? And what about her mother? She couldn't imagine genteel, cultured, delicate Ellen managing the big house alone.

Which only meant, of course, that she must do more to help. So many changes were coming for all of them!

Not returning to Wellesley would be the big change for Rosalyn, of course. And now she must also abandon her plans to someday enter the pharmaceutical field with her father. Then another dismaying thought occurred to her, one that made her feel guilty for being so wrapped up in herself. Charlie! How would Charlie, who cheerfully admitted to spending money "as if Daddy is printing it on a press in the basement," react to all this? At one time Charlie would have relied on the same spiritual foundation that Rosalyn and her parents had to sustain them. But Charlie had changed.

Oh, she needed Robbie! She needed his advice, the comfort of his confidence and experience...and the reassuring strength of his strong arms. But he wouldn't be home for several days, and she had no way to contact him.

Rosalyn tried to telephone Charlie after breakfast, but there was no answer. Later, just before serving time at the soup kitchen, she dashed out to a pay phone and tried again. Again no answer.

Rosalyn worried about Charlie all day, although there was one unrelated bright spot. Meg Moliveron happily confided that she would be starting full-time work the following week, a position resulting from the housecleaning job Rosalyn had helped her find.

A little later Rosalyn spotted the particularly ragged-looking boy she'd seen with his family a few days ago. He slipped along the line as if he'd rather not be noticed, but Rosalyn gave him a smile as she filled his bowl. "Where are your folks today?"

"They...uh...ate at another place."

That seemed odd, but just then someone spilled a bowl of potato soup on the counter, and by the time Rosalyn cleaned up the mess the boy had apparently gulped his meal and left.

At the end of the day Rosalyn regretfully told her supervisor that she wouldn't be able to volunteer full time after today, although she would continue to help out whenever she could until she found a job. The woman nodded sympathetically.

News about the collapse of Fallon-Richards Pharmaceuticals had traveled fast.

On sudden impulse, instead of going directly home, Rosalyn took the trolley that ran within a few blocks of the Richards' magnificent house. Charlie's Ford coupe was in the driveway, but Rosalyn had to ring the doorbell repeatedly before the door finally flew open.

"Will you please stop—Oh, Roz, it's you." Charlie blew on her fingernails, freshly painted in fiery red. Her hair gleamed in the late afternoon sunlight, glossy golden waves dipping jauntily toward her right eye.

"I've been worried! I haven't been able to reach you all day."

Charlie lifted a shoulder in a dismissive shrug. "Daddy let all the help go first thing this morning. Don't tell me you still ran down to the soup kitchen to chop and serve and clean?" She laughed, a tinkle as brittle and humorless as a shattering icicle. "Isn't that just a little ridiculous, now that we're as poor as all those miserable people standing in line?"

"I still want to help out as much as I can."

"How noble of you."

"May I come in?" Rosalyn asked, when Charlie still hadn't offered an invitation.

With an indifferent wave, Charlie motioned her inside. A spectacular crystal chandelier decorated the foyer of the stone and brick house that was the showplace of the neighborhood. "No one has arrived to haul off the furniture yet."

Uncertain if Charlie was being facetious or stating the actual situation about the furniture, Rosalyn said, "Do you mean—?"

"Yes. It's being repossessed. Not that it matters, I suppose." Charlie laughed bitterly. "Because we won't have a house to keep it in anyway."

The house, too! "Oh, Charlie, I'm so sorry—"

Charlie surveyed her with a certain surprise. "Aren't you losing your house?"

"No, I don't think so."

Charlie's eyes filled with tears. "Well, lucky you." She whirled and started up the wide staircase. Rosalyn followed. Once the airy bedroom had been filled with girlish, pastel ruffles, but now it was all sophisticated black and white, the bedspread a sleek gleam of matching satin diamonds. The only bright color was the blood-red splash of a spray of roses on the dressing table.

Sitting at her dressing table, Charlie began brushing on more fingernail polish. "Isn't this a gorgeous new color?"

"Charlie, let's talk about this." There was something hard and glittering about Charlie now, as if she were encased in a glossy shell.

"What's to talk about? We're paupers."

"It's awful. But we have each other. And God is still with us, Charlie."

Her friend's laugh was hard. "I don't need anyone. Besides, I already know what I'm going to do."

"You do?"

"I'm going to get married. And I'd advise you to do the same."

Rosalyn stared in astonishment at her friend's golden-haired reflection in the mirror. Charlie went out with a dazzling variety of men, but she hadn't been seeing any one of them steadily enough for—in Rosalyn's opinion—marriage.

"Married? To whom?" she finally asked incredulously.

Charlie made an angry growl of annoyance and with a fluff of cotton scrubbed furiously at some infinitesimal flaw in the polish. "Oh, I hate, hate doing this myself! But Daddy said I can't go to the manicurist any more. Or the hairdresser, either."

Rosalyn repeated her question. "Who are you going to marry?"

"I haven't decided yet. All I know is, he's going to be rich."

"Charlotte! Oh, Charlotte," Rosalyn murmured, reverting to that name of long ago. "You can't marry some man just because...because he's rich and you're terrified!"

"Oh, can't I? Just watch me." Charlie returned to the nail polishing with the determination of a soldier preparing his weapons for battle. "Has your father decided what he's going to do now?"

"I don't think so."

"Well, my father is planning to move to some miserable little town in Iowa and work in his cousin's drugstore." Charlie stabbed the brush into the bottle. "But I can't live poor, Roz. Trapped in some run-down apartment. Eating stew like that awful turnipy garbage at the soup kitchen. Wearing someone's cast-off clothes. I'll die like that!"

Charlie's closet held enough clothes that it would be years before she had to consider someone else's cast-offs. But Rosalyn had to admit that her own future didn't look quite as bleak as Charlie's.

"So, just like that, you're going to get married."

"Just like that."

"Do you have someone in mind?"

"I'm going dancing with Rex Overland tonight."

"Rex Overland! He's been a...a bootlegger!"

"Then he should be rich. He's also handsome, dresses elegantly, and has already sent me flowers." Charlie nodded toward the spray of blood-red roses. "I'm also considering Rodney Kilmer. His family is up to their ears in railroad money."

"He's also engaged to Ruth Warrenton!"

Charlie's shrug carelessly dismissed the ethics of stealing

Charlie's shrug carelessly dismissed the ethics of stealing someone else's man.

"Charlie, come live with us," Rosalyn begged impulsively. "We'd all love to have you. It will be almost like when we were girls. We'll both find jobs—"

"Wake up, Roz. There are no jobs. Even if there were, neither of us is qualified for anything worthwhile. And I'm not going to spend my life in some five and dime selling cheap perfume."

"But marrying someone you don't love can't be the answer—"

Charlie stood, her abrupt movement tumbling the stool to the luxurious carpet. She turned to her best friend with unexpected fury. "That's fine for you to say. You aren't being driven out of your home! You haven't already lost your mother! This takes *everything* from me, and it isn't fair. It just isn't fair!" she repeated with a blaze of passion.

Tears sprang to Rosalyn's eyes. Impulsively, she reached out to take Charlie in her arms, the way she had done when Charlie's mother died and her friend was beside herself with grief.

But Charlie pushed her away. "I suppose you're going to tell me that faith will sustain me." Her voice held a deep and bitter tone. "Faith! That and a nickel will get you a cup of coffee. Face it, Roz. We've gone to church and prayed and been good girls all our lives, but we're no better off now than some bum who's spent his life drinking and stealing. At least I'm not," she added, pointedly emphasizing the greater scope of her loss. "Now if you'll excuse me, I want to take my bath so I'll have plenty of time to do my makeup before Rex arrives." She scooped a white satin robe off the bed and headed toward the door of her private bathroom.

"Charlie, please, none of this means that the Lord has abandoned us. He still loves and cares for us—"

"You're not mad at God for letting all this happen?"

39

Charlie stopped at the door of the bathroom. Tears and anger had not altered her golden beauty, but the sweet innocence of earlier years had hardened to an impenetrable sheen. "You know what your problem is, Roz? You're too soft, just like I've always been. And you know what happens to soft hearts? The world uses them for pincushions. And so does God!"

The room vibrated as she slammed the bathroom door behind her.

Three

❧

Early Summer 1933
Castle Beach, Oregon

"Gate, Daddy, gate, gate, gate!"

Three-year-old Jessie burst out of the doorway and raced on churning legs to her father. Shea caught her up and swung her high overhead. The last rays of sun setting over the ocean turned her hair to a blaze of curly copper. She giggled as he held her close for a kiss and his red beard tickled her cheek.

"Now, what's all this about a gate?" he asked, more than a little bewildered that a gate could cause his small daughter such excitement.

Jessie opened a chubby fist and showed him her treasure, a smooth, translucent stone with a fiery, amber-red glow.

"Oh, an agate."

Jessie nodded as she settled into the curve of his arm. "Yes. A gate." She held the stone toward the sky, the side of her mouth scrunched upward as she tried to close one eye and squint through the stone. "Andy give it to me. Can we go find more gates, Daddy? Please?"

Andy was a little boy who lived down the street. Bonnie Lundford, the gray-haired, ruddy-skinned housewife who took care of Jessie while Shea was at the logging camp during the week, also took care of Andy occasionally. Now she stepped off the porch with a paper sack of clean clothes and Jessie's favorite toy. It was a four-legged, stuffed piece of cloth that Jessie called Lambie after Jesus' lambs in the Bible stories she loved.

"My sister took some of the neighborhood children to the beach yesterday. It was a good day for finding shells and agates," Bonnie explained. "I didn't let Jessie go because...well, I know how you feel..." Her good-natured voice trailed off awkwardly.

It was true. Shea had warned Bonnie, just as he had all the other good and helpful women who'd cared for Jessie since Molly's death: Jessie was not to go anywhere near the ocean. Not at any time. Not for any reason. He couldn't pretend the ocean out of existence, of course. In Castle Beach it was always there, and, unless rain or fog temporarily hid it behind a misty veil, always a visible presence, sometimes shining with deceptive innocence, sometimes dark and wild and angry. Even in deep fog it could be heard, endlessly booming and crashing, as if contemptuously taunting him. And sometimes, even back at the cabin fifteen miles inland, a certain breeze brought its unmistakable scent to him.

But he'd never actually touched those cold, killing waters since that day two and a half years ago. Never gone fishing, never crabbed in the harbor, never walked on the beach.

If he could have sold out and gone elsewhere he would have. But there were no buyers in these hard times of what was beginning to be called the Great Depression, and he didn't want to abandon his home, as others had done. Not that there were any jobs to be had. His own work in the woods was definitely shaky, although he had to admit that wasn't entirely due to the harsh economic conditions. Given his disagreements with the woods boss, he knew that if he wasn't one of the best high-riggers on the coast he'd already be out of work. But even if he lost the job, or work in the woods shut down completely, he'd still have a warm bed for Jessie here. If he had to, he could live off the land, hunting and gardening and selling a load of firewood occasionally.

Not exactly what he'd had in mind during the years he'd spent in college studying forestry, he thought wryly. But he'd heard there were former professors selling apples on the streets back east.

"Please, Daddy, I wanna find a gate," Jessie begged.

Shea answered with that noncommittal, evasive phrase used by parents everywhere, probably ever since the Lord created parents, he thought. "Well, we'll see."

He set Jessie on the sidewalk of weathered boards. Bonnie handed him the sack and Lambie. A silent sympathy in her eyes told him she knew he had no intention of going anywhere near the beach.

"We'll see you at church in the morning?" she asked.

He nodded. "Oh, I almost forgot to tell you, I won't be bringing Jessie back until Tuesday evening. Steam donkey broke down, so we're shut down until the middle of the week," Shea explained.

"Why don't you come to the church social? It's Tuesday evening." Bonnie smiled gently.

Shea hesitated. For weeks after Molly and Adam's deaths Shea had turned his back on God and anything spiritual, including church. His faith had been shaken to its very foundation. Why had his Lord let this happen? Why had he snatched away his beloved wife and brother? Why hadn't he answered Shea's frantic pleas for them there in the deathtrap of rock and water?

Shea never found answers to those questions. But he learned he couldn't go on, lonely and despairing, existing in a dark and bottomless place without his God. So after struggling alone through those raw and savage weeks, he finally cried out again to the Lord in agony, and began to cling to him in simple faith. He read from Isaiah 43, "I will be with thee…I will be with thee." He whispered the words again and again to himself, and the cold, dark place inside him began to fill with warmth and light. *"Fear not, for I have redeemed thee,"* he read. *"I have called thee by name; thou art mine. When thou passest through the rivers, they shall not overflow thee…hou wast precious in my sight, thou hast been honourable, and I have loved thee.… Fear not, for I am with thee."*

God hadn't promised that the waters, dangers, even death, wouldn't come. But he had promised to be there in the midst of it. He had been in the swirling, angry sea with Molly and Adam. And he had been with Shea all along. He was with him now, in his anger, in his sorrow.

So Shea had returned to his loving God, finally understanding that what had happened was a part of the mystery of the Lord's actions that sometimes must be accepted with simple faith. Now he attended Sunday services during the summer and as often as he could in winter if bad weather hadn't turned the mountain roads into a muddy quagmire. He immersed himself often in God's Word, seeking and finding comfort and guidance. He taught a bright and eager Jessie an occasional simple verse. He helped out when he saw someone in need: a load of firewood for elderly Mrs. Siikanen, roof repair for old Hank Bowman, some wooden toys he carved on long evenings at the logging camp as Christmas gifts for children at church.

But he wanted nothing to do with the social events of the church that he and Molly and Adam had once enjoyed. There were no church picnics or song-fests or potluck suppers. And he never accepted invitations to dinner after church. He did not, in fact, take part in anything that was just-for-fun. Not a movie or a ball game, not Fourth of July fireworks or a dance at the school gym. Never a frivolous afternoon of kite-flying. Molly had loved to fly a kite, her dark hair also flying in the breeze.…

"Shea?" Bonnie said, and he realized he was standing there with what must be an unfocused glaze in his eyes. "Are you thinking about the church social? There'll be games for the children, plus singing and lots of good food. We'd love to have you."

Especially, perhaps, Bonnie's niece who had recently moved down from Portland? She'd given him a very sweet smile at church last Sunday.

"Well, we'll see," he said.

He returned Bonnie's smile with a guilty grin. They both knew he was putting off her invitation just as he had put off Jessie's plea to go to the beach to find agates.

He stopped by the grocery store to buy fresh milk and a few oranges for Jessie, and to treat her to an ice cream cone. She had a hundred things to tell him on the long drive home.

"Me and Bonnie made cookies and we had a tea party. Then me and Andy put a doll dress on Pansy, and her scratched me. See?" Jessie held out a fair-skinned arm with a minuscule red mark.

He smiled at her busy chatter. Her three-year-old grammar could use some fine tuning, but he'd always talked to her like the small, bright companion she was, and she had a large vocabulary for her age. Or maybe, he thought as she launched into another story about Pansy having kittens, that was just a proud father's opinion.

"I guess Pansy didn't want to wear a dress," he said.

Jessie giggled. "Was an ugly dress," she agreed.

There were no fresh tire tracks on the road once they passed the cluster of houses near Deerfoot Creek. The dirt lane wound around hillsides and down into canyons. They crossed a couple of log bridges Shea had helped build, then headed through deep tunnels of forest where only lacy patches of sky showed between the interlaced branches overhead. When he and Molly had first married and started building their cabin, three other families had also lived out here. They were a tiny but gregarious community then, but gradually each of the other families, victims of the hard times, had moved on, abandoning the little houses they had built, hoping that things would be better somewhere else. Now only Shea and Jessie remained.

The road widened where it crossed a section that had been trampled flat and bare from use as a yarding area when this piece was logged. The entire hillside and valley were a devastation that Shea couldn't look at without getting angry.

Everywhere he saw logging practices that he found wasteful and destructive, but this was one of the worst, still a raw scar years after the logging. A steep hillside denuded and left to erode; trees, carelessly felled so they split and broke, left to rot; a stream choked with debris and eroded mud; no attempt made at reforestation. When he had his own logging outfit, it wouldn't be done that way, he vowed.

A few miles farther on Jessie pointed a stubby finger at a blue flash that crossed the hood of the truck. "Bluebird," she said.

"Bluejay," Shea corrected. "See the crest on its head?"

The feisty bird, raucously scolding them for some infraction of its bird rules, landed on a faded sign near a road leading off to the left. Shea had always been curious about this property. There was an old log house back in there; he'd run across it when he was hunting. It was a big place, two stories, but empty of furniture and crumbling now from lack of care. In a canyon beyond the house was one of the prettiest spots he'd ever seen, a slim, graceful waterfall plunging into a deep pool. He'd heard the property was owned by some rich man in the east, but in the years he'd lived out here no one had ever come near the place. The name on the sign, after the first letter "F," was too faded and blurred to read.

At the cabin, Shea got a fire going in the stove he'd built himself. The summer days were warm now, but the coastal nights still held an occasional chill. After he had the woodbox filled and other chores done, Jessie, in her pink flannel nightgown, curled in his lap with Lambie and a tattered book of Bible stories. This night, however, instead of instantly opening the book, she made an unexpected announcement.

"Andy's getting a new mama."

Shea blinked. "He is?" Fisherman Jim Borman's wife had walked out on him and her small son Andy last year. He was a good man, dependable and hard working. It wasn't surprising he'd remarry, but this was the first Shea had heard of it.

"Who is she?"

"A lady," Jessie replied airily, as if that were sufficient information for anyone. "Will I get a mama?"

With a twist of heart, Shea realized Jessie hadn't said "new mama" for herself. She'd never known any mother.

Would there ever be a new wife for him, a new mother for Jessie? He tried to picture it, briefly inserting the faces of various women acquaintances, but somehow he just couldn't imagine himself falling in love and marrying again. There was a kind of unreality to it, like imagining himself flapping his arms and flying.

"Do you want a mama?" he asked carefully.

Jessie puckered her lips thoughtfully. "Maybe." Shea was about to put her off with some variation of "we'll see," when she added, with surprising persistence for a three-year-old, "Mostly, I wanna find a ag-ate." She said the word carefully, as if proper pronunciation were perhaps the key to success.

Shea swallowed. The last thing he wanted was to go down to that beach where he'd washed in after the boat accident, but that was the only good local place for finding agates. He didn't want to smell the sea's briny tang or see the advancing scroll of white surf or hear the crash of waves around the Sisters. And most of all he didn't want a single drop of seawater, the water that had stolen Molly and Adam, ever touching Jessie or himself.

At the end of Sunday's church service, Shea headed directly for the door, as usual, but Bonnie Lundford intercepted him. With a matchmaking gleam in her eye, she motioned for her niece Elaine to join them.

Elaine Wiseman was an attractive young woman with a sweet smile Shea had noticed before. Bonnie mentioned that Elaine had offered to take care of the babies at church every other Sunday, information obviously meant as a clue to what a wonderful mother she'd make for Jessie. "And Elaine is bringing her marvelous lemon pie to the church social Tuesday night," Bonnie added brightly. Another clue, this time to Elaine's assets as a capable wife and homemaker.

Elaine had the good grace to look embarrassed by her aunt's unsubtle efforts on her behalf, but that didn't stop her from adding with nervous shyness, "I hope you'll be there." She peered at him as if trying to discern what was under the heavy red beard.

Shea murmured his approval of Elaine's commendable church activities, but, seeing the two of them converging on some church social trap for him, added hastily, "Nice meeting you, Miss Wiseman. But if you'll excuse us now, I'm—"

I'm what? He couldn't tell some outright lie. But something came to him, something that he suspected even Bonnie would approve.

"I'm taking Jessie agate hunting."

He doubted there was a mother in Jessie's future but he could at least help his daughter find an agate or two. And they needn't actually touch the seawater. The two women looked disappointed, but Shea grabbed Jessie and fled before they could switch targets and try to hoodwink him into inviting Elaine along today.

On the front seat of the truck Shea helped Jessie exchange her Sunday dress for faded overalls, and at a gas station he ducked into the restroom to change out of his suit into an old shirt and trousers he had in the truck. He stopped and bought crackers, cheese, and oranges for their lunch, and they ate on a grassy slope above the beach. Shea kept his back to the sea, ostracizing an old enemy, but Jessie chattered about birds and waves and something else that was out there. Finally he had to turn and look. Three dark, sleek heads bobbed in the water just beyond the surf.

"Sea lions," he said, reluctantly impressed with their graceful agility. He didn't want to admire anything about the sea, including its occupants.

Jessie repeated the words carefully, storing them up for future use, and they laughed together as the animals cavorted like mischievous children in the water. They tossed the scraps from their lunch to the sea gulls and left their shoes lined up in a neat foursome on the grass so they could walk barefoot in the sand.

"Now you have to promise to hold on tight to my hand, and not let go," Shea instructed as he got a good grip on her little hand. "Okay?"

"Okay."

They found shells and a half-dozen agates in the patches of

gravely rock along the long, curved beach, colors varying from fiery amber-red to a smoky blue. Jessie dug her feet in the sand and giggled delightedly as the grains spilled between her toes. She poked gingerly at a cluster of orange starfish clinging to a rock exposed by the low tide. She occasionally glanced yearningly at the foaming surf, cocking her head to listen to the swoosh of rolling water, but Shea had already told her they weren't going wading, and, though Jessie could be extremely persistent, she wasn't one to whine. She found a graceful swirl of driftwood with a round hole in it and peeked through the hole as if it were the opening to a whole new world. Which, he had to admit, this was for her.

He felt a certain guilt that he had denied her the joy of all this, but that didn't weaken his compulsion to keep her away from the water. He also determinedly avoided a direct gaze at the rough cliffs of the Sisters.

But he didn't realize one thing he was doing until Jessie plaintively complained, "Daddy, you're hurting me," and he realized he was clutching her small hand in his big, callused one the way he'd clutched the oars that tragic day.

He swept her into his arms. "Oh, sweetie, I'm sorry. Hurting you is the last thing I'd ever want to do."

Jessie giggled and held out her scrunched hand for him to kiss and make "all better," wiggling her fingers afterward to show him that it was indeed healed. Shea could see she was getting tired and sleepy, and he carried her back to the truck. She curled up on the lumpy seat, head tucked against his thigh, and promptly fell asleep, the small "hurt" already forgotten.

Yet the moment was less easily forgotten by Shea. Was it possible, he wondered uneasily, that he was hurting her in other ways that he didn't realize?

Reluctantly, as if meeting some wordless challenge, his gaze lifted to the Three Sisters and open sea beyond. Again he relived the terror of that day, the plunge of the boat going over, his frantic, futile efforts to reach Molly, the terror in her eyes as she hung there pinned to the cliff, and then his descent into the wild darkness of rocks and crushing currents. He'd been washed through a narrow hallway of stone between the Sisters, and was halfway to shore before he regained consciousness. A commercial fishing boat had picked up Molly's body that same evening; Adam's body had washed in a day later. Now Molly was buried beside her mother in a town farther north on the coast; Adam was in the Castle Beach cemetery.

He did not now ask, as he had shouted with fury and resentment in those first painful weeks, *Why, God, Why?* His faith was now as strong as it had ever been, stronger, perhaps, because he'd learned the Lord was his only refuge.

Looking down at his small, sleeping daughter, he wondered if anything could ever shake his faith again. He gently twined his finger in a shining coppery curl spilling softly across her temple. He loved her, and seeing her strong and healthy made him happy.

But where was the joy he had once felt? Where was the exuberance that had once filled his life?

He worshiped, prayed, and gave thanks. But he went through his days as if life were some dark punishment to be grimly endured.

Why? Because Molly's absence was still an empty hole in his life, as was Adam's. He and Adam had been best friends as well as brothers.

But there was more.

The guilt. Sometimes it still washed over him like an invisible tidal wave of the heart, powerful as any storm of the sea. If only he hadn't pulled the crank rope so hard. If only he'd checked the tool box to see if there was an extra rope before they left the dock. If only they had never gone fishing that day, or come in sooner....

Is my lack of joy part of that guilt? he wondered with a unexpected jump in perspective, as if he'd suddenly leaped from a narrow valley to a mountaintop with a new and revealing panoramic view.

Did he, deep down inside, feel that if he enjoyed life now, he'd be betraying both Molly and Adam? That if he acknowledged life could still be worthwhile he'd be committing a raw act of disloyalty? That if he looked on the sea with anything but fury and hatred he'd be a traitor to their memories?

Oh, yes.

But life wasn't a punishment, he thought with a certain confusion; it was a gift from God, a gift to be used for his purposes, not plodded through as if it were some dark and joyless tunnel! Spiritually, he'd accepted his loss and reconciled with the Lord. Yet had he ever truly reconciled with himself?

He crossed his arms on the steering wheel and stared openly at the scene of sea and sand and off-shore rocks as if seeing it for the first time.

Gulls wheeled above the rough tops of the Three Sisters, and a breeze brought the faint, discordant music of their squawks and cries. Water crashing through the gaps between the rocks exploded in glittering rainbows. Slanted sunlight lit one side of the walls with sparkling flashes, illuminating droplets of water as if they were small jewels, and the opposite cliffs rose in magnificent shadow. A golden path of sunlight shimmered across blue water; a translucent lift of wave turned to crashing white water. A sleek head bobbed to the surface right in the midst of the surf and disappeared with a frisky flip of tail. White scrolls of surf rose and fell on the beach, the turn of tide writing graceful new lines on the sand with airy bits of frothy seafoam.

Not some wrathful entity with a malicious will of its own, as he had so long viewed the sea. Nothing evil or ugly or sinister.

Only beauty and grandeur, from tiniest grain of sand to

crashing waves, from flat horizon to soaring rocks. God was in charge and the sea was simply a part of his creation, a mystery that was somehow always the same and yet endlessly changing as it followed his majestic plan in its rhythmic sweep of tides and cycles of storm and calm. As life also followed those cycles.

He'd denied Jessie all this, denied her the thrill of touching a strange orange creature from beneath the sea, denied her the tickle of sand on her toes and the joy of finding a mysterious seashell or glowing agate, denied her the close-up touch of beauty God had created. He'd been a grown man before he saw the sea, but he could still recall the thrill of wading into it for the very first time, feeling the power of the waves surging and lifting him...

"Jessie." Shea jiggled her sturdy body lightly. "Wake up."

He took joy in her sleepy awakening, the push of small fists into half-closed eyes, the yawn, the half-grumpy, "Huh?"

"How'd you like to go down to the water and stick your toes right into those waves?"

She came wide awake. "Me and you both?"

"Of course."

"Okay!"

They turned up their pantlegs and raced to the beach together, pausing only as a wave rolled up to meet them. Jessie's blue eyes grew large with wonder as its frothy edge crept almost delicately to her toes. Shea held her hand loosely as the moving water engulfed her ankles, smiling reassuringly even as he battled a powerful urge to snatch her up and out of its reach. Then the wave receded, and she giggled as the ticklish suction swept sand from beneath their feet, an oddly delightful sensation he had to admit.

In the gravely area below the sandy stretch where they stood, the receding wave made a busy, whispery chatter as it swirled and rearranged small rocks and pebbles, and Jessie cocked her head to listen.

But on the next incoming wave Shea panicked as Jessie plopped down and the water surged above her waist. He snatched her into his arms. "Are you all right? Did the wave knock you over? Do you want to go back to the truck now?"

"Daddy, I sat down." She spoke almost reproachfully. "I wanted to sit in the water. I'm not cold," she added as if anticipating his next worried question.

When the next wave came he impulsively sat down with her. "You know, we're getting our clothes soaking wet," he remarked conversationally. "And covered with sand. We may find little fishes in our pockets."

Jessie giggled, as if this were some happy secret. "I know."

"I know something else we can do in the water," he said.

"What?"

"Dance!"

And dance they did, Shea holding both her tiny hands in his big ones as he swung her up and over an incoming wave, letting her toes barely touch the froth before he whirled her upward again, the next time swooping her low into the water. They frolicked and romped and raced the waves up the sand. They jumped and cavorted, and once Shea even turned a clumsy cartwheel that left him upside down in the sand and both of them laughing. Seawater turned his already curly beard into wiry red springs.

Jessie pretended she was a master choreographer of the sea, grandly telling a wilting wave, "Go 'way, now!" and motioning a fresh new one to surge inward. Sunlight sparkled on the sea and in Jessie's bright hair. Shea gave Jessie a sea monster ride on his back while he crawled on the sand, and he balanced her on his shoulders as he spun and whirled in the surf. He had the feeling that if anyone was watching they'd think the two of them had gone crazy as they danced and frolicked and whooped and sang in joyous abandon.

And he didn't care!

In their happy play, Shea gradually felt a curious sense of release come over him. Not a forgetting—no, never a forgetting. There would always be pain of loss and bittersweet memories, and he felt a brief, sharp sting of tears, but with the tears came a gentle loosening of the bonds that had so long imprisoned him. Betrayal? Disloyalty? Shea looked at his bubbling daughter. He looked at the sea and rocks and sunshine. No, not betrayal or disloyalty; simply a turning, like the turning of the tide, from eyes fixed on the dark tunnel of the past to the sunlight of the future.

"We'd better go in now, before you start turning blue." Shea took off his shirt and wrapped it around his wet, goosebumpy, laughing daughter to carry her back to the truck.

"Can we come back?"

"Yes, we'll be back."

And they were also going to the church social Tuesday night!

Five

Summer 1933
Gideon, Indiana

Rosalyn started looking for work, but as Charlie had pointed out, she wasn't qualified for any high-paying jobs, and even the few low-paying openings had lines of applicants with more experience and skills than she. After job hunting every morning, she hurried to the soup kitchen to help with the tail end of serving and cleanup.

At home, she and her mother explored the mysteries of the kitchen, and, despite bullet-hard biscuits and rubbery-textured casseroles, it was a time of companionship and laughter. Hattie had gone back east to live with her sister, and Geoffrey would be leaving soon for a job on a horse farm.

Robbie stayed out of town several days longer than he had originally planned, but after hearing about the collapse of Fallon-Richards Pharmaceuticals, he called with immediate concern and sympathy. Even though it was almost nine o'clock the night he got back into town, he came to the house immediately, ignoring polite proprieties as he wrapped his arms around Rosalyn at the door. He murmured tender reassurances and endearments, and she felt cherished and protected.

They went for a drive in the country, and, with a cool stream of night air tossing her hair, Rosalyn felt some of the tensions and worries slip away. Robbie parked near an old-fashioned covered bridge, and they watched the moon rise together. Rosalyn told him all the things she hadn't been able to tell him on the phone, especially her concerns about her father, whose guilt about what he felt were his terrible errors in judgment seemed to weigh more heavily on him each day.

"I know I shouldn't be frightened or discouraged. The Lord will provide and see us through. But sometimes..."

Robbie reached across the seat and squeezed her hand. "I'm here. You can always count on me."

His eyes were warm and tender, and the thought of gently manipulating him into a proposal was suddenly a sweet temptation. If she were married to Robbie, she could forget all the unpleasantness of job hunting and rejection. And she loved him so very much! He looked wonderful, lean and bronzed from hours of summer golfing, but it was the loving concern in his eyes and the reassuring promise of always being there that were like a luminous bubble shimmering protectively around her.

But she couldn't hurry him into a marriage to solve her own problems. She leaned over and kissed him lightly on the cheek. "Thank you, Robbie. You don't know how much that means to me."

"Apparently the collapse of the business didn't hit Charlie too hard," he commented unexpectedly. "Old family money?"

Rosalyn concealed her surprise by asking, "Why do you say that?" While she had no hesitation about confiding her own changed situation to Robbie, she didn't want to gossip about the Richards' even greater problems. Or Charlie's wild talk of snaring a rich husband.

"I ran into Charlie today when I was lunching with a business associate at Horton House, which isn't exactly the most economical place in town to eat. She said she was on her way to play golf this afternoon, and she was laughing about some incident with a policeman. Apparently she'd managed to flirt her way out of a speeding ticket. She made a very amusing story out of it."

The following week Rosalyn surprisingly saw Robbie only once, when he took her to dinner, and then he acted oddly uneasy and distracted. Could Grenwich Enterprises also be in financial difficulty? He didn't confide in her, however, and she didn't pry.

She kept up her search for a job, determinedly not thinking that, if circumstances hadn't changed so drastically, she'd be getting ready to return to college now. She got a few days' temporary work in a commercial laundry and came home at night reeling with weariness. At home, the repossessed Packard disappeared, and Oliver started driving the rough pickup truck that had formerly been used only for yard and garden work. He was still going to the office to finish up details, but Rosalyn knew that he was putting out feelers about management positions elsewhere. And, she suspected, he was not getting any more job offers than she.

She tried to call Charlie several times, but she soon came to suspect that her old friend was deliberately avoiding her. She could almost think the same of Robbie. They had a movie date, but he canceled with an excuse about not feeling well. Then, on Friday evening he stopped by, apologizing profusely for being so busy. He also, to her surprise, had a lovely gift for her—a delicate silver bracelet set with an amethyst.

Then, silence. Rosalyn heard nothing from him the following week. She felt bewildered by these abrupt reversals in attitude and actions. She tried to assure herself that none of this was significant, that he was probably just preoccupied with business matters. But by the middle of the following week, there was no escaping the alarming realization that something was definitely wrong between them.

She agonized about what to do. Confront him and demand an explanation? Silently wait and hope? The happy bubble of love that had so recently shimmered around her now seemed to have little more substance than a vapor. Had there been more than business involved when he was seen earlier with the beautiful woman reporter?

The ominous and ever-more-obvious possibility that she had lost him churned up her days and savaged her sleepless nights. But she wouldn't let it end in this bewildering silence, she decided resolutely. She loved him.

She placed the call from a pay telephone after finishing with cleanup at the soup kitchen. She'd called Robbie before, when things were right between them, but this time her palms felt damp and a nervous muscle jumped in her jaw. The switchboard operator at the radio station put her through to his office, where a sing-song voice said, "I'm sorry. Mr. Grenwich isn't in now. May I take a message?"

"No." She hesitated. "Do you know when I may reach him?"

"Not for several days. Perhaps longer."

"He's out of town on business?"

"Well…"

"Do you know where I could reach him by long distance?" Rosalyn asked, growing impatient with the young woman's evasiveness.

"I doubt that Mr. Grenwich would want to be reached." A hint of a coy giggle invaded the rather smug voice.

"Why is that?"

"I wouldn't…if I were on my honeymoon."

Rosalyn removed the receiver from her ear and looked at it in disbelief. What kind of strange joke was this? "You must be mistaken," she finally scoffed.

"Oh, no. He got married." The young woman sounded very sure of herself, even a bit superior as bearer of such important news.

"When did this happen?" Rosalyn demanded skeptically.

"A few days ago."

"And who did Mr. Grenwich marry?"

"I'm not at liberty to say." The young woman now turned prim and a little nervous, as if she suddenly were afraid she'd already said too much. "But I understand there will be an announcement in the newspaper within a few days."

Rosalyn hung up the phone feeling dazed. It couldn't possibly be true! *I'm here,* Robbie had promised. *You can always count on me.* And she loved him! No, she commanded herself fiercely as she stepped out of the phone booth, she would not believe unfounded gossip. She would not fall into tears and panic. This was just some strange, malicious rumor stemming from his business meetings with the beautiful reporter.

At home, Rosalyn entered the house through the side door. She avoided the kitchen because her mother would know something was wrong the instant Rosalyn walked into the room, and she didn't want to give substance to the rumor about Robbie by repeating it even to her mother. She was on her way upstairs when her father called to her from his office.

"Rozzie, is that you? May I see you a moment, please?"

A quick dread flashed through her. Only recently had he started using that old name for her. And every time he'd used it he'd had bad news to give.

She brushed damp tendrils of hair away from her temples and tried to plant a cheerful smile on her face as she walked into the office, now cluttered with files and records transferred from the company offices. She would not burden him with her worries

61

about Robbie; he had enough problems already. His face looked gray and gaunt.

"Rozzie, Henry was just here to see me. He gave me some—" He paused as if uncertain what words to use, and Rosalyn saw that all-too-familiar blend of compassion and despair enter his eyes. "—some surprising information." Rosalyn swallowed. Had Henry Richards somehow also heard the shocking story about Robbie and come to tell her father so he could break the news to her? News that made Oliver Fallon look as if he'd rather walk across hot coals than have to tell her.

Awkwardly, she tried to spare him some of the pain. "It's that gossip about Robbie, isn't it? The rumor that he got married."

"I don't know what to say, Rozzie. He seemed like such a nice, trustworthy young man—"

"But it isn't true! You know how gossip is!"

Afternoon sunlight, filtering through the curtains swaying gently at the open window, hit a metal paperweight on her father's desk and skittered a bright flash across the ceiling. She felt a peculiar skittering dizziness within herself.

He shook his head. "It's true, Rozzie. And Henry is as surprised and shocked as anyone. He knew nothing at all about what was going on until Charlotte called him from Atlantic City."

"Atlantic City?" Rosalyn repeated blankly, unable to see any connection between Charlie and Atlantic City and this terrible rumor. Her father's face turned a shade more gray. He came around the big oak desk and wrapped his arms around her. "Oh, my dear Rozzie, you don't know, do you? Robbie and Charlotte are married! That's why she called from Atlantic City. To tell Henry they eloped."

Rosalyn stared at him, momentarily unable to assimilate the words. Robbie and *Charlie*? Charlie and Robbie married? "No! That's preposterous!"

"It's true. Rozzie, I'm so sorry—"

Rosalyn sagged against him, burying her face in his shoulder, the tears she had desperately held back since the phone call now trickling through her dam of control. The trickle became a torrent flowing down her cheeks and into her father's shirt. Rosalyn's shoulders shook with sobs, and her legs threatened to buckle. Her father helped her to the leather sofa and held her, stroking her hair and rocking her as he had done when she was a child, making wordless murmurs of support and comfort. This explained so much. Why Charlie had been avoiding her. Why Robbie had been too busy and uneasy and distant.

She remembered his promise: *I'm here. You can always count on me.* Now ringing false and empty through her mind, it mocked her. *I'm here. You can always count on me.*

And this time the hollow promise had an echo, Charlie's words, spoken so airily that day at the soup kitchen. *I can get any man I want to propose.*

Her best friend and the man she loved.

The two strands of betrayal wound like barbed wire around her heart.

Six

The announcement of Robbie and Charlie's marriage appeared in the newspaper a few days later. The double-ring ceremony was described as "private" rather than an elopement. The bride wore white silk and carried orchids. The new Mr. and Mrs. Grenwich had honeymooned in Atlantic City and would shortly be "at home" in a newly-constructed house on Winston Street.

Rosalyn had steeled herself for this, but the tears started once more, driven by a ragged mixture of pain and bewilderment. Fiercely she repeated the words she had already said to herself so many times that they were a white-hot brand on her brain and heart. If that was the kind of man Robbie was—deceitful, dishonest, unreliable—she was better off without him. She was also better off without a knife-in-the-back friend such as Charlie.

Yet in spite of everything, she couldn't tell herself she was no longer in love with Robbie. She desperately did not want to love him. It was unthinkable that she should feel anything but contempt for him after what he had done. She recognized now what the gift of the amethyst bracelet had been; an attempt to buy his way out of a guilty conscience for sneaking around behind her back! In the dim mists of the future she could see that maybe eventually she wouldn't love him.

But that wasn't now. Now the brilliant, treacherous strands of love still wove through the dark tapestry of hurt and betrayal. Love that bewildered, frightened, and angered her. Why didn't the love just die, instantly and completely? Why couldn't she just yank out those glittering strands and stomp them into oblivion?

She also didn't want to feel anything but contempt for Charlie and the greedy expertise and astonishing speed with which she had manipulated her situation. New rich husband, new home, new life. No turnipy stew or rundown apartment for Charlie! Yet even there the bright strands of long years of friendship still glowed treacherously; she would miss the friend who had once been as close as a sister.

It was still so difficult to comprehend that the two of them could do such a thing. Sneaking around to see each other, hiding from her, hiding from everyone, or surely gossip about them would have trickled back to her. The raw dishonesty of it!

Robbie and Charlie, she thought with a bitterness unfamiliar to her, had indeed used her naive, trusting heart as a pincushion.

Yet she couldn't simply stop her life and give in to her churned-up emotions. Her parents daily gave her their love and support and sympathy, but the practical problem of finding a job remained for both Rosalyn and her father. Sometimes they even job-hunted together, Oliver driving the rough pickup as they widened their search to neighboring towns and urban Indianapolis.

Added to the emotional turmoil was Rosalyn's inevitable encounter with the newlyweds. She braced herself for it, as she had for the newspaper announcement, but still it was a shock when it happened.

She had gone to the country club to apply for a job she had heard might be available in the dining room, and there they were, just coming into the club after playing golf. Laughing, Robbie's arm around Charlie's shoulders, her arm around his waist. Charlie, hair a shimmering golden halo, was in a fashionable, pleated golfing skirt. Robbie wore stylish, colorful plaid pants and Argyle socks. They looked lighthearted and happy, the epitome of a high-spirited, carefree young couple.

Part of Rosalyn wanted to confront and challenge and accuse them, but the part that wanted to run and hide won out. She frantically ducked out a side door without waiting to see about the job.

Outside, her heart pounded as if she'd just run, and lost, a long-distance race. She struggled with the anger and bitterness that felt like acid searing her heart. She leaned against the wall, hands clenched, and turned her closed eyes upward. *Lord, please don't let this eat away at me! Help me to be forgiving and handle this according to your will.*

Yet it was beyond her to go back inside and calmly offer them gracious congratulations.

She and her father drove downtown together the following day. He had an appointment for a job interview at the bank. He seemed cheerful, but Rosalyn had a small, nagging suspicion there was further bad news he hadn't yet told them. She'd brought sandwiches, to avoid spending money on lunch, and he parked the pickup at Dutton Park, where they agreed to meet for lunch.

Before they parted, Rosalyn leaned over and impulsively kissed him on his smooth-shaven cheek. He might be driving a battered pickup, but he presented a smart appearance. Pin-striped suit, white shirt, dark hat, shoes gleaming with fresh polish. Although, unlike the old days, Rosalyn knew this was polish he'd applied himself. "That bank had just better consider itself lucky to get you."

At lunch time, still jobless, Rosalyn retrieved the lunch sack from the pickup and sat on a sunny park bench to await her father. A squirrel immediately scampered toward her looking for a handout.

She was feeding the squirrel a bit of bread crust when the tranquillity of the park was shattered by the sounds of a skidding car...a scream...a crash. It came from the direction of busy Morrow Avenue, just a block away. Then there was more noise. The blast of a horn. Shouting.

Rosalyn's hands froze on the sandwich sack. The sounds had nothing to do with her, she instantly assured herself. Just another wreck of some sort in the busy traffic. There was more shouting. People running to the scene. Like hungry vultures to the scene of an accident, she thought.

Yet only a moment later she was running, abandoning the sack of sandwiches forgotten on the park bench, fear and dread pounding in her blood. She knew, somehow she *knew*.

Rosalyn rounded the corner onto Morrow Avenue. A growing knot of people clustered at mid-block. More yells and shouts. Traffic at a standstill.

Rosalyn discarded any pretense of courtesy and shouldered her way through the crowd. "Let me through! I have to get through!"

She broke into the open circle where a policeman was holding the crowd back. A crumpled figure lay on the pavement. A few feet away an automobile had its bumper buried in the fender of a parked car.

"I didn't see him!" a man yelled wildly. "He stepped right out in front of me! Like he wanted me to hit him! Like he wanted to die!"

"We'll get your statement in a minute," the officer was saying. Another officer was waving traffic around the accident scene. Rosalyn stood there motionless staring at the body whose face was turned away from her. Pin-striped suit, one gleaming dark shoe flung to the curb, a pool of blood.

Not her father! No! He was a much larger man than this broken figure lying on the street. And he was wearing a hat.

Then she saw it. A hat, or what had once been a hat, lay in the far lane of traffic, flattened to a dark smudge on the pavement.

Rosalyn ducked under the officer's outstretched arm, ignoring the whistle he instantly blew at her. A siren whined somewhere in the distance. She knelt, and she knew then what she had known from the moment she saw the crumpled figure. Perhaps even from the moment she'd heard the screech and crash.

"Miss, please, you'll have to—"

"I tried to miss him!" the man raged on in rising hysteria. His arms windmilled and he stomped his foot on an invisible brake pedal in wild pantomime of how he'd tried to stop his vehicle. "I tried!"

"It's my father," Rosalyn whispered brokenly as she knelt on the pavement, her silk-stockinged knees grinding unheeded into the city grime. "My father."

College...Robbie...Charlie...none of it mattered now.

Her father was dead.

Except for the searing pain of that horrifying scene, telling her mother was the most wrenching experience of Rosalyn's life. The only thing that kept her from collapsing in stunned shock herself was the knowledge that Ellen would not survive unless she was strong.

Ellen cried, not a hysterical sobbing but a quiet, desperate grief that went on and on, as if some essential life force were draining out of her. She went to bed crying; she woke crying. Until now, she had been bearing up cheerfully under all their adversities, exhibiting a remarkable strength and resilience, but with Oliver gone, Rosalyn had to help her through the days as if she were a lost and helpless child.

All the decisions that follow a death fell on Rosalyn. She even had to deal with heartless bill collectors who didn't let the accident deter their harassment. The funeral was a series of painfully sharp images with blurs between: the old hymns Oliver had loved, the heavy scent of flowers, the words of praise and loss, the gleaming casket, her fragile mother beside her, the cemetery, the brilliant sun and blue sky at odds with the stark scene below.

Rosalyn went often to the Lord, and he comforted and sustained her, but so many times she thought, with a ragged mixture of despair and anguish, *Oh, Robbie, Robbie, where are you when I need you? This is too much for me! And Charlie, I need you, too....*

But neither Robbie nor Charlie were there, only an elaborate, impersonal bouquet of flowers and a sympathy card with both their names on it.

Later they were in the office of Frank Lassiter, her father's lawyer, in a room that smelled faintly of furniture polish and leather-bound books. He was Oliver's age, dressed in a conservative dark suit with a vest, hair combed back over a balding spot. Ellen sat rigid as a store-window mannequin in her hat and black dress of mourning, not so much staring straight ahead as unseeing, withdrawn into herself.

"I'm so sorry to be meeting with you under these circumstances," Mr. Lassiter said. "Such a terrible, tragic accident."

Accident. Did he believe that? Did she?

That was how the newspaper had reported it, and that was how Rosalyn desperately wanted to believe it had happened. A terrible, tragic accident. She didn't want to think that her father had deliberately chosen this way out of the problems engulfing them. Yet she kept hearing the anguished cries of the driver of the car. *Like he wanted me to hit him! Like he wanted to die!*

Had something happened at that interview at the bank to push him over the edge, some final defeat that was more than he could bear? That he might have taken his own life went against everything Rosalyn believed in, everything she thought he believed in about trusting the Lord and leaving matters in his hands.

Mr. Lassiter went through details of the estate with tactful sympathy. With the assets already gone, the will was almost irrelevant. Rosalyn had held out hope that life insurance might still be in force, but the large policy had been borrowed against and then canceled when premiums weren't paid. "And it's most unfortunate, of course, about the house—"

A peculiar panic roared in Rosalyn's ears, like a freight train bearing down on her. "What about the house?"

Mr. Lassiter's lawyer-calm looked shaken. "Oliver didn't tell you?" Rosalyn shook her head, and he swallowed roughly. "He found out himself only a few days ago. We couldn't save it after all…"

Rosalyn suddenly had a vivid glimpse of the panic Charlie had faced in this situation. This was how people wound up homeless on the street, standing in line for a meal at the soup kitchen. She thought of that odd feeling she'd had that her father had more bad news he hadn't yet told them. And perhaps simply hadn't been able to face telling them.

With a certain irrelevance, she also thought of how she'd always planned to be married on the curving stairway there at the house, long white dress swirling around her, Charlie as a bridesmaid. In her girlhood, when she and Charlie played a giggling game of "wedding" on the staircase, the bridegroom had been a blur, but in recent months he had taken on face and shape. A tanned face with an irresistible grin and reckless blue eyes, a tall figure with lanky grace…

But she reminded herself fiercely it was, after all, only a house. An earthly structure of brick and wood, pleasant but inconsequential in the Lord's eternal scheme of things. And Robbie was another woman's husband.

Delicately Mr. Lassiter probed to see if Rosalyn and her mother had other financial resources. Yes, Ellen had indeed been born into a wealthy southern family, the only child. But after her mother's death, her father had remarried, his new wife a greedy and aggressive widow with four sons to match. When he died the widow and stepsons managed to grab everything. Rosalyn didn't explain all that; she simply shook her head no in response to the question and cut to the core of their situation.

"What is left?"

There wasn't much. A small, paid-up policy that covered burial expenses. The household furnishings and the pickup. Anything that belonged to Ellen or Rosalyn personally? Jewelry, perhaps? No. Expensive jewelry had never been of interest to either Ellen or Rosalyn. And what did Rosalyn herself own? A closet full of college clothes and a bicycle. An amethyst bracelet and a broken heart.

"There is a piece of property out west where your father used to go hunting. None of the creditors were interested in bothering with it." Awkwardly, as if he felt apologetic that there was so little to offer, Frank Lassiter pushed a file across the desk. "You might be able to get a little something out of it eventually."

There were papers to sign. Rosalyn read them and guided her mother's hand to the proper lines. When she asked Mr. Lassiter about his fee, he simply said it was already paid many times over.

Back home, Rosalyn glanced through the Oregon property file. It was located near a town named Castle Beach on the Oregon coast. Red ink outlined an eighty-acre oblong plot on a small map. An idea popped into Rosalyn's head. She instantly rejected it. Preposterous.

She hurried down to the soup kitchen to help out for a few hours while her mother napped. She hadn't been there since her father's death, and there were people she was concerned about. Elderly Mrs. Reutger was in line, and someone said Benny and his wife had moved west, but she didn't see the ragged boy with the huge, dark eyes. She did see something on the way home that left her shaken: Robbie and Charlie coming out of a department store together, gaily tossing an armload of parcels into the Studebaker. Charlie glanced up, saw Rosalyn in the battered pickup, and looked right through her.

Back home, Rosalyn asked her mother if there was a photo of the Oregon property around somewhere. After some searching Ellen produced a photo that showed a corner of the lodge behind Oliver in hunting clothes. All Rosalyn could discern was that the lodge appeared to be made of logs and had a front porch.

They had to be out of the house in two weeks. She had no job and no prospects of finding one any time soon. Somewhere in Oregon was their hunting lodge and eighty acres of land. And Oregon was two thousand miles away from any possibility of encountering Robbie and Charlie ever again.

Was it really such an outlandish idea?

Seven

August 1933
Castle Beach, Oregon

Roman Baylor, the last of the fire crew to be dropped off, climbed from the back of the truck at four o'clock in the morning. They'd left Tillamook before dark, but the narrow, crooked coast roads made slow traveling.

He stopped at the driver's side window which Shea had opened to let in the cool, rain-drizzled air. "How about something to eat? I'll get the wife up and have her fix us some bacon and eggs." The man's weary face was still soot-covered, his eyes white-circled where he'd rubbed them, and he reeked of smoke and sweat.

Or maybe that was himself he could smell, Shea thought wryly. His beard was as wiry and tangled as the stuffing spilling out of the truck seat, and his pants stiff with dirt. The crew had been in too big a hurry to get home to hang around camp and clean up.

"Thanks, but I'm too tired to eat." Shea held a hand out the window, letting the welcome raindrops speckle his palm.

"I've never been so glad to see rain in my life," Roman declared. "We could've been fighting that fire 'til winter if it hadn't started to rain."

Shea nodded wearily, waved, and put the truck in gear. The smart thing to do would be to go home, rest, clean up, and come back to town for Jessie later. But he hadn't seen her for two weeks, and he didn't want to wait any longer.

He would have to wait a little longer, he realized as he stopped the truck in front of the Lundford's weathered cottage. At this hour the occupants were all soundly asleep. His sense of time was off, not unusual, he supposed, considering that he'd put in several twenty-hour days on the firelines, with night and day often blending into one fiery haze.

He crossed his arms on the steering wheel and rested his head on his smoke-scented sleeves. He'd close his eyes for just a minute.

In what seemed no more than a blink, a light pounding on the side of the truck woke him. "Daddy! Daddy!"

Shea shook his head to clear it and carefully opened the door. Daylight had arrived, although a damp fog obscured any hint of sun. Jessie, still in her nightgown, clambered over the running board and into his lap. She wrinkled her nose and poked a finger at his tangled beard.

"You smell awful," she observed.

He laughed and stretched his neck in various directions trying to work out the kinks from his peculiar sleeping position. "You smell wonderful." And she did, all clean and sweet, with a faint scent of lavender soap clinging to skin and hair. "But you're barefoot!" He squeezed a small, cold foot.

"I ran out soon as I saw you."

Her tiny feet were wet from the heavy dew she'd scampered through, and she giggled as he rubbed them on his shirt. He lifted a foot and kissed the sole. She giggled again and squirmed away, but then she thrust the foot back at him. "Do it again, Daddy."

"I missed you, sweetie," he said huskily.

"You put out the fire?"

"Well, I did along with about fifteen hundred other men—and the rain." Although there were places, he knew, that could smolder for months yet.

By that time Bonnie, in a pink bathrobe, with curling rags tied in her graying hair, also had come out of the house. "We heard men were getting killed up there," she said. She squeezed his arm in a small gesture of relief that he wasn't one of them.

He nodded. "They were."

There had been some seventy firefighter deaths, he'd heard. And over 300,000 acres burned. The Tillamook fire was already being called the worst forest fire in Oregon's history. The woods boss at the logging camp had been angry when Shea said he was going to take off and go up north to help fight it, but he'd gone anyway, rounding up a crew of volunteers to take along. They'd fought the fire alongside other firefighters both experienced and green, including several hundred CCC "boys," as they were known, men from all over the country who were now a part of the new Civilian Conservation Corps. One of President Roosevelt's better ideas for coping with the depression, Shea had decided. Many of the men had never even seen big timber before, let alone a wildfire crowning from treetop to treetop, but they'd fought the fire with courage. He might not have come back himself if one lanky farmboy from Kansas hadn't yanked him out of the way of a falling snag.

"You run in and get dressed," Shea told Jessie, "and—"

"No, no," Bonnie interrupted firmly. "You're dead on your feet. You're going to have breakfast and then bed down right here."

Shea didn't argue. He had hotcakes and eggs with Bonnie and her husband, Hank, with lavender-scented Jessie perched on his lap. He took a bath in the Lundford's clawfoot tub, washing out the various bits of debris that had collected in his hair and beard. He then scrubbed furiously to get rid of the embarrassing dark ring of dirt and smoke left in the tub. Afterward Jessie tucked him in bed, proud to be doing for him what he usually did for her.

The drizzly fog had turned to solid rain by the time Shea woke, and he hoped it was pouring just as hard up north to forestall any possible new outbreaks of fire. Bonnie gave him coffee and sandwiches and they talked about what had been happening in Castle Beach during his two weeks away. The sawmill had shut down, but would reopen from time to time to fill orders, if any came in. Elderly Mrs. Siikanen had passed away, and Shea felt bad that he'd missed paying his last respects at her funeral.

"And Rachel was over a couple of times, wondering if we'd heard anything of you," Bonnie added. "I think she was a little hurt that you didn't say goodbye before you left for the fire."

Yes, he should have done that, he admitted guiltily.

"She's a lovely girl, you know, and Jessie is very fond of her." Shea smiled. Rachel was Shea's age, twenty-eight, but any woman younger than herself was a "girl" to matchmaking Bonnie. And friendly little Jessie, as they both knew, liked almost everyone.

"I'll be back to town in a day or two to see her," he promised, and Bonnie nodded approvingly.

Good-hearted Bonnie hadn't held any grudges when he hadn't been able to work up any romantic interest in her niece Elaine, and Elaine had returned to Portland after a few weeks. Then Bonnie had produced pretty Rachel Morgan, the daughter of an old friend. Rachel, a widow with a little girl Jessie's age, had moved up from Brookings and was doing quite well, especially considering the hard economic times, giving music lessons on the piano and violin in her small apartment over Thomason's Drugstore. She also played the organ at church now, occasionally with more spirit than some oldtimers thought appropriate. Shea liked her spirit and had taken her to a church picnic and a few other social events.

"Rachel even took care of Jessie one night when I had a...bad spell," Bonnie said.

"Bad spell?" Shea repeated, alarmed. Bonnie had never mentioned a physical ailment, but he'd noticed she had lost weight recently, and some of the ruddiness had faded from her complexion.

"I've been having these...pains now and again," Bonnie said, something in her tone warning that this was something about which a gentleman should not make too-personal inquiries of a lady. She took a sudden deep breath, as if she hated to say something that must be said. "Shea, I'm not going to be able to keep Jessie after next week. I have to go up to Portland for surgery, and the doctor says I'll not be able to do much for quite a while after that."

"I'm so sorry to hear that. About Jessie, of course, but even more about you! Will everything be all right?"

"I think so. And I doubt there'll be any problem finding someone to take care of Jessie. I'm sure Eunice Williams would be glad to do it, and she could use the money."

He nodded. Someone to care for Jessie truly never had been a real problem. The women of the church had always generously looked out for him and his motherless baby. One of the women who lived out near the cabin had taken care of Jessie until the family moved away; then Mrs. Siikanen had welcomed her, until her arthritis got too bad. After that had come various other good women, some with children, some without. Jessie had always managed to adjust.

But that wasn't the way it should be! His daughter shouldn't have to keep "adjusting," shouldn't be shuffled around from one caretaker to another, always the small outsider.

On the drive home, with Jessie snuggled up beside him and chattering about going "swimming" in a creek with Rachel and Rachel's little daughter, Mira, he came to a decision. There was a logical, practical solution to this problem, and he was going to do it.

The following day, while working around the cabin, Shea was surprised to find cougar tracks behind the woodshed. He occasionally caught a glimpse of cougars when he was out hunting, but they rarely came close to human habitation. Jessie trailed him everywhere he went, interested in everything. Together they checked the small trees he'd transplanted from an overcrowded section of forest to an area he'd logged when they were building the cabin.

In the late afternoon he heated water for baths. He'd laid pipes from a spring to the house to provide running water for faucets and the toilet, but for hot water he still had to crowd pans on top of the wood stove. He dressed carefully in a white shirt and slacks, not the ragged-around-the-ankles "stagged" pants he wore for work, and trimmed a few straggly curls from his beard. He dressed Jessie in a little pink dress Rachel had made for her.

As soon as he parked the truck in front of Thomason's Drugstore, Rachel flew down the outside stairs to meet him. She was tall and willowy, with a flashing smile and dark hair cut in a sleek cap, the kind of woman who invariably drew second looks.

"Shea! I'm so glad to see you!" Without recriminations for his not saying goodbye before he left, she threw her arms around him in a vivacious welcome.

An openly affectionate, good-humored woman. He liked that. She knelt to add a hug for Jessie, and he liked that, too. He gave Jessie a friendly swat on the bottom to send her upstairs to meet little Mira, who was wearing a blue version of the dress.

Rachel was an accomplished seamstress as well as music teacher.

She linked her arm in his. "I talked to Bonnie, and I was hoping you'd come in this evening. I put on a roast and made apple cobbler. You must be exhausted after fighting fires for two weeks." She tilted her head to press it briefly against his shoulder.

The small apartment, which Rachel had made cozy with pillows and dried flowers and braided throw rugs, smelled of rich pot roast and apples and cinnamon, plus Rachel's own subtle scent of jasmine cologne. He liked all that, too.

After the meal, they strolled down to the city park and listened to the veterans' band play a rousing trio of marches, Rachel wincing only slightly when the trombone hit an off note. They stopped for ice creams on the stroll home, Rachel playfully offering him a lick of her black walnut in exchange for a bite of his chocolate. Her eyes shone with a warm affection when they met his over the cone.

Back at the apartment, Shea settled uneasily on the sofa. A nice porch swing would be the appropriate place for this, he thought, but Rachel had neither porch nor swing. The outside steps, then, away from the girls, who, he had discovered, tended to be listening to adult conversations even when they appeared to be engrossed elsewhere. At the moment they were playing with teddy bears and dolls.

He took Rachel's hand and led her outside. The rain had stopped at midday, and the air smelled clean and sweet. They leaned against the weathered wooden railing on the landing. A bit of the harbor was visible from here, a fishing boat just crossing the bar.

"Rachel—"

"Yes, Shea?" Her tone was encouraging, as if she knew what was coming.

"Rachel, I—" He paused and swallowed.

She slipped her slim-fingered hand under his and entwined her fingers with his. "Yes, Shea?"

"Rachel, I'd like to—" Another pause. He ran his fingers, the ones Rachel wasn't holding, through his thick hair. This was more difficult than he'd expected. But he had gotten four words out this time, and that was progress. Now all he had to do was get the rest of them out. He mentally rehearsed the lines he wanted to say. *I love you, Rachel. I want to marry you. Will you marry me?* Yet the words stalled in his mind like some recalcitrant Model-T hub-deep in mud.

What words were moving in his mind? In dismay, he saw them pop up like tin targets in a shooting gallery. *Rachel, I want to be in love with you, but I'm not. Rachel, I wish I wanted to marry you, but I just don't.*

"Is something wrong?"

Shea sighed; he just couldn't do this. He liked Rachel. He liked her cooking and her jasmine fragrance; he liked her fondness for Jessie and he liked her daughter, Mira; he liked her spirited organ playing at church. He needed a mother for Jessie, and Rachel would surely make a fine one.

But he didn't love her, and he couldn't make a mockery of the Lord's sacred joining together of husband and wife by marrying Rachel on the basis of a vague liking and a hurried need for a caretaker for Jessie. Saying goodbye to her before he left to fight the fire hadn't occurred to him; he hadn't even thought about her. Nor had she crossed his mind more than a few times during the entire two weeks on the firelines. Those were not, he thought unhappily, the actions or thoughts of a man in love, a man eager to make a woman his wife. Marrying her wouldn't be fair to any of them.

"I just wanted to tell you...what a fine dinner that was, Rachel. A fine dinner," he repeated enthusiastically. A trifle too enthusiastically, he thought guiltily.

"Thank you." If Rachel had an organ to crash on a discordant note, she would, he suspected, have crashed it at that moment. A compliment about her dinner was not what she had expected.

"I'm sorry," he said with uncharacteristic helplessness. He didn't have to explain what he was sorry about; she knew.

"Yes, I am too. Is the problem that I...don't measure up to Molly's memory?"

He started to shake his head but paused, considering. Was he, somewhere deep inside, holding Molly's memory on some unreachable pedestal that no other woman could possibly attain? No, he'd loved Molly and a part of him always would, but he'd let her go; he'd made that turn from past to future.

He completed the shake of his head and, with no doubt about the genuine honesty of his words, said, "No, it isn't that. It's just that there's no..." His sentence trailed off helplessly. No what?

With empathy and regret and even a small, surprising touch of wry humor, Rachel supplied a word. "No spark?"

That was it. No spark. Just as there had been no spark with Elaine Wiseman or the other women in whom he'd taken a tentative interest.

"I'm sorry," he said again. He didn't want to say anything unkind or hurtful to Rachel; she didn't deserve that. Yet at the same time he felt an almost embarrassingly giddy sense of relief that this hadn't gone any farther.

"I suppose now is when I'm supposed to be a good sport and say I hope that someday a wonderful woman you can love will come along for you." She inspected him critically, as she might the hands of a pupil arriving for a piano lesson. "Because I think you are capable of very great love indeed. But I'm not that good a sport."

He grinned. "Yes, you are."

She sighed, but her mouth quirked in a rueful smile. "A dish of apple cobbler?"

"Thanks, but...well, I guess not." Impulsively he leaned over and kissed her lightly on the forehead, a kiss they both knew meant goodbye. "One of these days a man will come along who loves you the way you deserve to be loved."

She smiled again, a bit more sadly this time.

He retrieved a sleepy Jessie, and as they drove the silent, deserted mountain road home, he felt sorry things couldn't have worked out differently with Rachel, sorry that Jessie would have to adjust to yet another caretaker. And yet the sense of relief that he'd barely avoided some catastrophic mistake was greater than either sorrow.

It was quite possible, he realized with a feeling that was as much resignation as regret, that he'd never feel the spark that led to the flame of love again.

Eight

❧

September 1933
Gideon, Indiana

After a sleepless night of wrestling with the idea of moving to the lodge in Oregon, Rosalyn presented the possibility to her mother the following morning when she served her a cup of tea in bed.

The suggestion was apparently so startling that it momentarily evaporated the apathy that usually engulfed Ellen these days. She jerked upright and looked at her daughter as if Rosalyn had just suggested paddling across the Atlantic in a rowboat.

"The two of us leave here? Move to Oregon?"

"Yes. And live in father's hunting lodge."

For a moment Ellen looked as if she might rise up in protest, but then she settled back against her pillow, her brief spark of interest quickly dying. "Whatever you think best, dear," she murmured. She patted her daughter's arm gently. "I'm sorry. Nothing seems to matter much any more. Whatever you decide is fine with me."

Rosalyn put in two more days of job hunting, but all she got for her efforts was a glimpse of Charlie trying on a pair of frivolous dancing shoes at a downtown store.

That day, after she got home from an hour of cleanup at the soup kitchen, she called a dealer to come look at the furniture. The offer was discouragingly low; too many people were selling out in these hard times. But Rosalyn thought it was enough to get them to Oregon, and, if they were very careful, sustain them for a month or two.

And then what?

Bit by bit, other ideas came to her. It was a hunting lodge; they could take in guests during hunting season as a source of income. They could plant a garden and raise chickens. She carefully detoured the undermining thought that this was all as unfamiliar to both her and Ellen as setting up housekeeping on the moon. There were also the trees; she remembered her father speaking lovingly of the magnificent forest. But he would understand if they must log some of the trees to survive. The Lord knew how to grow more trees!

Rosalyn accepted the dealer's offer; his trucks would arrive in a week. She started her mother sorting through personal belongings, warning that space in the pickup was very limited. She told Frank Lassiter about their plans and gave him a forwarding address of General Delivery in Castle Beach, Oregon. He was shocked. No, more than shocked. He was obviously appalled at what he considered a reckless leap to the edges of civilization. But he had no better solution to offer.

Rosalyn resolutely pulled a curtain over all thoughts of Robbie. She donated clothing to a charity, her father's books to a school, and the food they couldn't carry with them to the soup kitchen. She sold some glassware and the good silverware. She took what company records Mr. Lassiter thought should be preserved to his office and destroyed the remainder. Geoffrey gave her a hasty course in care and feeding of the pickup, and her mind whirled with spark plugs, oil changes, and overheated radiators. She had occasional moments of wild doubt, moments when what she was doing hit her like an electric shock, stunning her into a frozen statue. How could they simply launch themselves into the unknown like this?

With the Lord's help, that's how!

The day before the trucks were to arrive, Rosalyn put in her final hours at the soup kitchen. Once more her heart ached for all the hurting, discouraged people shuffling through the line. Near the end she spotted the dark-haired, ragged boy again. He was sidling along trying to blend in as part of a large family. With a notable lack of success, however, because they were all tow-headed Scandinavians.

Rosalyn waited until he gulped his meal and intercepted him as he headed, alone, for the door. "Hi. I'm Rosalyn. Who are you?"

"None of your business." He tried to dart away, but Rosalyn grabbed his shirt collar and held on. "Lemme go!"

"Look, I want to help. I see you first with one family and then another. The truth is, you don't have any family, do you?" A yank to test her hold was the only answer. "Where do you live?"

"None of your business."

"I'll buy you an ice cream cone, and we'll talk about it, okay?" Rosalyn dragged her unwilling captive to a nearby soda fountain and pried out a name, Benjamin J. Harkanson—athough he said with a shy smile that he preferred B. J.—and an appalling story about his parents splitting up, his mother taking up with another man, and B. J. running away after the man beat him for knocking over a bottle of whiskey. He'd been trying to make it appear he belonged with a family because he was terrified of being picked up by the police and put in a "home." The stepfather had told him sadistic tales of what happened in such places and threatened to send him there. He'd rather live in his culvert under the highway, B. J. said, even if rats did run across his blankets at night. He reluctantly admitted that he had grandparents

85

in Tennessee, but he'd never met them and was as suspicious of them as of some institutional "home."

Rosalyn hesitated. She still had so much sorting and packing to do. The practical thing would be to turn B. J. over to the proper authorities and let them locate his grandparents.

She also knew she couldn't do that. B. J. would bolt and run from anyone who looked even marginally official. She took him home with her and started trying by telephone to locate the grandparents in a town with a "funny-sounding name" in Tennessee. By bedtime she'd still had no success, but gave B. J. the guest room, which rather awed him, and another hearty meal.

The next morning, Ellen was surprisingly helpful, gaily setting up an old croquet set on the front lawn and keeping B. J. busy with a lively game while Rosalyn, amidst the flurry of furniture removal, continued her phone search. Absentmindedly she noted the pieces as they were hauled out...her four poster bed....the console radio...her father's oak desk. Once she'd have been stricken, but now they were just things, already emotionally dismissed. Around noon she finally located the Harkansons in Chattanooga, Tennessee, and with relief found they were overjoyed with news of B. J.'s whereabouts. And of course he could live with them.

"Wonderful. I'll send him by bus—" Rosalyn broke off as B. J. paused on a dash to the kitchen, his dark eyes locked on hers. He'd never reach Chattanooga by bus; he halfway suspected even now that all this was just some trick to dump him in a "home." She saw only one solution. Not a convenient one.

She could almost hear Robbie and Charlie's scornful comments about putting herself out for a homeless boy when she was close to homeless herself. "You have to look out for yourself first when times are tough," Robbie had said.

No. When times were tough was exactly when you had to look out for each other.

"We'll bring him," she said firmly to the grandparents.

So all that remained now was to load the pickup, sweep the house clean, and be on their way.

No, one more problem. In dismay Rosalyn surveyed the astonishing mountain of belongings that remained in Ellen's bedroom after the dealer's workmen had gone. She opened a box and saw the set of delicate, gold-rimmed dishes that had been a wedding gift from Ellen's mother. There were cartons of Rosalyn's baby clothes and old dolls, letters, photograph albums, scrapbooks, diaries, mementos of family trips to Florida and Europe. Even the wedding dress both Ellen and her mother before her had worn, the white satin now mellowed to a candlelight sheen.

Nothing of great monetary value…and yet irreplaceable treasures. All that was left of life as Ellen had known it.

"One box," Rosalyn said finally. She hated herself even as she said it, one more harsh, unfeeling person snatching something Ellen treasured. But the pickup, even with the wooden sides Geoffrey had built, would never hold all of it. They had to concentrate on necessities for setting up housekeeping two thousand miles away. "One box is all we can take."

Ellen didn't argue, and, in the end, Rosalyn didn't know what went into that one heavy wooden box they loaded into the pickup. She didn't really want to know, because she, too, mourned the loss of all those irreplaceable accumulations of a lifetime.

She made room in the load for one item that she didn't mention to her mother: her father's hunting rifle. It was not a sentimental decision, however. Although she'd never fired a shot in her life, their destination was a hunting lodge. And if she had to, she thought resolutely, she'd learn to hunt to provide for their needs.

They visited Oliver's gravesite one last time and set a vase of roses, the very last Geoffrey had coaxed from the bushes at home, on the still-fresh mound. Yet, even as the tears fell, she didn't feel despondent about moving so far from this spot. Her father's body was there, but he was not. He was with his Lord.

And so, on a brilliant, frosty morning in October, Rosalyn locked the door one last time and squeezed into the pickup cab with her mother and B. J. She sat there briefly, saying goodbye to the home she had always known, the life she had always known. At that moment she was painfully aware how sheltered that existence had been, how basically ill-equipped she was for the venture ahead.

Then she resolutely started the engine and let out the brake. An unexpected spirit of adventure and exhilaration surged through her.

Oregon—after a small detour through Tennessee—here we come!

Nine

❧

September 1933
Logging camp outside Castle Beach, Oregon

At a hundred feet in the air, Shea paused to catch his breath, leaning back to brace himself against the wire-cored rope that encircled the bare trunk of the tree. He breathed deeply, inhaling the scents of bark and warm pitch and feeling the heat of the sun and the good trickle of sweat on his back and chest.

Overhead a hawk circled lazily; he saw it almost every day. For no particular reason he grinned and waved at it. To the east the ridge broke off sharply, slanting in a steep jumble of loose rocks and trees to a creek far below, its twisting curves and white-water rapids like a ragged blue snake hiding in the trees. To the west, the shaggy green carpet of treetops sloped gently, and on this glorious morning he could see all the way to the gleaming silver-blue ocean in the distance. Over the hill, cables screeched as the steam donkey lifted a log from where it had been felled to the pile that would eventually be turned into lumber at a sawmill. The thunder of a crashing tree shook the ground; Shea felt the vibration through his metal climbing spurs spiked deep into the tree's bark.

Many men would rather eat nails than tackle this high-altitude job, but Shea liked the exhilarating climb and eagle's-eye view.

And he much preferred this work to standing on a springboard and working the "misery whip," the two-man crosscut saw used to fell the trees.

Breathing slowed, he started upward again. At a hundred and fifty feet he reached the first limbs and chopped them off flush with the ax he carried attached to his climbing belt. Thirty feet higher he chopped the undercut in the trunk, then pulled up his saw to do the backcut. As the forty foot top began to topple, he braced himself for the inevitable reaction. It came, a reeling, punishing, wilder-than-any-roller-coaster ride as the trunk whipped in a frenzied, twenty-foot arc. Now, as always, were the few wild seconds when he closed his eyes and dizzily wondered what had made him decide to be a high-rigger. No longer did the tree trunk stand straight and solid; now it flexed and bent like some powerful spring. Rushing air roared in his ears as gravity spun out of control. He feared he'd be catapulted into space, flung to earth, crushed between rope and tree—! He dug his spurs in deeper, clutched the rope harder. Exhilaration replaced the dizziness, and he rode the whipping, bucking whirlwind to fierce victory.

A few minutes later he was fifteen feet below the sawed-off top, now a "spar pole," calmly chopping away the bark to clear a space to hang the rigging for the cables that would be used to move the logs.

When the whistle shrieked for the midday meal, Shea took the fast route down the tree, letting himself drop ten or fifteen feet at a time before briefly breaking his fall with spurs, looping the rope downward. As usual, conversation was limited as the men gulped their lunches. Shea had just started back to the ridge when he heard Lester Wiggins, the woods boss, tell the scaler to do a rough estimate of the timber on the steep side of the slope. He was appalled.

He waited until Lester was alone before protesting, "Surely

you're not planning to take the timber on that east side."

"Yes, I surely am," Lester mimicked snidely. He was a short, rather wide man, and he surreptitiously moved to higher ground so Shea wouldn't tower over him. "No point letting it go to waste."

"Leaving it isn't wasting it! Those trees are holding that slope intact! If the timber is cut, and we tear the ground up getting the logs out, that whole hillside is going to erode into the creek. There isn't really enough timber there to bother with anyway, and half of what is there will wind up in the creek."

"And I suppose you're worried about all the little fishies in the creek, too, aren't you?" Lester said with mock solicitousness.

Shea gritted his teeth. "It's a spawning area. But it won't be if it's filled with dirt and debris."

"Well, I know that's how you fancy college boys think with all your book learning. If it were up to you, there'd have to be a committee meeting before we cut every tree and a feather bed for it to fall on."

Shea clenched his fists. It was not the first time Lester had taken a dig at his education. Nor was it the first time they had squared off on opposite sides of a disagreement. Lester, of the rough, grab-all-you-can-and-get-out school of logging, thought Shea's ideas about selective cutting, stream preservation, and reforestation were frivolous nonsense. Only an overruling by the company owner had kept Lester from firing Shea when he took off to fight the Tillamook forest fire. Let 'er burn, was Lester's philosophy. They're just trees and there's always more of 'em.

But Lester was woods boss, and the company owner was up in Seattle now, so it was Lester's opinions, not Shea's, that mattered here. *Shut up, Donahue,* Shea muttered to himself. *You need this job, and talking to Lester doesn't do any more good than yelling at a tree stump. Maybe less.* And there was a mean glint in Lester's little eyes that said he'd like nothing better than firing Shea on this fine day. Silently Shea turned and stalked off.

"Hey, Donahue," Lester yelled. Shea turned and Lester motioned to a big, blond logger everyone called Swede. "I've changed my mind," Lester said. Shea eyed him warily. Was it possible something had actually penetrated that stubborn skull? Then Lester grinned maliciously. "We won't bother scaling that east slope. Swede, you, and Carl just start cutting there this afternoon."

The slope was so steep that the two men had to tie a grab-rope to a tree on the ridge and hold on to it to work their way down to the timber. From his perch on the spar pole Shea could hear their voices occasionally and sometimes a squawk as the saw hung up. A crash came a couple hours later. Shea paused. It wasn't a big enough crash to be a falling tree.

A moment later he heard a call for help. He plunged down the spar pole in record time, pausing at the bottom only long enough to strip off the big spurs and climbing belt. He followed the rope down the slope, slipping and sliding on the loose rock.

Swede lay on the ground, his partner frantically trying to drag away a massive dead branch, a "widow maker" that had crashed down from another tree. Shea added his muscle, and together they freed Swede. A gouge over his left eye showed why he was unconscious, but it was the blood spurting from his gashed left arm that frightened Shea. Frantically he grabbed his handkerchief and used a stick to twist it into a tourniquet above the elbow.

He looked down at the unconscious man and hesitated. He knew all the good advice about not moving an injured man. He also knew Swede would die here if he weren't moved. Medical help was miles away.

Together he and Carl, slipping and sliding, got the limp man to the top of the ridge. They caught their breath after the hard climb and then carried him on to the landing where logs were piled. Lester came over and frowned at the blood-covered figure.

"What happened to him?" Lester asked, and Carl explained. "Well, lay him over there in the shade. Someone can drive him into town this evening if he needs a doctor."

"What do you mean, if he needs a doctor?" Shea exploded. "The man is unconscious. He's spurting blood from an artery! He can't wait until tonight to see a doctor."

"We aren't losing time just because some dumb Swede got himself hit on the head. Never knew a Swede yet whose head wasn't harder than any log," Lester tossed carelessly over his shoulder as he walked away.

Shea supposed he shouldn't be surprised at this callous attitude. It was common practice that if a man got killed in the woods, his body just lay there until the workday was over. Accidents got much the same treatment. He hesitated. The head wound might or might not be serious. But that tourniquet couldn't stay on all afternoon. He'd lose his arm.

"I'm taking him to a doctor," Shea said.

"Yeah? Somebody all of a sudden made you boss?" Lester challenged.

Shea didn't answer. He looked to Carl for help carrying Swede down to camp, but Carl, with a nervous shake of head, backed off. He had a big family to support.

Okay, so he'd do it alone. He might give in where a tree was concerned, but not when a man's life was involved. He leaned down and hoisted Swede over his shoulder like a sack of beans. Again, he knew this was no way to treat an injured man. But neither was leaving him unattended on the ground for hours with a tourniquet around his arm.

"What'd'ya think you're doing, Donahue?" Lester roared.

Swede had to weigh almost as much as he did. "I told you. I'm taking him to camp. I'm putting him in my truck. Then I'm hauling him to a doctor."

"You got work to do, Donahue."

Shea just started walking, trying not to stagger under the dead-weight burden.

"You leave here now, Donahue," Lester warned, "and you can just keep on going."

Shea half-turned. "You're firing me?"

"Another step and you are fired."

Shea took that step. And another and another. He was weak in the knees and shaky by the time he finally draped Swede in the seat of the truck. By then the man was groggily aware of what was going on. Shea drove the long miles to Castle Beach in a conflict over wanting to get to the doctor as fast as possible but knowing every bump jarred Swede like another blow to the head.

It was after dark by the time Shea returned to camp to pick up his belongings. The doctor had patched up Swede's arm and thought he could save it, although he probably wouldn't have been able to, he said, if that tourniquet had been on there all day. Shea went to the timekeeper and picked up the wages he had coming.

He then drove away from the camp again. He was in no way sorry he'd done what he had, but that didn't change the fact that he was now unemployed. Now what? There was only one logging outfit still working within a hundred miles, and it was only working its men half-time, two crews working alternating weeks. And they probably had ten times as many job applicants as they had jobs.

When he fought the Tillamook forest fire with the CCC boys, he'd talked with a supervisor about the possibility of getting on as an instructor or leader with the forestry work. The supervisor had sounded encouraging, but Shea hadn't heard anything more. Government programs came and went; maybe this one was already on its way out. Perhaps, he reflected, it was time to re-think his determination to stay here. He still had family back in Michigan. Maybe it was time to pack up Jessie and move on.

October 1933
On the road!

N ow they were truly on their way.

B. J. was safely delivered into the welcoming arms of his grandparents, and Rosalyn knew that even B. J. could see what good people they were. Grandma Harkanson's kitchen— and Grandma herself—smelled deliciously of vanilla and cinnamon, and Grandpa Harkanson knew how to carve a hunk of wood into a whistle. When Rosalyn saw the well-worn Bible beside a rocking chair in the living room, she knew B. J. was in good hands.

They sailed like kings of the road across Tennessee and Missouri, spending nights in cheap, small-town hotels. But it was too soon for Rosalyn to enjoy the sense of adventure and freedom, not with her mother's withdrawal and indifference, not with the loss of her father and the haunting thought that he might have killed himself. And not with the betrayal of love and friendship that still ravaged her heart.

Often, when something especially reminded her of Robbie— a marquee, blazing the name of a movie they'd seen together, or the sight of a young couple gazing at each other adoringly—she felt an almost breathless jolt of anguish. Painfully she pictured

Robbie and Charlie together in their lovely new home on Winston Street, smiling and happy. Did they laugh at her? Pity her? Feel an occasional twinge of guilt? Or, in their self-centered enjoyment of their carefree life of golfing and dancing and parties, did they even think of her at all?

Yet, paradoxically, it was also impossible not to feel a growing sense of anticipation when she woke each morning wondering what new adventures the day would bring. Not so long ago she'd thought she might like to see Oregon. These were far from the circumstances she'd have preferred. But she was going to see Oregon! And every mile on the road took her farther from the pain of the past.

They were not the only travelers in these hard times, Rosalyn quickly discovered. Often she saw battered trucks loaded with belongings, or cars with boxes tied to running boards and mattresses flapping on top. Once she gave a ride to a desperate-looking young couple, but their perch on top the loaded pickup was so precarious that she didn't dare do it again.

Rosalyn's twentieth birthday arrived somewhere in eastern Kansas, unfortunately marked by a wrong turn as they left a small town. They wandered most of the day in what seemed an endless flatland maze of arrow-straight roads. Rosalyn kept driving, however, hating to waste time and gasoline returning to the point where she had gone astray. Eventually, worried that if they didn't turn back they'd be caught out on the prairie after dark, she pulled into the yard of an abandoned farmhouse to turn around.

A big dog of no determinate breed, with backbone and ribs showing through the tangled knots of its tan-brown hair, slunk around a corner to look at them, tail wagging. Rosalyn hesitated. They had enough problems without taking on some homeless, hungry creature. But she couldn't just leave it there, obviously starving. Grumbling to herself about her own softheartedness, she fed it most of a loaf of bread and rearranged the load to make a space for it just inside the tailgate. She'd give the poor thing to some good home as soon as they reached town.

That, of course, turned out to be like trying to give away a case of warts, and by the end of the day they were still in the town they'd passed through earlier, only now they had the addition of one bedraggled dog with a peculiar habit of pulling back her lips as if trying to smile.

After the wasted day spent wandering on miles of dusty Kansas roads, plus wrestling the dog in and out of the pickup several times, Rosalyn felt grumpy, hair-covered, and dirty. When they reached the Oregon lodge, she vowed, she was going to crawl in the bathtub and not get out for a week.

"This is just temporary, you know," Rosalyn warned as she fed the dog some of their supper leftovers. "Tomorrow we'll find you a home. We don't have room for hitchhikers."

The dog smiled and wagged its tail.

They were in Colorado, with the jagged, silver line of snow-capped mountains glittering ever larger on the western horizon, the dog still in the back of the pickup, when they zipped past a lonely figure standing beside the road. A girl, Rosalyn realized as the young woman lifted her hand to thumb a ride. What was she doing all alone out here? The girl had a suitcase at her feet and a bundle strapped to her back, but there was no house, no car, nothing to indicate how she had arrived at this desolate place.

She was probably just waiting for a friend or relative to pick her up, Rosalyn assured herself. No need to stop. They were already running late on the schedule she'd planned for reaching Oregon, and the cramped pickup cab certainly wasn't large enough to add a third person.

Yet if the girl was all alone, stranded and desperate, they couldn't just ignore her.

Rosalyn sighed, braked at the next wide spot, and turned around.

Ellen rolled down the window as the pickup pulled up beside the girl. She looked no more than sixteen or seventeen, a small-boned girl with a freckled pixie face and sandy hair, probably pretty if she weren't so wan and weary looking. The bundle on her back unexpectedly moved.

Rosalyn's jaw dropped in astonishment. "Is that a baby?"

"Yes."

"Yours?"

"Yes." The girl's blue eyes stared at them with wary suspicion, as if she were prepared to protect her baby no matter what the odds. "Are you waiting for someone?"

"No. I need a ride."

Rosalyn peered past the girl at the barren landscape of skimpy grass and scrubby brush. "How did you get here?"

"A man gave me a ride from St. Louis." She put a hand on the window frame, her grip making pale marbles of her cold knuckles. "He...wanted me to do some things. I wouldn't, and he dumped me out here."

"You shouldn't accept rides with strange men!"

"I know. But I have to get to Twin Falls, Idaho. My husband's got kin there." Desperation flooded the girl's voice. "We've nowhere else to go."

"Where is your husband?"

"He lost his job in St. Louis and went to find work in California. When the rent came due I couldn't pay. They kicked us out."

"How long has he been gone?"

"A while." She hesitated and added reluctantly, "A month or so."

"You've never heard from him?" What kind of man went off and left his wife and baby stranded and penniless?

"No. But I figure he'll know to look for us with his people in Idaho, because we talked some about moving there." The girl glanced at the load. "I could ride in back. I don't mind."

Rosalyn felt a sinking sense of dismay. First a stray dog, which, in spite of several efforts, she had not yet been able to give away. Now a stray girl. And a baby.

"We can't take you all the way to Twin Falls," she said firmly. No, definitely not. She vaguely remembered seeing the name on the map, and it was not on the route she had planned. "But we can give you a lift to the next town."

"Okay."

"But you're not going to ride in back with that baby," Ellen said indignantly, the first flare of emotion she'd shown in a long time. "You'll both catch your death of cold."

Ellen stepped outside and held out her arms for the baby. The girl hesitated briefly but then granted Ellen her trust and slipped the straps of the makeshift carrier off her shoulders. Rosalyn got out and wrestled the girl's suitcase onto the load.

The young woman's slight build didn't take up much space, and neither Rosalyn nor Ellen were large women, but the three of them plus the baby filled the cab like the dolls stuffed into Rosalyn's closet when she was a child. Rosalyn had to scrunch her elbows into her ribs to keep from jabbing the girl, whose name they learned was Nadine Bailey. The baby was Andy, short for Andrew Patrick Bailey, Jr., age six and a half months. Free of the confining carrier, Andy turned out to be a squirmy, inquisitive handful.

Soon, however, Nadine's eyelids sagged and she fell asleep

with her head on Rosalyn's shoulder. Minutes later the baby was sleeping peacefully in Ellen's arms.

Over their passengers' heads, Rosalyn's eyes met her mother's with a certain helplessness. Now what? If they dropped Nadine off in the next town, she might wind up in an automobile with a man who would do worse than dump her in some isolated spot.

As it turned out, the next town, where they spent the night, was not a place Rosalyn's conscience would allow her to abandon anyone. It consisted solely of a gas station, auto court, and tavern/cafe, a place that, if it had a name, wasn't proud enough to reveal it. The cabin had only one double bed, but the owner grudgingly hauled in an extra cot. Rosalyn felt grimy and depressed as they trudged back to the ramshackle cabin after hamburgers at the grease-fogged cafe, but Nadine seemed cheerful.

"What's the dog's name?" she asked as she breast-fed the baby before putting him down for the night. The dog lay curled at Rosalyn's feet. A cutting wind rattled the windows, and the night was much too cold to leave her in the pickup.

"She doesn't have one." Rosalyn had, in fact, carefully refrained from calling the dog anything, uneasily suspicious that conferring a name somehow implied ownership.

"You could call her Smiley," Nadine suggested. "Because she always looks like she's trying to smile."

Rosalyn had no intention of doing so, but an idea suddenly occurred to her. If the dog wasn't so scruffy looking—and so doggy smelling—perhaps she would be easier to give away!

Improving the dog's appearance started out as a simple enough project. She didn't object when Rosalyn whacked out the tangled knots with scissors, and she liked being combed. But she definitely did not think much of being held in the old tin shower, drenched in the chilly spray, and soaped up. Within seconds Rosalyn was as wet and soapy as the squirmy dog, and moments later the shaggy, sopping creature slithered out of her arms and dashed around the room, pausing only to shake suds and drops everywhere.

Nadine, who had tucked the baby in bed, said, "I'll get her!" and made a dive for the dog.

The dog saw a path of escape, between Nadine's legs, and took it. Nadine sprawled on the floor, upended and soapy.

The dog sat on her haunches and grinned cheerfully, obviously considering this a great game. Rosalyn scooped a wet strand of hair out of her eyes and determinedly marched toward the animal. The dog responded with a flying leap into what apparently looked like a safe haven, Ellen's lap.

Rosalyn looked at the strange scene in astonished dismay. Her genteel, delicate mother, accustomed to fine furniture and an orderly life, now sitting in a ragged, overstuffed chair with one large, wet, soapy dog practically smothering her.

"Oh, Mother, I'm so sorry!" Frantically, Rosalyn tried to get the hairy mass of wet dog off her mother.

But instead of helping, Ellen unexpectedly started laughing, and then Rosalyn and Nadine were chuckling too, and the dog was smiling. Once they started they couldn't seem to stop. Nadine pointed to a smear of suds on Rosalyn's face and laughed. Rosalyn pointed to Nadine's undignified position on the floor and laughed. Ellen wrapped her arms around the dog and put her cheek against a wet ear and laughed.

And Smiley, Rosalyn knew with resignation, had a home.

Later, after Smiley was rinsed and dried and the mess cleaned up, Rosalyn spread her frayed map of the western United States under the room's single bare bulb. The trip would take longer, she finally concluded, and the road across eastern Oregon appeared a bit doubtful, but, yes, they could reach Oregon by way of Twin Falls, Idaho.

They crossed the glistening mountains and swept past the Great Salt Lake in Utah. They were cramped so tightly in the pickup cab that they joked they had to take turns breathing, but a small bonus was that Nadine occasionally could relieve Rosalyn at the wheel.

On the outskirts of Twin Falls, Nadine produced a tattered envelope with the name and address of her husband's relatives. Rufus Bailey, 2715 Union Street. They got directions at a gas station and found Union Street in an area of dilapidated houses with straggly fences. Cans and trash littered the yard at 2715.

"I'm sure they're good folks, just poor like us," Nadine said hopefully, although Rosalyn had her doubts.

"I'll go with you," she said after retrieving Nadine's suitcase from the load. Smiley went too, growling warningly at another dog as she walked stiff-legged beside Rosalyn to the drooping gate.

A man in dark pants, suspenders dangling around his hips, answered Rosalyn's knock. "Yeah?" he growled through the ragged screen door.

"I'm Nadine, Andrew's wife," Nadine said quickly. She lifted the baby to eye level. "This is Andy's son, Andrew Patrick Bailey, Jr."

"So?"

"Don't you remember? You invited us to come visit when your wife wrote last Christmas?" Nadine's voice turned squeaky with panic.

Rosalyn looked at the scrap of paper again. "You are Rufus Bailey, aren't you?"

"Nope. The Baileys used ta live here, but they don't no more." He banged the door closed in their faces.

Rosalyn, surprised by the unexpected rudeness, indignantly

pounded until the door opened again. "Where did the Baileys go?"

"I dunno. Landlady might know. Three doors down." He jerked a grease-blackened thumb to the left.

Three doors down they found the henna-haired landlady. She didn't know where the Baileys had gone. "But they must of left town. They wouldn't dare stick around, owin' everybody like they did. Worthless no accounts, that's what they were," she added with surly venom.

Nadine's slender shoulders sagged, and Rosalyn reached for the husky baby that suddenly looked too heavy for his mother's arms. The door closed, and Nadine twisted the thread-thin golden band on her left hand.

"I've just been fooling myself," she said bitterly. "Andrew didn't leave just to look for work in California. He left us. He's just like these Baileys here, no good, no account."

"Oh, Nadine—"

"I've been too scared to let myself admit it, but that's what he done." Rosalyn didn't know what to say, because this had been her awful suspicion from the start. Nadine lifted despairing blue eyes to Rosalyn's. "What am I going to do?"

Rosalyn shook her head helplessly. A girl and baby alone, what could they do?

Then a dismaying thought struck her. *Oh, no, Lord,* Rosalyn protested vehemently. She'd gone hundreds of miles out of her way to find a boy a home; she'd accepted the stray dog. But not this. There must be another way. She had too many problems and responsibilities already. *Surely, Lord, you don't expect me to take care of a stranger and her baby.*

The baby bounced in Rosalyn's arms and gurgled and smiled as he flailed a fist toward Smiley's outstretched nose.

Yes, she knew with a feeling like an iron ball plunging to hit bottom in her stomach, that was exactly what the Lord expected.

For long moments she looked despairingly at the pickup and its load, the canvas tattered and flapping now. She thought about the little money they had and the problems they still faced.

Then she thought about being alone and abandoned, with nowhere to go and no one to turn to. She thought about how the Lord had given them a place of refuge in Oregon. With all the confidence she could muster she said, "You're coming with us."

"Oh, I couldn't do that! You're not kin. You hardly even know me!" Rosalyn handed the baby back to Nadine and patted her shoulder. "We'll manage." *We will manage, won't we, Lord?* she added silently.

So onward they went. The endless miles of sagebrush and rocks in eastern Oregon surprised Rosalyn. This dry and barren land was not the lush countryside she had expected! But eventually they did reach the forests and mountains: trees so thick the road cut like a narrow canyon between them, the green on either side an impenetrable wall reaching so high she had to crane her head to see the stately treetops. And often she couldn't even see their crowns, because the branches met in a tangled canopy overhead. There was a magnificent timelessness to the forest, a peaceful dignity, an assurance that only God could create something so majestic.

They saw deer, once a proud buck with antlers like some barbarian king's headdress. A bear, black and shiny, scooted across the road, and birds swooped and sang.

There were no roads directly across the state to Castle Beach. They had to travel up the coast on a winding and precarious road. More than once Rosalyn clutched the steering wheel, well aware that misjudging just a few inches could send them plunging into the wild surf below. Yet their spirits remained high; Rosalyn found herself singing "Blessed Assurance" and

"Heavenly Sunshine," and Nadine kept time by clapping the baby's hands together.

Then the rain began. It started as a misty drizzle, clouds dropping to conceal the mountains crowding the road on one side and the roaring sea on the other. The drizzle turned to a silver-gray curtain, and then to a windswept downpour. Passing vehicles shot blinding fountains of spray across the windshield. The windows steamed from the warmth of their breath, and from time to time Rosalyn swiped her sleeve across the fogged-up glass to see the road. Wind tore one side of the tarp loose, and by the time she and Nadine got it retied both they and the load were soaked.

In spite of its rather grand sounding name, Castle Beach, when they reached it about midafternoon, did nothing to lift Rosalyn's wet spirits. Weatherbeaten, unpainted buildings flanked a harbor with a few boats, and mixed scents of ocean and fish and fresh-cut lumber and woodsmoke hung in the air. Tangled piles of green-brown seaweed littered the beach. The few vehicles on the street resembled their own pickup, tired and battered. The kind of place, Rosalyn thought with a certain grim amusement, in which Charlie would "die" if she had to live.

She stopped at a gas station to fill the tank and ask directions. The older man studied her map and, with an abundance of hand gestures, outlined a route for her.

"Pretty wild country out there," he added dubiously as he eyed the motly trio and baby. "Ain't nobody much lives out that way."

The man looked honest and trustworthy enough, but Rosalyn quickly decided that letting everyone know three women and a baby were going to be living out there alone probably wasn't a good idea. So all she said was a vague, "Thanks. You've been very helpful."

They passed an occasional house after turning inland, but a

cluster of buildings beside a creek seemed to mark the end of civilization because there were no more after that. The country grew ever wilder and the road rougher, winding around hills and rocky outcroppings, rising to crest a hill or ridge, dipping to cross a steep valley or rough canyon. The rain continued to fall. No, it didn't just fall, Rosalyn thought unhappily, it hammered the earth in angry assault.

She slowed the pickup, puzzled, as the thick, lush forest through which they had been passing suddenly vanished. It looked as if some tree-eating monster had chomped great bites from the woods, carelessly trampling what it did not eat. What in the world, she wondered, appalled, had happened here? Everything looked wounded. Old trees, trunks shattered and broken, lay under the scrub brush starting to grow around them. Great piles of wood debris rose like rough sweepings of the careless giant. Ragged rivulets cut deep into a raw hillside denuded of trees.

Then Rosalyn saw the cut stumps, many of them five or six feet across, and realized the area had simply been logged. She shivered. No wonder her father hadn't wanted this done to his property.

Beyond the logged area, the road narrowed even more. Rosalyn had to navigate cautiously around mudholes, and sometimes branches brushed the side of the pickup as she tried to keep away from a dropoff on the other side.

"Are you sure we're not lost?" Nadine asked doubtfully.

No, Rosalyn wasn't certain. But in several places blown-down trees had been sawed away to make passage possible, and narrow log bridges spanned the rushing streams, so there must be people out here somewhere.

And in spite of her doubts and the continuing rain, she felt a certain exhilaration as they pressed on. Home! They were almost there now! They were again in the midst of the lush forest.

Wild-flowing creeks spilled over rocks in spectacular crashes of white spray, and everything was incredibly green. She recognized fir and pine, and there were beautiful trees she didn't know, with sleek, branching russet trunks and glossy leaves. Another tree growing along creek bottoms had silver-gray bark dappled with black, the leaves shivering delicately in the rain. And everywhere was thick brush, an impenetrable barrier of brambles, twining vines, and lacy fronds.

Suddenly Nadine pointed to something at the edge of the road. "Is that a sign?" It wasn't much of a sign, just an unpainted board tacked to a tree beside an overgrown road, the lettering dim, but it was the first sign of any kind they'd seen in miles. Rosalyn edged the pickup across the muddy ruts for a closer view. Did it say what she thought it said?

Yes! The lettering was barely visible, little more than the "F" and dim lines that could be "on" remaining. But if you filled in the missing letters the name was unmistakable. Fallon!

"This is it," Rosalyn said, her voice unsteady. The promised land!

"The road doesn't look as if it's been used for years." Nadine wrapped both arms protectively around the baby as if some unseen danger suddenly threatened him.

Rosalyn peered at the road—if it could be called that—through the rainswept dimness of early evening. Grass grew as high as the hood of the pickup, and dark branches formed a ragged canopy overhead, but she didn't see any downed trees. Carefully she edged the pickup past the sign, breathing easier as the tall grass bent without resistance and brushed the underside of the pickup with a whispery rustle. Low branches dragged the sides and top of the pickup, and all three women automatically ducked every time a branch hit the windshield, laughing nervously afterward. In places small firs and pine had started growing in the roadway, but none were so big that the pickup couldn't

108

push them over. Smiley, bored with their slow progress and unmindful of the rain, jumped out and ran ahead, invisible except for the waving grass marking her route.

Rosalyn was concentrating more on branches and trees crowding the narrow road than what was underfoot when suddenly she realized the solid ground no longer felt solid. It was soft and spongy. In dismay she opened the door and peered at the wheels. They were half buried in soft black ooze, the tracks of the front tires rapidly filling with water.

Hastily, she tried to back out of the soft bog, but the pickup was already in too far to escape. Ahead, then. Frantically she stepped on the gas pedal, jamming it all the way to the floor.

Not the right thing to do, she realized in dismay, as the spinning wheels simply dug deeper and deeper into the soft earth.

Rosalyn slid out of the pickup and looked around apprehensively. The forest had taken on a sinister look, with its dark branches reached like threatening arms to ensnare them. The rain had let up, but the tops of the trees were lost in a foggy mist. Something rustled in the wet underbrush. Anything, Rosalyn thought with a surge of pure panic, could be hiding in there. A wet branch spilled a shower of water down her neck, and a blackberry bramble snagged her arm. Her feet were already wet, and she had the wild feeling that if she stood too long in one place the muddy ooze might swallow her up.

What now? They couldn't get the pickup un-stuck by themselves. Neither could they spend the rapidly approaching night in it, cramped and shivering.

She stuck her head into the pickup cab. "I'm going to walk up to the lodge." Nadine looked momentarily undecided and then scrambled across the seat with the baby. "I'm not staying here. It feels...spooky."

Ellen didn't say anything, but she got out on the other side. Running water tinkled nearby as Rosalyn led the way across the muddy bog, aware that she must maintain an aura of calm and confidence to keep her mother and Nadine from panicking. She stepped from one clump of grass to another trying to stay out of the ooze, but they were all muddy-footed by the time they reached solid ground. Within seconds they were also wet from toes to chest from pushing through the tall, rain-soaked grass. Except Andy, whom Nadine, with a surprising show of strength in her slender arms, held safely above her head.

"Snakes?" Nadine asked uneasily.

"If there are, I'm sure we're making enough noise to scare them away." Rosalyn carefully did not point out the tracks she noted when spreading the grass to make a pathway, tracks of something large and clawed. Smiley sniffed the ominous indentations and growled softly.

Rosalyn's thoughts echoed Nadine's earlier words; it did indeed feel spooky here. But they had no choice, so instead of grumbling she made a determined vow: I will learn to shoot that gun. She just hoped she wouldn't find herself needing it before she did learn how.

She was holding a heavy branch aside to let her mother and Nadine pass when Ellen suddenly stopped short.

"There it is."

Rosalyn let the branch go and desperately tried to keep her heart from plummeting down to her wet feet as she took her first dismaying glimpse of the lodge.

Had she misunderstood the Lord's will? Had she recklessly acted on her own desire to get far away from Robbie and Charlie and called it the Lord's will?

Surely he hadn't sent them two thousand miles for this.

Eleven

❦

October 1933
The Lodge

The hulking, two-story building was constructed of logs and topped with an impressive pair of chimneys. But the generous size was its only asset. The roof showed gaps between the wood shingles. The porch running the width of the building sagged and leaned. An outside stairway leading to a door on the second floor had collapsed, leaving steps dangling in mid-air, and a clump of tall fir trees, like unfriendly sentinels, crowded close to that side of the house. Something had dug an ominous-looking hole under the porch, and a general air of abandonment hung over everything. The front door stood wide open, but the dark oblong was more threatening than welcoming.

"It looks like nobody's been here for a century," Nadine said.

"Ten years," Ellen said. "Oliver hadn't used the lodge for ten years."

Rosalyn could see that it had undoubtedly been a rather impressive structure at one time, but now the word "lodge" sounded foolishly grand. With an effort at cheerfulness she said, "There's certainly plenty of room. Let's look around inside." Briskly she started toward the open door, but she stopped before she reached the sagging porch. "But first we should thank the

Lord for bringing us safely here."

Nadine said nothing, but her doubtful expression told Rosalyn what she was thinking. *How safe are we, with the pickup stuck in the mud, and this house that looks like something out of a scary movie?* But Rosalyn offered thanks anyway, adding a silent prayer that the Lord give her the strength to face whatever lay inside.

She crossed the porch carefully to avoid several broken planks. At the door, with a stiff-legged Smiley by her side, she paused to give her eyes time to adjust to the dim light trickling through the dirty windows.

She needed the strength for which she had prayed.

The entire front half of the building consisted of a single, cavernous room with fireplaces like yawning mouths flanking each end. Once there must have been furniture, but the huge room was empty now, its contents apparently stolen long ago. Cracks of light showed between the logs where the chinking had fallen away. A musty, animal scent permeated the air, and piles of sticks and twigs, apparently the lair or nest of some wild creature, filled the corners. Something rustled overhead, and Rosalyn jumped as a handful of disturbed bats streamed out the open door.

A doorway that looked large enough to accommodate a grizzly bear led to a dining room, which held a large table made of thick wooden planks, another long slab on each side forming attached benches. A table not stolen only because it had been too large and heavy to steal, she suspected.

Ellen's fingertips lifted to brush her throat as the women advanced to the kitchen, separated from the dining room only by a countertop. "Oh, my," she said faintly.

Like everything else here, the rust-covered iron stove was enormous. The deep sink had no familiar faucets to supply water; instead there was a hand pump, also rusty. The tall cupboards disappeared in the gloom of the ceiling. Cuts and gouges scarred the long, high countertop.

"Where are the lights?" Nadine asked.

Rosalyn hadn't thought about this before, but she knew the dismaying answer immediately. No electricity. She turned around slowly, realizing more unhappy facts. There was also no telephone, no refrigerator, none of the modern comforts she had taken for granted back home. An old metal washtub hung on the wall near the back door. She cautiously lifted a rusty lid on the stove and saw the ashes of some ancient fire clumped in the bottom of the firebox. She and her mother had barely been able to cook on the efficient, gas-burning stove back home. How were they ever going to manage on one that must be fed sticks of wood? When she tentatively worked the handle on the pump the only response was a protesting squawk.

Another dismaying thought struck her. Where was—? But she knew the answer even as she searched. No bathroom. She peered out the window over the sink, the dirty glass so high she had to stand on tiptoes to see out. Yes, there it was: an outhouse, unpainted, leaning, and ugly. Her fantasy of luxuriously soaking in a tub of hot water vanished like a pricked bubble.

The stairs to the second floor squeaked as Rosalyn cautiously climbed them. Smiley ran on ahead, but Rosalyn kept a firm hand on the rough pole banister in case the steps gave way. Upstairs she found only a single huge room with exposed upright roof braces, perhaps used for dormitory-style sleeping when Oliver and a crowd of friends stayed here. The beds had rusty springs, but what must once have been mattresses were now only piles of shredded stuffing, homes of a small army of mice that scurried at the sound of her footsteps. Overhead, slits of sky, darkening but still pale over the dim gloom of the room, showed through the roof.

Downstairs again, she went out the back way, alone. Near the outhouse was a woodshed, complete with an old chopping block and a rusty ax with the head buried so deeply in the block that she couldn't budge it. Attached to the woodshed was another small room with big hooks hanging from the ceiling and sawdust spilling out of cracks in the thick walls, its use a mystery to her. Another big hand pump, perhaps with a well beneath it, stood in the yard. More large, clawed tracks shivered her spine and raised the hackles on Smiley's back. Slowly she turned and looked back at the looming "lodge."

So this was it. Home.

She knew she should be grateful. It was a roof over their heads, of sorts. The woodshed held enough old wood to last them for a while. They'd arrived safely and in good health. They still had a little money plus food and supplies to start house-keeping.

Yet the things they didn't have and the enormity of the problems facing her, problems unanticipated even in her darkest moments, suddenly felt like a cloak of iron dropping on Rosalyn's shoulders. She sagged to the chopping block. Her father gone, her mother changed, her college education vanished, her love and friendship betrayed. To be replaced by this—this hollow wreck of a "lodge" and a mountain of unfamiliar, overwhelming responsibilities. How were they ever going to manage here? She couldn't do it. She just couldn't!

Fiercely Rosalyn rejected self-pity. She rubbed her sleeve across her eyes to banish a hot sting of tears. She had neither the time nor energy to waste on feeling sorry for herself. She stood, resolutely straightening her back. She was here with two women and a baby depending on her to figure out what to do now. And, she reminded herself, they had one great and glorious asset that always more than balanced whatever they might lack, one powerful strength. The Lord was always there to lean on; the Lord would see them through.

Inside, Ellen was sitting on one side of the table with her

elbows braced on the wooden slab. Opposite her, Nadine jiggled the baby to soothe him. Or to soothe herself. Both were obviously waiting for Rosalyn to lead the way.

So where, on the mountain of problems that must be tackled, should she start?

Ellen suddenly shivered and pulled her sweater more tightly around her, which served to identify the top priority for Rosalyn. Heat. They must have heat to dry themselves and their wet clothing, warmth to hold back the chill and dampness of the night. In surprise, she realized she had not the vaguest notion how the big house back in Indiana had been heated. It was simply something that Geoffrey took care of in the basement. But here?

She eyed the monster-sized kitchen stove that was little more than a dark hulk in the fast-falling darkness. She'd learned to build a campfire at summer camp; this couldn't be much different.

"We'll need matches," she said, talking to herself more than her mother or Nadine. "Wood. Paper to get the fire going."

Other immediate needs were food, cooking and eating utensils, bedding and water, all of which would have to be carried in from the stuck pickup. She did not probe all the other problems looming in the future, problems of long-term survival; right now all she could manage was tonight.

Crisply she issued orders. "Mother, you take care of Andy. Nadine, you go out to the woodshed and carry in several arm-loads of wood, enough to last all night."

Ellen reached for the baby, but Nadine held on to him. In a small but defiant voice she said, "I don't want to go out there. It's too dark. And spooky."

"Would you rather hike back to the pickup to get everything we need for tonight?" Rosalyn suggested pleasantly. "Your choice."

Silence, and then an even smaller voice saying no. Rustling noises followed as she handed the baby to Ellen. An oblong of faint light at the end of the kitchen silhouetted Nadine's slight figure as she opened the door and hesitated before stepping into the unknown.

Impulsively Rosalyn ran and hugged her. "I'm sorry. I didn't know it would be like this. Would you believe that I had big plans for taking a week-long bubble bath when we got here?"

Nadine smiled at the foolish fantasy. "I'm sorry I grumbled. This is better than standing alongside a road waiting for a ride, and I'm glad you let me come. I just wish I was as smart and brave as you." She squeezed Rosalyn's hand and stepped into the deepening darkness.

Rosalyn turned and made her way through the shadowy cavern of the front room. She paused on the sagging porch to gather her courage. The forest looked dark and alien and impenetrable, and at the moment she felt neither smart nor brave. Smiley stuck a wet nose in her hand, and she was suddenly grateful for the animal's reassuring presence. Yes, the Lord had known what he was doing when he added the dog to their party of amateur pioneers!

Smiley confidently forged ahead, and Rosalyn followed, grasping the waving plume of tail so they wouldn't become separated. She screamed once when a branch touched the back of her neck like a furry hand. Her imagination ran riot when something jumped in the brush, but a few minutes later the pickup's shadow loomed ahead. Rosalyn hurried toward it, anxious to get her hands on the flashlight.

A jutting stone caught her toe. She tried to regain her balance, but slipped and fell, crashing face first into the mud.

When she got to her hands and knees, her entire front side was covered with the slimy muck. Mud on her eyelashes, mud in her mouth, oozy mud trickling down her neck and under her shirt and into her trousers. She scooped handfuls of the sticky stuff off her clothing and disgustedly flung them into dark forest.

What else can go wrong? she wondered as she got to her feet, wet, dirty and shivering.

Then the flashlight, which she finally located under the seat after several minutes of blind searching, wouldn't work. She clicked the switch; again and again she clicked it. She shook and jiggled everything she could find to shake and jiggle, but nothing had any effect. She finally slammed the useless instrument to the ground and left it.

Digging her way blindly through the wet load, Rosalyn found the jug of water and a big, damp lump that had to be bedding. In the boxes of food supplies she dug out a couple of cans and boxes of what she hoped was something edible. She found newspaper that had been used to wrap dishes, a rattly jar that sounded as if it held matches, and then her fingers closed around an unexpected treasure. A candle!

She yearningly thought about lighting it then and there but regretfully decided it must be saved for use back at the house. Smiley had helped her find her way in the darkness; the dog could also lead the way back. She loaded herself down with as much as she could carry at one time and left the remainder in the cab of the pickup. She didn't even try to stay out of the muddy ooze on the return trip. She simply slogged through it.

At the house she lit the candle, the slender taper of wax casting a surprising flare of light around the high-ceilinged room. The three women blinked and stared at each other, and unexpectedly they all started laughing.

"You look like you've been slopping around in a pigpen," Nadine declared when she looked at Rosalyn.

"You should talk! You have enough bark and twigs in your hair to build a bird's nest," Rosalyn retorted.

Ellen held out a wet, muddy foot and laughed. "And I feel

like the child who didn't listen when her mother told her to wear galoshes."

Rosalyn first tackled the task of getting a fire started in the big kitchen stove, using the newspaper and some twigs plucked from a corner pile that she uneasily suspected was a rat's nest. It took a dozen matches to get the damp newspaper going, but finally a tentative flame licked at the small sticks.

"It's burning!" Nadine cried as if it were some near-magical feat.

Smoke briefly puffed ominously from several joints in both stove and rusty stovepipe, but after a few minutes the small twigs crackled merrily. After the fire was safely established, Rosalyn hiked back to the pickup for another load, again grateful for Smiley's reassuring presence.

They draped the bedding over some rough wooden chairs Rosalyn found in a storage room at the end of the kitchen. They dried their wet clothing simply by huddling around the stove. Dinner turned out to be cornmeal mush, burned, accompanied by canned applesauce. At the time, Rosalyn appreciated it more than any expensive restaurant meal she'd ever eaten. Smiley happily cleaned up the leftovers.

Afterward, prowling with the candle, Rosalyn made some interesting discoveries. The kitchen cabinets held some cast iron skillets, several big dishpans, a blue enamel coffeepot and various other pans and buckets, apparently missed or unwanted by the furniture thieves. Even more helpful was finding a half dozen lamps with some oily liquid in each.

Rosalyn's only knowledge of kerosene lamps was for emergency use when the electricity went off back home, but she figured out how to take the lamps apart and get enough oily liquid from several to fill one lamp. The old, dry wick didn't want to burn, but after several tries she finally managed to light it. Once Rosalyn would have scorned such primitive lighting, but now she delighted in the steady glow that was so much more generous than the candle's flicker.

Afterward, giggling like schoolgirls, they all trooped to the outhouse together, the kerosene lamp throwing light far up into the surrounding trees. Rosalyn caught her breath as the light gleamed on a pair of eyes glowing in the darkness, but they disappeared before anyone else spotted them. Back in the house, they settled on chairs around the fire, occasionally rearranging the damp bedding. The baby, content after his breast feeding, was already asleep in his mother's arms.

In spite of clothes caked with drying mud, the prospect of a night sleeping on the hard floor, and an intimidating mountain of problems that must be faced tomorrow, Rosalyn also felt surprisingly at ease. And both amazed and pleased with what she had managed to accomplish. They were there, warm, fed and safe.

The feeling of well-being suddenly vanished. The women looked at each other in terror as a loud and heavy pounding shook the back door.

Twelve

⁂

The three women froze. Nadine's eyes grew huge in her pale face. The drumming at the door stopped and then started again. Smiley growled.

"You bring the lamp," Rosalyn said softly to Nadine. Ellen took the baby and held him close, arms protectively wrapped around him. Rosalyn looked frantically for a weapon and finally grabbed a chunk of firewood.

Together, Rosalyn leading the way and holding the wood like a baseball bat, they advanced toward the door. It didn't have a knob or lock, just a wooden bar that dropped into a metal holder to hold the door shut. Thankfully she had dropped the bar into place.

The pounding stopped again, and Rosalyn held her breath as she put her ear to the door. A deep voice suddenly boomed on the other side. Startling her, she jumped backward, crashing into Nadine. The kerosene in the lamp sloshed dangerously.

"Are you folks okay in there?" the voice repeated.

Rosalyn didn't want to call out, letting him know that she was a woman. But she had the awful feeling he might smash through the door if she didn't respond. A moving flicker of light outside the window indicated he had a flashlight. Smiley growled again.

"Who are you?" she asked guardedly.

"A neighbor—Shea Donahue. I saw tracks turning in on this old road and none coming out, and wondered if someone was in trouble. Saw your pickup stuck in the mud. Thought I'd see if you need help."

Rosalyn and Nadine exchanged glances over the glow of the lamp. Rosalyn didn't want to turn down help, but she wasn't about to throw the door open to a deep-voiced stranger. She had no way of knowing whether he was a friendly neighbor, as he claimed, or an ax murderer.

"We're fine," she finally said cautiously.

Silence, and she could feel the man's curiosity as plainly as if it were arrows shooting through the door.

"I'll come back in the morning, then, and help get your pickup out of the mud."

Rosalyn hesitated. They needed help, that was certain. But she wasn't about to issue an open invitation to a stranger. They were three women and a baby, miles from anywhere, and the chunk of wood in her hands felt like puny protection against a male intruder.

"Thank you, but that won't be necessary," she said, putting all the aloof confidence she could collect into her voice. "We can manage by ourselves." She had no idea how, but she'd worry about that later.

She held her ear against the wooden door, waiting for a reply, but all she heard was the sound of heavy-booted footsteps trailing off.

"Is he gone?" Nadine's voice shook.

"I think so." But would he believe her hollow proclamation of self-sufficiency? Or would he return, for some far less noble purpose than "help"? At the moment, he couldn't know that there wasn't a husband or brother or father present to confront him. But the revealing light of day would leave no doubt.

Shea hiked back to his truck, following the trail of crushed grass apparently made by the occupants of the old house on several trips to and from the pickup. The tarp on the pickup had been left loose, and he retied it. If wind and rain returned in the night at least the load wouldn't get wet. Wetter, he corrected, as his hand contacted a soggy cardboard box beneath the ragged canvas.

Who was in the house? These surely were not the rich owners from the east. Although the woman had certainly sounded snooty enough. He scraped the mud off the license plate. Indiana. Squatters? He'd heard of people simply moving into a vacant place.

Well, none of his business. He'd offered help and they'd rejected it. He stamped his boots against the running board to loosen the mud before stepping into the cab of the truck. He'd stopped in town to pick up Jessie, but she had a cold so Eunice had put her to bed early and he hadn't wanted to wake her. He'd pick her up tomorrow when he went in with a load of firewood. He was backing the truck down the overgrown road before a thought occurred to him. Why hadn't the husband or father responded to his knock? Was it possible that a lone woman was at that crumbling wreck of a house?

He braked, the cluttered pickup still in his headlights, and thought back over the brief conversation. She'd sounded young, cultured, her voice cool and haughty. Or was it not so much unfriendly as scared? Puzzling, very puzzling.

The women spent an endless, uncomfortable night. They slept in their clothes under sheets that were reasonably dry. But only a few of the blankets were beyond the soggy stage. So they huddled together, the baby and Ellen in the middle, Nadine and Rosalyn on the outside, Smiley at their feet.

The floor was mercilessly hard, and Nadine, for all her fragile appearance, was no weakling when it came to yanking blankets in her sleep, and Rosalyn kept waking to find herself uncovered and chilled. The house was alive with rustles and creakings and patters of tiny feet, but once she was certain she heard something much larger scratching outside. Uneasily, she remembered the open front door. It had sagged so heavily into the floor that she hadn't been able to budge it. When she got up to feed the fire she carried a chunk of wood back to bed and kept one hand securely wrapped around it.

The last remnants of storm and clouds swept through during the night, and in the morning cheerful fall sunshine streamed through the tall windows in the kitchen and dining room. No one, including the baby, was in good spirits, however. They had more cornmeal mush for breakfast, again burned because Rosalyn had no idea how to regulate heat in the wood stove. She couldn't get anything but that protesting squawk out of the pump, so they had to conserve every drop of water for drinking and had none to spare for washing. She felt dirty, unrested, sore from the hard floor, and grumpy.

The firewood Nadine had carried in the night before was gone now, so after breakfast Rosalyn went out to get more. She knelt to gather a load and was just standing up when Smiley tore around the corner of the woodshed barking furiously. Rosalyn whirled and was so startled at what she saw that she dropped the entire armload.

A man stood before her. And such a man! Wild, curly red

hair, unruly red beard, astonishingly brilliant blue eyes. Tall, brawny enough to wrestle a bear, with a powerful aura of virile masculinity. He wore a red and black checked shirt, wide suspenders, and dark work pants that were ragged at the bottom and came just to the top of his heavy boots. His age was impossible to determine under all that red hair and beard. Smiley circled him warily, sniffing cautiously.

"I'm sorry. I didn't mean to startle you." The big voice of last night. He turned his hand to let the dog sniff his fingers. "I know you said you didn't need any help getting your pickup out, but I just thought I'd check—"

"That's very thoughtful of you, Mr....uh...Donahue," Rosalyn said, not voicing her suspicion that it was as much curiosity as helpfulness that had brought him back. He was between her and the door of the house. Could she make a dash for it and get around him?

"I found this. The bulb was loose so I fixed it." He flicked the flashlight switch to show her that it was working and handed the repaired instrument to her. He also smiled, a friendly white flash in the red beard, and suddenly he didn't look quite so menacing.

She cautiously extended a hand to take the flashlight. "Thank you. Thank you very much."

"My truck's back there by your pickup. I brought along a chain."

"A chain?" she repeated uncertainly.

"To hook between the two vehicles. I can pull yours out with my truck, but I'll need some help." He glanced toward the house. "Perhaps your husband or father?"

She was not about to give him the information that no such male protectors existed. While she was trying to think of an appropriately evasive answer he asked bluntly, "You aren't here alone, are you?"

"Oh, no, I'm not alone!" She waved her hand toward the house. "There are five of us," she added quickly, stretching their number to include both baby and dog.

"I can carry that load of wood to the house for you," he offered.

And have him see just how vulnerable they were? No. She wasn't quite as fearful of him now, and she was indeed grateful for the repaired flashlight, but she wasn't taking any chances.

"Thank you, I can manage," she said, looking at him evenly. "You said you live around here?"

"On up the road about a mile. There used to be several families out this way, but I'm the only one left now." Quite casually, as easily as if he were pulling a knife out of butter, he put a heavy-booted foot on the chopping block and with one hand yanked the ax free.

"Are you a...family?" Rosalyn asked. She stepped back uneasily when he didn't immediately drop the ax, but all he did was pick up a chunk of wood and start chopping it into kindling.

"There's just my little girl, Jessie, and me. She stays with a woman in town while I'm working." He glanced back at Rosalyn, sun glinting sparks of copper-red in his hair and beard, and apparently her sudden curiosity was all too obvious because he added quietly, "My wife was accidentally drowned three years ago. Jessie was only six months old."

"Oh, I'm so sorry," Rosalyn said, her natural empathy for someone's loss momentarily overriding her nervousness. "I lost my father just recently, too. In an...automobile accident. Actually," she added impulsively, surprising even herself, "his death and some...financial reversals are the reason we've come here."

"To stay?"

"Yes. My father used it only occasionally as his hunting lodge, but we intend to make it our permanent home."

He leaned the ax against the chopping block and regarded her with open speculation in those incredibly blue eyes. Speculation that she suspected included whom the "we" referred to. "It's a long way from town. And a little short on city conveniences."

"You seem to manage."

"I'm accustomed to roughing it."

Rosalyn lifted her chin determinedly. "Then we'll have to become accustomed to 'roughing it' also. Although I did assume there would be furniture. Father used to bring friends with him to hunt and fish for a couple of weeks. It's obviously been stolen at some time."

She didn't mean that as an accusation, but a slight narrowing of his eyes suggested that he may have taken it that way. His facial expression, under the heavy beard, was difficult to determine.

"The place has been bare ever since I've lived out here." Perhaps because that statement indicated he had been here before, he added, "I cross through here occasionally when I'm hunting."

He went back to chopping kindling, a powerful arm accurately wielding the heavy ax one-handed while he held the chunk of wood with the other hand.

"What do you do? Working, I mean?" she asked.

"I'm a logger. There isn't much market for lumber these days, but this one logging outfit is still working and I just got on with them a few weeks ago. They have alternating crews, each working a week at a time. It cuts each man's wages in half, but the company is trying to give as many men as possible some work. On my weeks off, I cut firewood and haul it to town to sell."

"Did you grow up around here?"

"No. I'm originally from Michigan, but I've lived here several years." He paused. "I don't recall ever seeing your father here. He must not have been here for several years."

"Ten, my mother says. Unfortunately, the lodge seems to have gone downhill in that time. But we plan to get it back into shape as soon as we can."

He glanced at the shabby house but made no comment. She could tell he was even more curious about who the "we" represented. In spite of slowly coming to believe he really was what he presented himself to be, a friendly, concerned neighbor, she didn't elaborate.

Unexpectedly, she was suddenly uncomfortably aware of her own dirty clothing and uncombed hair; she must look like a wild woman to him. She tucked a loose tendril of hair behind her ear and smoothed the front of the mud-stained trousers she'd been wearing for several days. Then she mentally chastised herself for the characteristically feminine gestures; how she looked to Shea Donahue was irrelevant.

"I see you have a furry friend hanging around," he commented.

At first she thought he meant Smiley, who was now lying by the woodpile with her nose between her paws, amber eyes lazily closed in the sunshine. Clearly Shea Donahue had met some acceptable character standard in her doggy estimation. But Shea wasn't looking at Smiley; he was looking at the tracks around the woodshed.

"A deer?" Rosalyn suggested hopefully. Deer were shy, harmless creatures. Yet even as she asked the question she knew deer did not come equipped with the clawed paws obvious in the tracks.

He shook his head, not quite laughing but definitely smiling. "No, not a deer. Cougar. Big one. I've seen him a couple times." He sobered. "Cougar usually stay away from people, but occasionally they can be dangerous. And this one may think he owns this place and you've moved in on his territory. You're from the city?"

"Is it that obvious?" Rosalyn asked with a reluctant smile. "Yes. Gideon, Indiana. It's near Indianapolis."

"I don't suppose you have a gun?"

"Oh, yes, we have a gun," she stated firmly, glad of this opportunity to let him know they were not defenseless. Against cougar or any other dangers. "My father's hunting rifle."

"Then you should keep it loaded and ready where you can grab it. It's good you have a dog, too. Cougar don't like dogs. Although they've been known to carry off and eat small ones."

Uneasily Rosalyn thought of the snuffling and scratching noises she'd heard during the night, and she was tempted to tell Shea Donahue she hadn't the faintest idea how to use the gun. But she was still hesitant about revealing any vulnerability.

Shea was watching her as if he sensed her fears, but when he spoke it was about the pickup. "We'd better get it unstuck before it decides to rain again," he said, glancing briefly at the sky.

That meant walking far away from the relative safety of the house with him. Rosalyn hesitated. He hooked his big thumbs in his pants pockets and watched her while she tried to decide what to do. She touched her hair, feeling more bedraggled and unkempt than ever under his appraising gaze. Smiley got up and sniffed Shea's pants legs again, plume of tail waving gently. He patted the dog's head, and Smiley offered that peculiar doggy grin of hers.

Rosalyn wasn't sure if it was Smiley's acceptance of Shea Donahue that made up her mind, or whether it was just desperation born of a knowledge that she must take a chance or the pickup could be stuck there all winter.

"I'll just tell the others I'll be gone for a few minutes." She went to the back of the lodge, and when Nadine unfastened the

128

bar and opened the door a crack, Rosalyn whispered what she was going to do.

"Don't come out," she warned. "I don't want him to know there's just us." Nadine nodded and quickly closed the door. Then Rosalyn joined Shea at the corner of the house where he was idly throwing sticks for an eager Smiley to chase.

"Your…uh…husband's not coming along?" Shea inquired as they set out.

She gave him a benign smile and simply said, no.

Shea had backed his larger truck up their road, so the two vehicles now stood tail to tail, her pickup looking as if it were rapidly taking root in the mud. He fastened the heavy chain between the trucks and, after checking that the engine of the pickup would start, gave her instructions.

"I'll pull my truck ahead a little, just enough to tighten the chain. Then you, when you feel it really starting to pull, give the pickup some gas. Just an easy push on the gas pedal. Don't jam it to the floor or the wheels will spin and dig in deeper." His gaze flicked to the half-buried wheels. She figured his experience with such things told him that was exactly what she had done before.

Still standing on dry ground, Rosalyn stooped to roll up her trousers. It was probably futile, but she wanted to keep them dry when she sloshed through the mud to the pickup.

She had no idea what Shea had in mind when he suddenly moved toward her.

Not until she was in his arms.

Thirteen

※

Pure astonishment made Rosalyn go rigid as an icicle. She stared into Shea Donahue's bright blue eyes that seemed not at all concerned that he was holding her like a new husband about to carry his bride across the threshold.

"What are you doing?" she finally managed to gasp. "Put me down!"

"I thought you shouldn't have to wade through the mud."

"I don't care what you thought! Put me down!"

When he didn't instantly comply, she kicked and struggled, flinging arms and legs and body in as many directions as a squirming cat. Her hand connected with his beard and hard jaw underneath, and her fingernails ripped into something softer. Her kicking feet collided with a muscular thigh. She got hold of a handful of hair and yanked as if she were pulling weeds.

At first her struggles only seemed to strengthen some instinctive male reaction in him to hold on to her even more tightly, but finally, like a man warily releasing a tiger, he set her upright on the ground and took several hasty steps backward. He rubbed his beard and the left side of his head, where a few loose, curly hairs floated as if in a spring shedding.

Yet despite feeling a spirited indignation at being so rudely manhandled, Rosalyn, surprisingly, wasn't afraid. He made no threatening move toward her, simply stood there rubbing his scalp. With all that red beard she couldn't see his facial expression, but his blue eyes looked as astonished as she'd felt when he picked her up. He also had a bloody streak just below his eye where her fingernails had connected.

"I suppose I should have asked first if you wanted to be carried to the pickup," he muttered. He pulled a red bandanna handkerchief out of his pocket and dabbed at the scratch.

Rosalyn stifled an inappropriate urge to laugh. Here stood this big, strong logger, who had picked her up as if she were no heavier than a kitten, this man who could overpower her in an instant if he chose to, now looking as if he were ready to take flight if she again bared her fingernails.

Instead of laughing she said in the most severe tone she could manage, "A gentleman does not grab a woman and pick her up as if she were a sack of corn!"

"If my actions appeared ungentlemanly, I apologize," he said, although his somewhat surly tone didn't sound overly apologetic. With unconcealed sarcasm he added, "Perhaps I should have flung myself into the mud and let you simply walk across me, like a bridge."

"I may have overreacted to your...helpfulness," she admitted reluctantly. "I am sorry I scratched you. Does it hurt?"

"Feels like I tangled with that cougar," he mumbled sourly. He slopped off through mud and water that apparently had little effect on his heavy boots, leaving her to fend for herself, and mud squished through her shoes and between her toes as she slipped and sloshed to the pickup. She had the impression, from his quick backward glance, that he took a certain satisfaction in this.

She got into the pickup, started the engine, and, following

instructions, eased her foot down on the gas pedal when she felt the pull on the chain. Slowly, ever so slowly, the pickup moved backward, the tires making big sucking, slurping sounds as they pulled free of the entrapping mud. Shea kept going until there was some twenty feet of solid ground between the pickup and the bog. She got out and watched him unhook the chain and toss it into his truck.

"Thank you very much." She felt awkward about their earlier confrontation.

Silently, and without explanation, he grabbed a saw out of the truck and within a few minutes had half a dozen small trees downed by the edge of the forest. He whacked off the branches with an ax. Rosalyn was completely puzzled by his actions until he dragged the trimmed poles to the mudhole and started laying them crossways in it.

"You're fixing the road so we can drive all the way up to the house! Oh, that's a marvelous idea!"

He didn't comment, just kept working, taking off his shirt as exertion heated his body. He also didn't ask for help and didn't appear to notice when she started working with him. But whenever she came to a larger, heavier pole he'd let her puff and grunt a bit and then, with little more than a ripple of smooth muscles, dragged the ten-foot pole along as if it were no more than a stick of kindling.

Rosalyn steadily got wetter and dirtier, and it wouldn't have mattered, she thought wryly, if she had combed her hair earlier this morning because it was straggly and dirt-streaked now. Shea also had blotches of mud on his beard and bare chest, plus bits of sawdust and shavings thrown by the saw he wielded so expertly. Smiley dashed around as if this were all a messy, joyful game.

"There. That should do it," Shea said finally as he surveyed the poles stretched in an orderly lineup across the mudhole. He took the bandanna out of his pants pocket and wiped his sweaty forehead. The blood from the wound had dried in a ragged streak across his cheekbone, and Rosalyn felt a small stab of guilt.

"Thank you again," she said. They had little money to spare, but what he'd done deserved much more than mere words of thanks. There was so much, she thought ruefully, that a man's strong hands could accomplish faster and more efficiently than her own. Even if she'd figured out that this was the way to repair the road, which was unlikely, it would have taken her days to do it. "We want to pay you, of course, for all your help—"

He glanced at the old pickup with its bedraggled load. "Unless I miss my guess, you haven't much to spare," he observed bluntly. Without waiting for a response he added, "Try driving across the poles and see if they're going to hold up under the weight."

"I'm sure they'll be just fine, and I do appreciate all you've done for us." She hesitated a moment and then said, "I don't believe I introduced myself earlier. I'm Rosalyn Fallon."

She held out her hand. He stepped forward and shook it with a big hand that was surprisingly gentle in spite of its rough calluses and obvious strength. For no reason at all she thought of Robbie's smooth-palmed hand that had never known the kind of work that built calluses. Then she could feel Shea's renewed curiosity, wondering where the men were and why she was the one out here doing manual labor with him. But she felt awkward at the idea of suddenly spouting the information that she had no husband. A fact that was basically irrelevant, of course.

"I do want to pay you," she offered again.

"Perhaps I'll think of something you can do for me."

His tone was casual, without any apparent sly undercurrent of meaning, but a certain hint of speculation in those brilliant blue eyes sent alarm jolting through Rosalyn. Just what sort of payment, other than money, might a big, tough logger living out here without a wife have in mind? In spite of feeling indebted to him, she did not encourage further thought along those lines.

"Well, again, thanks from all of us," she said with a hasty, bright smile.

The poles squished down a bit as she drove slowly over them, but they made a good, solid footing for the pickup. In the rear view mirror she saw Shea watch until she was safely across, then turn and head for his own truck as she drove toward the house. Smiley raced ahead, announcing their arrival with wild barking.

Nadine ran out the front door as the pickup approached. She clapped her hands as if Rosalyn had just put on a wonderful show. "I was afraid we were trapped here forever!"

As Rosalyn stepped out of the cab a roar from the driveway made both women turn. Rosalyn had assumed Shea was heading home, but his truck came bursting backward out of the trees with a blast of blue smoke from the exhaust pipe. Shea got out and Rosalyn saw his observant blue eyes gather another fact: two women, and still no male in sight.

Just then Ellen came through the doorway carrying the baby.

Rosalyn could see Shea mentally tallying their current visible number. Four. His eyes settled on Smiley, then returned to her, and their unexpected sparkle of amusement told her he knew she'd included the dog in her tally.

Almost defiantly she introduced everyone. "This is my mother, Ellen, and our friend, Nadine. That's Andy, Nadine's son, in Mother's arms, and the dog is Smiley. Mother and Nadine, this is our neighbor Shea Donahue. He cut poles and laid them across the mudhole so we can drive across it now."

"I'd have never thought of that!" Nadine gave him a wide-eyed look.

"You're planning to stay here alone?" Shea asked in obvious disbelief as he surveyed their feminine number.

There was no point in trying to continue some illusion of male presence, Rosalyn knew. "Simply because there is not a

134

man among us does not mean we are alone," she pointed out with spirit.

Her optimistic plans about how they were going to survive—living a pioneer existence off the land and taking in hunting guests—suddenly loomed as far-fetched as hoping to dig up buried treasure. But there were still the trees. She hadn't liked what she'd seen of logging so far, but it was, in a term Robbie had sometimes used, their "ace in the hole." If they got desperate enough, they could sell the timber.

Shea still hadn't responded to her admission that they really were planning to live here "alone." She studied him warily, wondering if some ugly side of his personality would suddenly surface now that he knew how vulnerable they were. His mud–and sawdust–spattered chest, bared by the shirt he'd put on but not buttoned, and red-hued eyebrows knit in a scowl, made him appear formidably dangerous.

But all he did was turn and glance at the mud-covered pickup. "I'll help you unload."

Rosalyn instantly thought about the unknown "something" he might yet demand as payment for favors done and started to tell him they could manage quite nicely from here. But Nadine had already clambered into the pickup bed and was handing boxes and cartons down to him. Rosalyn could hardly order him to drop everything and get off their property. She followed him into the house with a heavy armload of her own.

"Just put everything in here," she instructed as they entered the dim, cavernous front room.

He did as she told him, but she could see his observant gaze taking in everything. The high ceilings, the gaping fireplaces, the huge arched doorway into the dining room. "You're never going to be able to keep this place warm this winter."

"We all slept right by the stove last night." Though they still hadn't been any too warm in the big, drafty room.

"This winter is going to get a lot colder than last night."

"Snow?"

"Probably not, although it's possible. But definitely plenty of wind and rain." He studied their situation appraisingly. "It would be a bit crowded, but heating the place would be easier if you boarded up that archway and simply lived in the kitchen and dining room."

Rosalyn was ready to relinquish privacy and space for warmth. "That's a wonderful idea!"

"I think I saw some old boards out by the woodshed. I'll nail them up after we finish carrying everything in."

Rosalyn swallowed. "We can't ask you to keep doing things for us." She was getting deeper and deeper into debt with this big, red-haired stranger. "You have your own work to do—"

"You didn't ask. I'm offering." He headed back toward the pickup for another load, his long strides leaving her behind.

Shea, Nadine, and Rosalyn worked steadily until the pickup was empty. Ellen took care of the baby, who was cranky because of a rash on his bottom. The only interest she showed in the unloading came when Shea carried in her private box. She instructed him to take it upstairs, as if she feared Rosalyn might yet tell her she must get rid of everything it contained.

Afterward Shea got hammer and nails out of the truck, which seemed to be an inexhaustible source of whatever might be needed, and nailed up the boards to close off the big archway. There were cracks, because the boards were weathered and warped, but the difference was immediate.

"It's almost cozy in here now," Rosalyn said, pleased.

"It's hard to be cozy when you don't have a bathroom or beds or—" Nadine broke off without completing the list. She looked embarrassed for having complained and busily started unpacking a box of damp clothes.

From what Nadine had said about her past, Rosalyn knew the young mother hadn't grown up with the luxuries Rosalyn herself had enjoyed. But Nadine was accustomed to the basic comforts of city life, which were nonexistent here. Roughing it was also more difficult because she had the baby to care for. Rosalyn hadn't had much experience with babies, but she suspected Andy's rash was caused from not having a bath for several days. Nadine had done her best to keep his diapers clean, but they'd been getting only a minimal rinsing before reuse.

Rosalyn admitted with rueful honesty she wouldn't want to be raising a baby, especially without a father's help, in these primitive and uncertain conditions.

Shea tackled the pump on the well next, but it took him only a few minutes to determine it was rusted beyond repair.

"But we can't get along without water!" Rosalyn said in dismay.

She was, however, about to discover how resourceful Shea could be. He dug around in his truck, produced a shovel and short length of metal pipe, and, carrying the ax as well, headed back down the driveway. Rosalyn hesitated for a moment, then trotted to catch up with him.

He poked around the edges of the boggy area until he found the trickle of water flowing into it. He followed the trickle and Rosalyn followed him, crawling under and through the rough brush until they came to the water's source about a hundred feet away from the house.

"The water is flowing right out of the ground," Rosalyn marveled. Water, in her city-bred life, came out of faucets. She had a vague knowledge that digging a hole deep enough in the ground might also produce well water. But to see it burbling right up out of the ground!

"It's a spring," Shea said. "I knew there had to be one around here feeding that muddy area." With the shovel he dug a basin-shaped hollow in the ground and then arranged the pipe so the main trickle of water flowed through it and dropped into the catch basin. The flowing water was muddy at first, because Shea's digging had disturbed the earth, but within a few minutes it ran with transparent clarity.

"It's quite a distance to carry water to the house," Shea said. "But better than no water at all."

"It's good to drink, just like that?" Rosalyn asked doubtfully.

"Try it and see."

He showed the way by letting the water trickle into his cupped hands, and Rosalyn knelt on the damp ground to follow suit.

"It's wonderful!" The water was cold, fresh, and delicious. "I'm going to the house to get a bucket."

"I'll cut a trail through the brush for you."

Suddenly Rosalyn realized with some embarrassment that Shea had been here since morning, helping them with one task after another, and they hadn't so much as offered him a cup of coffee or tea, let alone lunch. And here it was, now late afternoon. She hadn't had anything to eat, either, her stomach told her with an unladylike rumble.

"Would you join us for supper?" For all her wary suspicions of him, they owed him that much for all he'd done. She smiled. "We haven't exactly mastered cooking on that big old wood stove yet, but if you don't mind taking the risk—"

"Thanks. I appreciate the offer. But I'm going to town to get Jessie to bring her out to spend the week with me." He tilted his head and gave Rosalyn a thoughtful look. "But there is something you can do for me."

Fourteen

❧

Rosalyn took a wary step backward. After crawling through the brush Shea's hair resembled a bushman's out of *National Geographic,* and his curly red beard stood out as if electrified.

She gulped. "And what is it that I might...do for you?"

"With all the families moved away, there's no one for Jessie to play with out here. She's just crazy about babies, and I thought perhaps I could bring her over?"

Rosalyn was so surprised and relieved at this innocent request that she laughed. She also felt guilty about her suspicions of this good man. His abrupt method of trying to keep her feet from getting muddy may have been a bit unorthodox, but never once had his actions been anything other than those of an honest, caring neighbor.

"We'd love to have her."

"I'll bring her over tomorrow afternoon, then."

"And you'll both stay for supper," Rosalyn said firmly.

He looked undecided, and she suspected he was thinking about the limited supply of food he'd seen when he helped unload the pickup. His next words confirmed that thought. "I'll bring some venison."

Oliver Fallon had brought home only antlers as trophies of his hunts, and Rosalyn had never eaten, much less cooked, venison. She had a momentary vision of Shea strolling in with something on the hoof slung over his shoulder, but she didn't let that deter her. It was time to learn how to cook wild meat. They might have to live off it. She might have to learn to shoot it.

"That would be wonderful. Thank you."

She crawled through the brush to the house. By the time she returned with a water bucket, he'd hacked a trail through the brush with his ax. He also carried the filled bucket to the house for her, and she once more thanked him for all he'd done.

"I'm glad I could help. It will be nice to have neighbors again."

"We'll see you and your little girl—Jessie?—tomorrow, then," she said, and he nodded.

As a final good deed, with a screech of wood against wood, he muscled the front door shut. It wasn't operable, and they couldn't open it again, but it was no longer an open invitation for any wild predator.

Shea Donahue, Rosalyn thought with a certain amusement as his heavy boots thumped across the porch on his way to the truck, was not a noiseless man who could sneak up on anyone. Yet, in spite of some rough edges, he was not an unattractive man. *Oh, no,* she thought with an unexpected quickening of pulse. *He's not unattractive at all!* She listened until the forest and hills swallowed the roar of his truck. It was, she realized, comforting to know he was only a mile away.

When she returned to the kitchen, Nadine looked at her knowingly. "He's sweet on you."

"Don't be ridiculous. We've barely met." Rosalyn brushed at the twigs and bits of brush still clinging to her hair and trousers. "Besides I look like something Smiley dragged out of the brush. He's just being neighborly."

"I didn't see him looking at me like I was a piece of chocolate cake and him a hungry man." Nadine grinned. "He might be a pretty good catch."

The word "catch" was an unpleasant reminder to Rosalyn of the past. That was how Charlie had described Robbie not long before she decided to grab him. Rosalyn still didn't know what to do with her feelings about Robbie—a confusing mixture of scorn, resentment, and leftover love. Several times she'd decided she should get rid of that amethyst bracelet, but she'd never quite been able to do it. But now a sharp awareness of all the differences between Robbie and this man she had just met unexpectedly jabbed her.

Never could she imagine smoothly sophisticated Robbie as roughly dressed as Shea, clumping around in heavy boots rather than handmade Italian shoes, or stripping off his shirt to do manual labor. Never could she imagine his face covered with an unruly beard or his hair untamed and shaggy. Never could she envision him driving a battered old truck like Shea's. Conversely, she couldn't begin to picture Shea ordering an elegant meal in a sophisticated restaurant or playing a game of golf. And it was difficult to imagine Shea's big voice booming over the radio!

Yet there was one more thing she couldn't see. And that was Robbie spending all day helping a houseful of new neighbors.

Rosalyn realized she was just standing there in the middle of the kitchen, with Nadine staring at her reflectively. Nadine knew a little of Rosalyn's heartbroken past with Robbie.

"What we need," Rosalyn said, with a firm change of subject to something more practical than speculation about Shea Donahue's romantic inclinations, "are baths."

Shea loaded the firewood he had already cut and then went into the house to clean up before driving into town to deliver the wood and pick up Jessie. In the bathroom, bare-chested, dabbing at the scratch on his face with a damp cloth, he suddenly put both hands on the sink and leaned over to inspect himself in the mirror. Something, he realized, he hadn't done for a long time.

And then he groaned.

He wasn't as rough looking as some of the men at the logging camp. His neck wasn't black with collected grime, his teeth felt the scrub of a toothbrush regularly, and his beard wasn't stained with tobacco juice. Basically, he was clean, other than today's surface accumulation of mud and sawdust and twigs.

But it was no wonder Rosalyn Fallon had dropped her armload of wood when she saw him. His appearance was enough to startle any woman.

Red beard bushy as some old hermit prospector's. Hair like Little Orphan Annie curls combed with an eggbeater. Even his eyebrows looked fierce and unruly. Why hadn't he noticed all that before?

Maybe, he had to admit, because it just hadn't seemed of any great importance. Jessie would love him no matter how he looked, and he hadn't been seeing anyone since he broke up with Rachel in August. Making wages cutting firewood wasn't easy and took long hours of hard work, especially when he gave away to needy older people at church almost as much as he sold. None of which was any excuse, of course, for letting himself look like something that had lumbered out of a cave after a winter's hibernation.

Neither was there any excuse for the way he'd picked Rosalyn Fallon up as if she were, in her own indignant words, a "sack of corn." Had he lost all sense of propriety and proper manners, living out here alone or cooped up with a gang of boisterous loggers? Yet he knew why he hadn't put her down instantly, as he should have. At first it was pure astonishment at her unexpected reaction. But then it was simply because she'd felt too good in his arms, slender and feminine but supple and strong, too.

He'd also had, he admitted as he stared at his reflection in the mirror, a strong urge to kiss her.

What kind of woman was she? She was beautiful. That was obvious, in spite of her disheveled appearance. Ginger-brown hair, gold-flecked brown eyes, and creamy skin, a figure that hinted at sweetly rounded curves in spite of the shapeless shirt and trousers.

Yet much more than just a pretty woman. Never once had she stopped to fuss about mud on her face or tangles in her hair as they worked on the road together. She'd struggled with dogged determination, dragging the poles without complaint even though he could hear mud squishing in her shoes with every step. Her mother and friend obviously looked to her for leadership. She'd known an easy life, he was certain. Her hands were soft and cared for, her astonishment at drinking water bubbling out of the ground almost laughable. She was obviously unsuited to a life balanced on the rough edge of civilization. And yet just as obviously determined to do it.

Suddenly he had to laugh at the bold audacity of her claim that there were five of them living in the old log house. Yes, technically, that was true. Two young women, one older woman, one baby, and one dog. Clever and courageous, she wasn't about to let him, a stranger—a wild and threatening-looking stranger—know how vulnerable they were.

But he sobered as he thought of her claim of having a gun for protection. What was it? Some old blunderbuss that couldn't hit the side of a barn? She'd carried the gun into the house herself and he hadn't gotten a good look at it. But, unless he was badly mistaken, she hadn't enough experience with guns to know which end to put the bullet in.

He'd seen the open Bible on the massive dining room table as he helped carry in their supplies. Was that the source of her strength in what had to be a hard time for her? Because if it were, he thought suddenly, she wasn't nearly as helpless as it appeared. She also, he realized with a sudden rush of protectiveness that surprised him with its intensity, had him for help.

He began rummaging in the bathroom cabinet for the razor he hadn't seen in months.

Rosalyn built up the fire in the kitchen stove, and she and Nadine made several trips to the spring with buckets. While the dishpans of water heated on the stove, Rosalyn dragged the big metal washtub to the center of the kitchen so she wouldn't have far to carry the hot water.

"It isn't very private." Nadine looked doubtful.

"If it's privacy you want, you can hike around until you find yourself a nice, private, icy creek to bathe in."

Nadine didn't have to consider that idea long. "I guess I can get along without privacy," she agreed, with a guilty laugh for being so fussy.

They bathed the baby first, directly in a dishpan. He gurgled and grinned and splashed, obviously delighted with the feel of the soothing warm water on his irritated bottom. Rosalyn and Nadine scrubbed diapers while Ellen bathed, and then it was Nadine's turn and finally Rosalyn's.

She remembered reading about pioneer families all taking baths in the same water, with the last family member in line getting the gray dregs. They weren't yet to that point, she decided, and resolutely hauled more buckets, saving one to do her hair. Afterward, she brushed it into a soft curl on her shoulders instead of carelessly tying it back as she'd been doing for days now.

"That looks really nice." Nadine smiled, then with a mischievous quirk of her mouth she added, "I'll bet Shea will like it, too."

"I certainly don't care what he thinks!" Rosalyn tilted her chin upward. "I didn't wash my hair for him."

"Of course you didn't," Nadine agreed, still grinning. "And you didn't douse yourself with all that wonderful-smelling talcum powder for him, either."

Rosalyn threw the brush at her.

They gathered at the dining room for a few minutes of Bible reading and prayer before bedtime. Nadine, as usual, listened but did not join in. Rosalyn offered thanks for all the blessings of the day. So much accomplished! Road opened, water supply made available, even that impossible-to-budge front door closed.

Yet, once in bed, she was uncomfortably aware that one thing they had not accomplished was an improvement in the sleeping arrangements. Getting the cold draft shut off was a start, but Rosalyn was certain she could feel the rough woodgrain in the floorboards through the blankets. And a rock, feeling like a boulder against her back, turned out to be pinhead sized when she got up and scraped it out from under the blankets. Tomorrow night would be different, she vowed.

Next morning, right after a breakfast of oatmeal and canned milk, Rosalyn sewed two blankets together, leaving one end open. Then she dragged a none-too-enthusiastic Nadine upstairs to help her sort through what remained of the stuffing of several old mattresses and pack the cleanest of the shredded bits into the sewed blankets.

"What are we doing?" Nadine grumbled. She shook a handful of stuffing fluff, and mouse droppings spattered the floor.

"We're making our own mattress."

Nadine looked appalled. "I don't want to sleep on something the mice have been crawling around in!"

"Then sleep on the hard floor!"

Nadine sighed and went back to sorting through the bits of mattress stuffing. "You used to be rich. How come you don't mind living like this?"

"I do mind. I didn't expect it to be like this when we decided to come here." Rosalyn couldn't really understand why the Lord had brought them to this, but since he had, she didn't see much else to do but make the best of it. "Isn't there some old adage about adversity building good character?" She raised an eyebrow in Nadine's direction.

"I don't see how mouse droppings in a mattress could do much for anyone's character," Nadine muttered, and they both started laughing.

In the end, Nadine decided she'd prefer a makeshift mattress, even if the contents had previously housed a few tenant mice, to sleeping on the hard floor, so they sewed two more blankets together and made a second mattress. At the same time, in a more serious vein, Rosalyn talked to Nadine about her Lord— how his love and comfort and guidance helped her through some of life's recent rough spots. Nadine didn't argue, but Rosalyn suspected that it was because the girl was drifting in her own thoughts.

That suspicion was confirmed when Nadine interrupted. "I wish you'd told me last night that Shea was going into town to pick up his daughter today. I'd like to of ridden in with him."

"Why?"

"Well, because we could use some fresh milk and..." Her voice trailed off. "And because it's so...wild and lonely out here. I don't like wondering what's scratching and prowling around outside in the middle of the night."

So Nadine had heard those sounds too; it hadn't just been Rosalyn's overactive, middle-of-the-night imagination.

In a longing voice, Nadine went on. "I like to go to the movies. Even if I don't have any money, I like to look in the stores. I like lights and music and ice cream. I get lonely for people."

"Nadine, we've only been here a couple of days! It isn't as if we haven't seen anyone for a month."

"I know," Nadine agreed unhappily.

"We have had one visitor. And how can you be lonely when you have your very own baby for company?"

Nadine gazed out a window of the slant-roofed upstairs room. All that could be seen was the rocky bluff rising beyond the house. "Sometimes I almost wish..." But she stopped in midsentence and didn't go on with what she almost wished.

As Shea and Jessie got out of the truck Smiley bounded out of the house to announce their arrival with fierce barking, but her warning quickly changed to tail-wagging welcome.

Jessie was excited about seeing the baby, but she kept her hand wrapped around Shea's forefinger as they approached the back door together. Shea had hoped Rosalyn might approve of his change in appearance, but he was unprepared for her astonishment when she met them at the door.

She didn't even say hello; she simply looked stunned, then announced, "You shaved off the beard!"

He touched his chin, the freshly-shaven skin feeling exposed and vulnerable, a sharp contrast with the weathered tan around his eyes and forehead.

"And got your hair cut!"

The red curls were still a bit unruly. Eunice, Jessie's present caretaker, was no professional barber, but she'd done her best when he asked her assistance last evening, and it was a big improvement. He was slightly embarrassed—but pleased—at the way Rosalyn was examining him with such apparent interest. He wasn't dressed up, but he hadn't worn stagged-bottom work pants today.

"I looked in the mirror after I went home. It's a wonder you didn't run screaming into the woods when you saw me yesterday."

"You were a bit intimidating." Rosalyn's smile did unlikely things to his usually rock-solid pulse.

"I brought the venison." He held up the burlap bag he carried.

Rosalyn took the bag and peered warily inside as if she expected something might jump out at her. She seemed relieved that it was a neatly cut chunk off the haunch. Just then Jessie spotted Andy lying on the makeshift mattress. She clapped her hands in delight. "There's the baby!"

"Would you like to meet Andy?" Rosalyn held out a hand. Jessie wasn't one to shy away from people, but neither did she offer her friendship or trust without careful consideration. Her inquisitive blue eyes gave Rosalyn a good going over.

With her dark trousers, Rosalyn wore a blouse the color of a winter sunset, and her hair, soft and gleaming, curved against her shoulders. She had tied it back with a pink ribbon, and wispy tendrils danced at her forehead. A hint of rose-hued lipstick tinted her mouth.

Rosalyn passed Jessie's inspection—and Shea's too—and his daughter transferred her grip to Rosalyn's hand. Andy, with that knowledge which seems instinctive to babies, immediately recognized Jessie was a different sort of person than the adults who always surrounded him. Jessie got down on the bed with him, held out her finger, and the baby immediately grasped it. In a moment she was chattering away to him, and he was answering in some indecipherable baby language.

Rosalyn and Shea exchanged pleased glances and smiled at

each other. He glanced around. She seemed to be alone.

"Nadine is out climbing the hill to see if town is visible from the top," she explained. "Nadine is not...crazy about the wilderness."

"And your mother? How does she feel about living here?"

"She doesn't say much one way or the other." A disinterested attitude which Shea had also noted about Mrs. Fallon. "At the moment she's upstairs, but I'm sure she'll be down later."

So far as Shea had seen, there was nothing upstairs but rusty old beds and the heavy box he'd carried up for her, which she'd treated as if it held precious jewels. Although he doubted that could be, given what appeared to be the precarious financial position of the family.

"I guess I'd better put the venison on to cook." Rosalyn peered into the bag again. "I suppose it should be...roasted?"

"Slow cooked in a covered pan with some water in the bottom." Shea made the suggestion tentatively. He didn't want to intrude on her kitchen domain, but Rosalyn nodded as if she were grateful for the advice. "Putting some slices of onions on top helps take away the gamy flavor," he added.

"I'm afraid we don't have any onions."

Shea instantly chastised himself for not bringing some from his own supply. "Just salt and pepper, then. This was a young buck and shouldn't taste too gamy anyway. I could slice off some steaks, if you'd like, so you could have them for a later meal."

"We don't have a refrigerator, so there's no way to keep them."

"Sure there is. There's the cooler out by the woodshed. The room with the thick sawdust walls?" he added, when her blank look told him she knew nothing about country-style coolers. "The sawdust acts as insulation. That's where hunters hang a carcass to keep it cool."

Rosalyn smiled and shook her head a little helplessly. "There's so much I don't know," she admitted. "I've always lived in the city—"

"In a nice home, with servants."

Rosalyn nodded.

"And it's especially hard on your mother."

"Mother hasn't been the same since my father was killed and our...circumstances changed," Rosalyn said hesitantly. "She takes some interest in the baby, but that's about all."

Shea had sliced off the steaks and Rosalyn had just placed the roast in the oven when Jessie tiptoed into the kitchen.

"Sssshh," she whispered. "The baby's asleep." She spoke in the mature, proprietary way she sometimes had, as if she were years older than Andy. "Me and the doggie—"

"The doggie and I." He'd recently started trying to do something about the grammar Jessie picked up from an assortment of playmates. "Actually, her name is Smiley. What about you and Smiley?"

"We're going out to play."

"Okay. Don't go beyond the woodshed."

He watched from the doorway for a minute. A sudden roar made him glance back at the kitchen. Rosalyn was looking with alarm at the stove as if she expected it might explode any minute.

"All I did was put in a few sticks of wood—"

"It'll be okay." He showed her how to regulate the draft and damper to get slower, more even heat.

"No wonder I've been burning everything I tried to cook." She sighed. "I'll bet your Jessie knows more about cooking than I do."

Shea chuckled. "Jessie does help me cook—when I'm home." He paused, thoughtful. "At least she's with me more now that I'm not working full time. We have some special times together.

150

But it still doesn't seem like enough."

Rosalyn nodded. "It must be difficult for you both." She got five plates from the cupboard and carried them to the dining room, where they barely filled one end of the massive table. She had to step over a corner of the beds on the floor to get around the table.

"If that table weren't so large, you'd have a lot more room in here. I could cut it down if you'd like," he suggested.

"You've done so much already and I didn't invite you over to work," she protested.

"I'd be glad to do it." Which was true. He'd made most of the furniture for the cabin, rough but serviceable, but he hadn't done indoor carpentry work since the day Molly died. The day he'd come home and smashed the bookcase he'd been building for her birthday.

He went out to the truck and got his handsaw. Within a few minutes he had the table reduced to a reasonable size. Together, he and Rosalyn scooted the larger, leftover piece outside for use as a summer picnic table. By the time the venison roast was giving off a delectable scent, and Nadine had returned from her hike up the hill with a disgruntled report that all she could see was "trees and more trees," he had most of the sharp edges rounded off with a file. Before the meal was ready he also filled the woodbox, carried a half dozen buckets of water, filled the lamps with kerosene he'd brought from home, and, noticing diapers draped everywhere to dry, made a clothesline out of wire he found in the woodshed. Jessie, as inquisitive as always, followed him everywhere until the baby woke and she went back to play with him.

Supper was a great success. Without any prior discussion, Shea bowed his head and offered a prayer of thanks. From the way everyone accepted it he knew that saying grace was customary in this household. The meat was tasty, not gamy, and the gravy Rosalyn made from the drippings served to soften the hard biscuits. The rock-solid nuggets of dough, which she had so carefully mixed, made him want to hug her; she was trying so hard. Dessert was canned pears. Rosalyn said their cook back in Indiana had put them up last summer, which again told of the privileged life she'd once lived.

Rosalyn didn't want him to rush off, and she was delighted when, after the meal, Jessie begged, "Let's sing, Daddy."

While Shea went out to the truck to get some unnamed instrument, Jessie chattered about everything from an interesting worm she'd found in the yard to how her daddy climbed to the top of trees that reached the sky to chop them down. That seemed a bit unlikely, but Rosalyn laughed, liking her. She was so bright and busy and serenely certain the world revolved around her daddy. She was sturdily built, her hair more silky and coppery than her father's, but the family resemblance was unmistakable.

Rosalyn wouldn't have been surprised if Shea had managed to wrest a piano out that unlikely treasure-chest of a truck, but what he did produce was a harmonica.

He smiled after he made a preliminary riffle of notes. "I can't say that it's my first choice of instrument, but in a logging camp you have to make do with what's available."

"What would have been your first choice?"

"My grandfather was a violin maker," he said, surprising her. She'd assumed he came from a long line of loggers. "I heard a lot about him and always thought I'd like to learn the violin, but he died when I was only five or six."

Shea knew dozens of tunes, most of them lively and rollicking, and Rosalyn enjoyed the unexpected entertainment.

Without the concealing beard she could make a better estimate of his age. Twenty-seven or twenty-eight, she decided. He was also a very good-looking man, even a "heartthrob" as Charlie might have put it. The beard had hidden a face more angular than she expected. Strong cheekbones, square jaw, faint laugh lines at the corners of eyes that were a deep sea-blue when he was serious or lit like sunlight dancing on the sea when he laughed. And an always ready flash of smile. He was also a man with keen powers of observation, she reflected, remembering how he had so quickly understood their situation.

Nadine surprisingly knew the words to many of the tunes he played, many more than Rosalyn did, and when Jessie didn't know words she cheerfully made up her own, often including a whirling dance. One song she knew by heart was "Jesus Loves Me," and she sang a sweet solo to Andy when it was time to put him down for the night.

When Jessie, too, got sleepy, Shea picked her up in his big arms and said they'd best be getting home. He seemed reluctant to go and Rosalyn was reluctant for him to leave. His cheerful masculine presence somehow changed the whole atmosphere of the gloomy house.

"I have some spare shingles at my place," he said as Rosalyn followed him to the door. "I'll bring them over tomorrow and see what I can do." He nodded toward the ceiling.

"Really, you've already done so much for us—"

"I don't want my new neighbors giving up and moving away just because of a leaky roof."

Rosalyn caught her breath, because his expressive eyes said more. They said he specifically didn't want *her* to move away. "Thank you, then. We'd appreciate that."

Observant Nadine picked up on the comment and the way his eyes held Rosalyn's. "I told you he was sweet on you." She said smugly as soon as he was gone. "He's courting you."

"He's just being neighborly."

"He didn't have to get a haircut and a shave just to be neighborly," Nadine pointed out.

CHAPTER

Fifteen

❧

Shea returned the following day with several armloads of sweet-scented cedar shingles in the back of his truck. He flatly turned down Rosalyn's offer to pay him. She learned that they were left over from the building of his own house, and that he'd cut them himself.

A man of many talents—talents to solve problems that Rosalyn had been too sheltered to realize existed. And what a disastrous situation they would have been in without his competent and willing assistance. She had known the Lord would see them through. Although she hadn't realized help would come in the form of one brawny, red-headed logger!

Rosalyn, Nadine, and Ellen watched as he put a ladder to the side of the house, clambered to the ridge of the roof and anchored himself with a safety tether to the chimney. He scarcely seemed to need the rope, however, as he worked his way back and forth across the roof with surprising agility, inserting fresh shingles to cover the gaps.

He finished by noon and had a midday meal with them. Jessie had spent most of the morning happily "taking care" of Andy. While they were lingering over coffee, Rosalyn noted that

Shea was absent-mindedly picking at something on his right hand.

"Did you hurt yourself?"

He looked down at his hand. "I probably picked up a sliver or two. It's an occupational hazard, when you're handling shingles."

"Let me see."

He held out his hand reluctantly, like a small boy caught at something, and Rosalyn could see several small slivers and a longer one embedded in his hand. Before thinking better of it, she touched the skin over the dark line of sliver at the base of his thumb with her fingertip, oddly feeling the contact with a peculiar jolt out of proportion to the feathery touch. She jerked away and then, embarrassed at the overreaction, determinedly studied the hand with a purposely clinical attitude, her own hands clasped behind her back.

"Those really should come out. Especially that big one."

"I'll work on them later," he said.

"How?"

"With a pocket knife and tweezers."

"It's almost impossible to use your left hand to get a splinter out of your right hand, unless you're left-handed," Rosalyn pointed out. "And you're not left-handed."

Shea dug into his trousers and produced a pocket knife. "How about seeing what you can do?"

Pocket-knife surgery was not something Rosalyn wanted to tackle, but she could hardly refuse after all he'd done for them. She found tweezers and a bottle of iodine and scrubbed both knife and tweezers in hot, sudsy water. She then rolled up Shea's sleeve and scrubbed his hand, looking up once to find him grinning as if he were enjoying the procedure.

He straddled the bench at the dining room table and draped his hand on the table. Jessie climbed up and squatted on the

156

table to watch, and Nadine knelt on the opposite bench and leaned across the table so she had a good view also.

There was nothing intimate about taking Shea's hand in hers, Rosalyn assured herself as she eyed the deeply lined palm. It was purely a medical procedure.

Yet it felt intimate, grasping his hand with her left one to steady it—and herself—while she gently slid the tip of the knife under the end of a splinter, then reversing hands so she held the knife in her left hand and used the tweezers with her right to extract the sliver. His skin felt warm against hers, rough with calluses but not unpleasant, the bones of his competent hand big and solid. A myriad of tiny nicks and old scars interrupted the fine lines of his fingerprints. Even as she worked, with her lower lip caught between her teeth in concentration, she was aware of the nearness of him, the compelling masculinity of his size and the glint of red-gold hairs on his muscular forearm.

The scent of cedar lingered on his clothes, and she felt the faint warmth of his breath on the back of her exposed neck as she leaned over his hand and her hair fell forward. The big sliver at the base of his thumb had broken off below the surface and she actually had to cut the skin to get to it, but he gave no indication of pain. When she was done, she doused everything with iodine.

"I hope I didn't hurt you too much."

"Not at all. It was a much better job than I could have done myself." Shea grinned as he rolled down his sleeve and rebuttoned the cuff, a sparkle of tease in his blue eyes. "You can be my nurse any day. Oh, I almost forgot, I have something out in the truck for you."

While he was gone, Nadine whispered mischievously, "Isn't there some old saying that if you save a man's life he belongs to you?"

"It's not a saying I've ever heard…and all I did was take out a few slivers, not save his life!"

"But if the slivers had gotten infected, he might have been a goner. First an infected finger, then an infected hand, finally an infected heart." Nadine projected the melodramatic progression solemnly, then giggled. "Except I think his heart is already infected. It looks to me as if he'd like to belong to you!"

"You've seen too many silly romantic movies," Rosalyn muttered.

Shea returned with a burlap bag holding venison, potatoes, fall squash, and big, yellow onions that he said were all from his garden.

"I have to get some firewood cut and hauled to town, so I probably won't be over for a couple of days. Before I leave for camp on Sunday, though, I want to make sure you know how to use that gun." He smiled gently. "You don't know how to use it, do you?"

"No," Rosalyn admitted. She'd vowed she was going to learn to shoot the gun to hunt for food if she had to, but the idea of actually wielding a deadly weapon definitely made her uncomfortable. Uneasily she asked, "Is there danger here?"

"I don't think so, but you should be prepared. I'll be back on Saturday to teach you. Do you have shells for it?"

Rosalyn nodded.

They made a trip to town the following day to pick up fresh fruit and milk and fill the pickup tank with gasoline, expenses that made Rosalyn aware of how rapidly their funds were sinking. Could she possibly get a job in town? She didn't see how, but she was soon going to have to figure out something.

She inquired about mail at the tiny post office. She had left the address of General Delivery, Castle Beach, with a few people, and there was a letter from the lawyer about final disposition of some of her father's business affairs. The postmistress was a talkative, inquisitive sort, wanting to know where Rosalyn was staying and how long they were going to be there. When Rosalyn said they were living out in the direction of Shea Donahue's place, the plump woman looked astonished. "Way out there? My goodness."

On impulse she stopped at the only hotel in town, an unimpressive, two-story, board structure, and asked if they ever had guests who inquired about hunting in the area, but all she got was a negative shake of head and an incredulous look that suggested she had, in a term Charlie had once used for her, turnips for brains.

Shea returned on Saturday afternoon. Jessie came in announcing importantly that she and her daddy had "forested" all morning.

"Forested?" Rosalyn repeated, puzzled.

"Re-forested. We planted trees," Shea explained. "I logged my place a few years ago, and whenever I get a chance I transplant new trees to take the place of those I cut. I don't think God gave us this land and forest simply to abuse and demolish. We're supposed to take care of it, too."

Rosalyn tilted her head, thinking of that devastated, logged-over area on the way to town. "You don't sound like a typical logger."

Shea grinned. "And you, of course, know all about 'typical loggers'?" he teased.

Rosalyn ignored that and led him to the table where she had set the gun and a box of shells, metal-nosed, viciously deadly things that made her nervous just looking at them. Shea expertly broke the gun open and squinted down the front end of the barrel.

He nodded approvingly. "Your father took good care of this."

He gave Jessie strict instructions to stay in the house while they were practicing with the gun and to keep Smiley in, too. Carrying a cardboard box to use as a target, he led the way to the base of the rocky hill Nadine had climbed.

"Never practice shooting where your bullets will just keep going," was his first instruction. "There's probably no one within miles, but we don't want to risk a stray bullet hitting anyone." He carefully explained the parts of the gun to her, how to open and load it, and how the safety worked. He made a practice shot to see if the gun was "sighted in" correctly. The printing on the box had an "o" in it, which the bullet neatly drilled dead center, not by accident, Rosalyn was certain.

He showed her how to brace the gun against her shoulder, line up the sights, and squeeze, not yank, the trigger, and finally told her to try a shot. She yelped in surprise as the gun's explosion kicked the wooden stock against her shoulder.

"Are you all right?" His big hands anxiously probed her shoulder and collarbone for injuries. "Maybe this gun is too big for you—"

"I'm fine," Rosalyn said, and his face reddened as he looked down and saw where his hands were. He withdrew them hastily. "What did I hit?" she asked.

Not the target. The bullet had chewed up a chunk of earth well in front of the box. She tried three more times, not getting much closer. Keeping the heavy rifle from wobbling while lining up the front and rear sights was much more difficult than it looked.

"We'd better give your shoulder a few minutes' rest," Shea advised. He took the gun and set it on a nearby rocky ledge.

Rosalyn massaged her shoulder. It was a dazzling fall day, brilliant sunshine, with scents of woodsmoke and an invigorating ocean tang in the air. Wild maples blazed golden among the green fir and pine, but the russet-barked madrone, which supplied most of the firewood they burned, didn't lose its glossy leaves in the fall.

"I'm going to worry about you while I'm away next week," Shea said.

Rosalyn could feel him watching her, but it was not an unpleasant feeling. She was, in fact, doing some studying of her own. The line between the tanned and untanned, recently shaven areas of his face was already beginning to fade, and the scratch she guiltily remembered raking across his cheekbone had healed. His clothes, as usual, were workaday rough, but they took nothing away from his rugged shoulders and lean hips. Quite a glorious specimen of manhood, she had to admit.

"Do you like being a logger?" she asked impulsively.

He braced a rough boot on the rock beside the gun and leaned a hand on his bent knee. "I like working out in the woods, and I'm certainly not opposed to all logging, but I'm frustrated by the methods of most companies. Although the outfit I'm working for now is better than most. But sometimes," he admitted ruefully, "I've had a most unchristian feeling of wishing I could knock together a few heads when I see so much unnecessary waste and destruction. Sometimes I think of what John Muir wrote: 'Any fool can destroy trees. They cannot defend themselves or run away.'"

So Shea read John Muir, the Scottish naturalist who wrote so passionately of his wilderness travels. She shook her head lightly. "You really aren't a typical logger, are you?"

He smiled and shrugged. "Maybe not."

"How did you happen to move here from Michigan?"

"My parents were both schoolteachers there." He smiled, this time with a haze of faraway reminiscence in his eyes. "Not a

161

common situation and many people were horrified that my mother kept on teaching after she married and had us boys. But it seemed natural enough to us. They were godly people and instilled their beliefs in my older brother Adam and me."

He spoke of his parents in the past tense, she realized, and his next words confirmed that observation.

"An outbreak of influenza took them both while Adam and I were still in school."

"Oh, Shea, how terrible for you!"

"Adam quit school immediately to go to work and support us. I wanted to quit, too, but he wouldn't let me." Shea laughed. "He was about half my size, but he could boss me around. After I graduated, we took off and bummed around the country for a couple of years, working a few weeks or months here and there. We saw everything from the skyscrapers of New York to the beaches of Florida. We even passed through Indiana. Finally we worked our way west, going from a logging outfit in Montana to one up in Washington and finally here to Oregon. Then Adam decided it was time I went to college."

"College?" Rosalyn repeated, surprised. But, on reflection, she wasn't so surprised after all. True, Shea had his rough edges...she suspected she also might acquire some, living out here like this! Perhaps it took rough edges to survive here. But his speech wasn't backwoods uneducated and there was somehow an air of confidence and self-assured leadership about him.

"Our parents had intended for us both to go to college. I'd always liked books and school, but Adam didn't and had no desire for higher education. Which didn't mean he couldn't be very stubborn and bossy about its value for me." His smile revealed affection, not resentment for his brother's attitude.

"You didn't want to go?"

"Oh, yes, I wanted to, but I didn't see how we could swing it financially. But we did. I enrolled at Oregon State and between

162

my working part time and Adam working in the woods to help pay my way, I was almost able to finish."

"And then?"

"Then Adam had both arms crushed in a logging accident. I quit college and went to work to take care of him and pay for the best medical care I could find."

"Didn't his employer help? Father's company back in Indiana had a system set up to pay any injured worker's medical bills, plus wages until he could return to work."

"Unfortunately, most companies are not so concerned about their workers. Which is something else I'd like to change. I'm afraid it will only get worse, with new mechanized saws and equipment I hear are coming. I've planned for quite a while to start my own logging company after the depression is over, but sometimes—" Shea hesitated and then glanced at her as if suspecting she might laugh at his next words. "Sometimes I think I might eventually go into politics."

She didn't laugh. She nodded reflectively. "That may be the only way to make real changes. Where is your brother now?"

Shea's throat moved in a rough swallow. "He died in the same boating accident that killed Molly."

"Oh, Shea, you lost your wife and brother the same day?"

"I was the only survivor." For a moment an unfamiliar bitterness clouded his voice. "Sometimes the Lord's will and workings are difficult to understand."

"Yes."

The fervency of Rosalyn's response brought Shea's gaze from the blue haze of faraway hills back to her face. "You, too?" he asked softly.

She nodded. "Have you ever really understood?" she asked with a hint of wistful longing.

"No," he admitted. "I regretted and mourned my parents'

passing, but it was losing Molly and Adam together that really shook my faith for a time. I went...wild for a while. But eventually I came to an acceptance and peace with what happened."

"My faith isn't...shaken," Rosalyn said slowly, as if she were trying to sort through her own her thoughts. "But..."

"Your father's death?"

"More than his death." She filled in the details, then, of all the drastic changes in their lives that had led them to this isolated refuge. The collapse of her father's company, her lack of funds to continue her education at Wellesley, the loss of their home, and the final, agonizing uncertainty about the circumstances of her father's death. "I don't want to believe he deliberately stepped in front of that car. I don't want to think that at the end he lost faith and abandoned his beliefs. But..." Again her words trailed off and she shook her head helplessly.

"Oh, Rosalyn." He wrapped his arms around her almost fiercely, holding her close, wishing he could take away the pain and uncertainty and ease the devastating changes in her life. He felt her slim body tremble and her tears seep through his shirt. He put a hand on her soft hair and held her face close to his shoulder and his cheek on the top of her head.

Finally she leaned her head back and looked up at him, the glitter of tears bringing out the gold in her brown eyes. "There's something else I should tell you."

He listened in astonishment and growing anger at what she next told him, about the man she'd been in love with and her best friend eloping together. How could this guy, this Robbie, have been not only ruthlessly cruel and unethical, but stupid? To have Rosalyn in love with him and carelessly toss her love away!

Finally, she retreated from his arms. Reluctantly he let her go. She accepted the clean handkerchief he pulled from his pocket.

"And the worst part," she added, sounding bewildered and unhappy, "is that in spite of everything, I'm not over loving him."

From the moment she'd started telling him about the other man, Shea had had a sinking feeling this was true. He didn't know what to say. *Be patient; you'll get over him. He betrayed your love; forget him!*

But what he did, almost without thinking about it, was take her in his arms again. She didn't resist and he was glad he could comfort her. Yet, oddly, it hurt to know she was thinking of this Robbie even while she was in his arms. Even while he was falling in love with her.

No. He'd known her only a few days. He didn't believe in careless, impulsive "love" generated more by physical attraction than genuine emotion. Not that Rosalyn wasn't physically attractive! The other day, when she'd been working on his hand and her soft hair had fallen away from her neck, he'd almost leaned down to kiss that lovely patch of exposed skin. But she was also sweet and loving and generous. Look how she'd taken in Nadine and her baby, how she devotedly cared for her mother! She had a powerful sense of responsibility plus a fierce determination and an unwavering confidence in the Lord.

Yes, even though the time was very brief, his love for her was deepening. Wryly he thought of Elaine and Rachel. They would've been delighted to have been the recipients of such affection…and instead he was falling for the one who was still in love with another.

He sighed and again set his mind on the shooting lesson. She was no expert by the end of the afternoon, but she did manage to hit the box twice, in opposite corners. He felt reasonably certain that, in an emergency, she'd be able at least to scare off a predator, animal or human.

He was pleased when, before he and Jessie went home, Rosalyn brought up the idea of attending church together the following morning.

Sixteen

Rosalyn woke with the glorious feeling that something wonderful was happening this day. Yes, they were going to
church. And they were going with Shea! Even the blue-black
bruises and soreness of her shoulder couldn't dampen the bright
hope of this beautiful day.

But the feeling quickly disappeared when Andy woke cranky
and his breakfast came up all over Nadine's one good dress. Ellen
didn't think Andy's problems were serious, just teething pains
that had brought on an upset stomach. She gave him a rubbery
spatula to chew on, which seemed to soothe him, but taking him
on the rough ride to town hardly seemed a good idea.

Shea looked surprised when he arrived and found Rosalyn in
a rumpled shirt and trousers and Nadine and Ellen still in their
robes. It was the first time Rosalyn had seen him in anything
other than work clothes, and she had to admit the midnight blue
suit, white shirt, and polished dark shoes made an impressive difference. His tie had a pattern of narrow, dark red diagonal lines,
certainly nothing flashy, but the bit of color added a definite flare
of style. She knew the suit couldn't be as expensive either in fabric or cut as the custom-made suits Robbie wore, but it couldn't

have looked any better on Shea if every inch had been measured and fitted.

"If you're going into politics today," she teased lightly, feeling breathless, "you have my vote." The only incongruous note was the burlap bag in his left hand.

"Clothes make the man?" he suggested, with an amused quirk of lips and questioning arch of red eyebrow.

No. In Shea's case, the clothes looked good on him and were an attractive change, but it was definitely the man who made the clothes. Rugged shoulders, trim midsection, long legs. It suddenly occurred to Rosalyn that such an attractive man must have women in his life. Not that this mattered to her, of course.

Jessie looked sweet and lovely, too, in a pink dress, the gleam of her copper-red curls showing Shea's loving care with a brush. And the burlap bag this time contained a big ham Shea said he had gotten in part payment for a load of firewood.

When Rosalyn hesitated in accepting another gift, he grinned. "I'm counting on being invited for dinner and eating my share of it."

Rosalyn smiled back. "You're invited for dinner."

Rosalyn briefly explained Andy's teething and upset stomach. "I suppose we could leave Nadine and the baby here, but I really don't think that's a very good idea."

She doubted that Nadine was particularly disappointed about missing church, but the glum-faced young woman was definitely disappointed about missing a trip to town. Ellen would probably have stayed home with Andy, but Rosalyn felt just as uneasy with that alternative. Ellen often helped care for the baby, but she frequently had a vague air of not knowing what was going on. The baby really shouldn't be left alone with her.

"No reason we can't have our own worship service right here, is there?" Shea suggested.

167

The idea appealed to Rosalyn, and she sent Shea outside while she changed into different clothes to give some dignity to the occasion. Her enthusiasm unexpectedly infected Nadine and Ellen, and by the time Rosalyn called Shea back inside they were all in Sunday best, Nadine in a fresh dress that Rosalyn lent her. The soft, orchid-colored wool drooped a bit on Nadine's slight frame, but a few appropriately placed pins helped.

They sat at the dining room table, Shea at the head. He read from Matthew and they discussed the verses, Jesus' words about not worrying about your life or what you would eat or drink or wear. Verses that Rosalyn suspected Shea intuitively knew she needed, because she definitely did tend to worry. They sang some of the old hymns they all, except Nadine, knew by heart. Shea's voice, if not as polished as Robbie's professional radio-announcer tones, rang with conviction and strength. With a prompting in places from Shea, Jessie sweetly sang a simple song that Rosalyn had never heard before, about Jesus answering prayers.

After the improvised service, Rosalyn, following Shea's cooking instructions, put the ham on to cook. By that time Shea had loosened his tie and unbuttoned his suit jacket.

"Look, would you mind if I went home and changed?" he finally asked as he rolled his shoulders against the restraint of the dress clothes. He laughed as he looked at Jessie who was happily astride a cheerful Smiley. "Jessie, too. I spent almost half an hour ironing that dress and I'd rather not have to wash pawprints off it and do it again."

A task he could probably do better than she could, Rosalyn thought, remembering how a hired laundress had always taken care of such things back home. Where there had also been Hattie to cook and maids to fuss over you. The kind of comfortable life Charlie was living right now.

Let it go, she told herself fiercely. *Let it go.*

"When I get back, I'd like to take you someplace and show you something special," Shea added.

"Where is there to go out here?"

"You'll see. But you should change clothes, too."

By the time he returned, Rosalyn had changed out of her lovely pink dress, which instinct more than experience told Shea was probably expensive silk. Now she was in her customary shirt and trousers.

He found her equally appealing in either, but the trousers were definitely more practical for what he had in mind.

He led the way out past the woodshed. At the point where the ground fell away steeply, taking her hand in his seemed the natural thing to do, and he was pleased that she didn't object. Her fingers clasped his, her hand so much smaller than his yet her grip wiry and firm.

"Where are we going?"

"You'll see," he repeated.

It was rough going on the steep, rocky hillside, but he knew a well-worn deer trail that zig-zagged around some of the worst places. He helped Rosalyn over an occasional rock or log, although he suspected she let him help more out of politeness than because she really needed assistance. On the flat below the hill, the tall trees stretched like magnificent spires longing to touch the sky and a soft moss covered the rocks with green velvet. Here, the scent of forest untouched by the saws of man was damp and lush, a little mysterious. Vine maple added a blaze of red and copper-brown, the colors deeper than the yellow-gold of full-sized maple trees. Once something crashed through the brush to their left and Rosalyn stopped short. He could feel the thud of her heartbeat as she pressed close to him, her hand clutching his arm like a small vise.

"The cougar?"

He had to admit a small temptation to tell her yes. What better excuse for protectively wrapping his arms around her! But honesty made him say, "No. Just a deer or two we scared up. They like to bed down in here during the day."

"How can you be sure it's deer?"

He smiled. "It's one of the things experience in the woods teaches you."

After a moment Rosalyn's stiffness relaxed. He was glad for her trust but sorry to lose that sweet pressure of her body close to his. They could hear the creek through the veil of trees before they saw it, the musical bubble of water over rocks and the steady splash of the waterfall. He pulled a curtain of prickly brush aside so Rosalyn could step through to the flat ledge of rock above the pool of water formed by a natural rock dam. The creek was higher now than it was at midsummer, when he'd come here a few times to swim, but there hadn't yet been enough fall rain to give it the whitewater roar of winter flow.

"It's beautiful!" She sounded awed.

"I thought you'd like it."

The creek swirled and danced through the rocks upstream before falling in graceful, silver-white ribbons to the deep pool just below them. Miniature waves rippled beneath the waterfall, but the far end of the pool was calm except for the glassy swoop through a cleft in the boulders. Sunlight slanting through the trees lit the depths of the pool with a golden glow on one side, while the other side lay in mysterious shadow. A trout darted from darkness into light, snapped a frisky bite at a bug on the surface and disappeared again. Rippling circles widened around the spot where the fish had broken the surface, colliding with the larger ripples from the waterfall.

"Oh, I'd love to go swimming here!" Rosalyn exclaimed eagerly. An unexpectedly reckless look sparkled in her eyes, as if she were halfway thinking of plunging in. She looked at him and laughed, apparently suspecting he was reading her mind. "But the water is much too cold now, of course," she added demurely.

"There's a good place to sit right over there." Shea pointed to a higher ledge right next to the waterfall, and they scooted to the edge so their feet dangled above the pool.

They simply sat in companionable silence for several minutes.

Finally Shea asked gently, "Are you sorry you came here, Rosalyn?"

"To see the creek and waterfall? Of course not!" She leaned over, letting a vagrant spray from the waterfall spatter her hand with clear drops.

"No, not the waterfall. Here. To this place and life."

"It doesn't really matter how I feel," she said slowly. She tucked her hands beneath her thighs, and he briefly wondered if the gesture, conscious or subconscious, was to keep him from taking her hand in his. Which was exactly what he wanted to do. "We had no choice. Although I sometimes wonder how we're going to survive here."

"You have—" He paused. He felt uncomfortable prying in this area and yet it concerned him. Everything about Rosalyn, he realized, concerned him. "Financial complications?"

She laughed. "That's putting it mildly. Back in Indiana I had all these live-off-the-land plans that seem so foolish now. How we'd have a cow and raise a garden and chickens." She shook her head.

"That's not impossible. I can help you with a garden."

"But it's not enough to exist on completely. I also had this grandiose idea that my father's 'hunting lodge' would be suitable for taking in hunters as paying guests, to provide us with income.

171

Which, considering the reaction I got from a man at the hotel in town, was probably a crazy idea even before I discovered that what we have here is more an overgrown shack than hunting lodge."

It wasn't a crazy idea. In Montana he'd known of easterners staying as paying guests at ranches or lodges while hunting or fishing. But she was right; at this point it was not a workable idea.

A totally different idea briefly darted into Shea's head. *You could marry me!* But it was much too soon for that, of course. He might be certain he was falling in love—falling as inevitably as a sawed tree plunging to the forest floor—but she was still too tied to the pain of recent heartbreak, not yet ready even to consider loving again, much less actually marrying.

"I suppose what I need is a job," she went on. "But living way out here, I don't know how I could get to a job even if I could find one. Father never wanted to log the property, and I can certainly see why. But it may come to that eventually." Her gaze followed the brilliant, red-headed flash of a woodpecker swooping into a dead tree on the far side of the creek. She nodded as if assuring herself of something. "The Lord will see us through."

Looking to the future, Shea posed a careful question. "If your financial situation wasn't so...uncomfortable, could you be happy here?"

"I certainly have no desire to go back to Gideon and run into the bubbling newlyweds every few days!" Sounding guilty, she added, "I know that being angry and bitter isn't right. But I— I was so much in love with Robbie..."

"*Was* in love?" he repeated lightly.

"I'm trying very hard to make it 'was.' I don't want to feel anything for him. He's married to someone else." Rosalyn sighed. "But love isn't always rational or sensible or right. Sometimes it just won't go away even when you want it to. It clings on and on, like a splash of cheap perfume." Unexpectedly she smiled and added, "Although sometimes I think I miss my best friend as much or more than I miss Robbie. I worry about her. She rushed into the marriage so impulsively."

Carefully Shea asked another question. "What kind of man is Robbie?"

"Deceptive and deceitful, obviously! A man not to be trusted. Definitely not the kind of man I want to love! Or did you mean, what does he look like, what does he do for a living?" She tilted her head and looked at him with curiosity. "Why do you want to know?"

The blunt question caught Shea by surprise. The answer was simple: He wanted to scout out the competition for Rosalyn's heart! But he didn't want to scare her off or make her reluctant to accept any help he could give her, so he simply said, "I'm interested."

She told him, then, and he listened with growing dismay. Robbie Grenwich was wealthy and handsome, Princeton-educated and world-traveled. His future in his family's business of radio stations and movie theaters, a business he was in line to take over eventually, was secure.

In short, he was all the things Shea Donahue was not.

However, Shea thought with a bit of grim satisfaction, there was one irrevocable point in his favor.

Unhappy and painful as the situation might be for Rosalyn at the moment, Robbie Grenwich was married to someone else.

Later, after dinner, they had a Sunday-evening family prayer time around the dining room table together. Shea hated to leave, especially knowing he wouldn't be back for a week. But finally, there was nothing to do but gather up Jessie and go, giving her time to kiss Andy goodbye first, of course. He carried her upside down, her arms dangling so she could "walk" on the floor with her hands, a bit of foolishness she loved, and then swung her up into his arms at the door.

"I will worry about you," he said from the step to Rosalyn, who was standing at the open door. "I wish there were some way you could get in touch with me if you needed help."

"We'll be fine. Thanks for teaching me about the gun. And everything else you've done for us."

Unexpectedly, Jessie turned and held out her arms to Rosalyn. "Kiss?" she said.

Rosalyn looked momentarily startled, but then smiled. Jessie smacked her on the cheek and Rosalyn returned the kiss on Jessie's plump cheek.

Boldly Shea said, "Me, too?"

But if he thought he was going to sneak in a kiss with that lame ploy, he was mistaken. Rosalyn just laughed and shook her head.

Seventeen

❧

That week everything went wrong. Andy's teething kept him fussy and Nadine grew impatient and grumpy. A drenching rain set in. The repaired roof didn't leak, but wind and rain blew in around the drafty old windows. While stuffing rags in the cracks, Rosalyn tripped on her own shoelace and broke a dining room window. She tried to board up the window, but she had no hammer, and she hit her thumb trying to pound a nail with a rock. The chair she had carried outside to stand on sank a leg in the soft ground and dumped her in a puddle. She finally draped a blanket over the broken glass, which was about as effective as carrying soup in a sieve.

She found fresh cougar tracks around the woodshed and, more ominously, under the broken window as well. She hung the gun by the door, where she could grab it easily, but, worried about a possible accident, kept it unloaded.

Finally, partly because their supplies were running low, and partly because they were getting on each other's nerves, Rosalyn decided Thursday morning that it was time for a break.

The trip to town bore no resemblance to the pleasant drives in the country that the family gaily took back in Indiana.

Rosalyn's hands clamped white-knuckled around the steering wheel most of the way to town. Water running in the road had deepened the ruts to canyons. The puddles were small Red Seas that did not part. Twice she had to get out and pull blown-down branches from the road. In several places, small rivers of mud had cut into the roadway, treacherously narrowing it. Ellen, as usual, said nothing, but Nadine dramatically gasped or held her breath.

In town Rosalyn selected her purchases carefully. Where once she blithely ignored dollars, now she considered pennies. They must have kerosene for the lamps, soap and matches; food that wouldn't spoil easily, bacon, oatmeal, coffee, and canned goods, plus yeast and more flour for the bread she intended to try making. They were all sick of her soda biscuits that inevitably turned out like concrete nuggets or doughy blobs.

Her only small indulgences were some fresh apples and a few pink peppermint candies, but the money seemed to melt away. At the post office the only mail was a property tax bill the lawyer had forwarded and a few scrawled lines from Geoffrey, both inspected with friendly inquisitiveness by the postmistress as she handed them over. On the way out of town Rosalyn braked at a sign she hadn't noticed earlier. Chickens for sale. Fried chicken would taste so good!

She was a bit taken aback when she discovered they weren't the ready-to-eat variety. These were laying hens. She peered doubtfully at the feathered creatures scratching in their pen. Having chickens to supply eggs had been one of her earlier plans. But what did she know about poultry?

Well, why not? she challenged herself. She'd learned to shoot a gun. She could certainly cope with a few chickens! And this wasn't really an expense, she pointed out to herself; this was an investment.

She bargained on the price and got a sack of feed and a movable pen included. The owner even threw in a Bantam hen named Topsy who had raised the family of ten hens that now dwarfed her. A husband and son rounded up the squawking flock and loaded the coop into the back of the pickup.

Back at the house, Rosalyn made the unhappy discovery that she and Nadine couldn't unload the bulky load by themselves.

"Shea'll be back Saturday night, won't he?" Nadine asked. "He can do it."

Rosalyn didn't want to become any more dependent on Shea than they already were, but she didn't appear to have much choice in this. She opened the door of the coop and the hens scattered in a flurry of squawks and feathers. She had the sinking feeling she'd never see them again.

Smiley, however, took as protective an attitude toward the chickens as she did the other members of the family, and when one wandered too far into the woods she went after it. By evening, Rosalyn was delighted with her purchase. With Smiley's nose-sniffing help she had located half a dozen eggs scattered in unlikely places, and Topsy, like a small, feather-footed general, had paraded her flock back into the coop for the night.

The next morning, as they enjoyed scrambled eggs for breakfast, Rosalyn's thoughts rosily expanded to a new possibility: Why not turn this into a chicken and egg farm? Her optimism increased when the egg output rose to nine the following day. If ten hens produced nine eggs, then twenty hens could lay eighteen eggs, and fifty hens—! At how much per dozen?

Yes, things were looking up!

Her blooming optimism lasted until the following day when she braved wind and rain to let the chickens out about mid-morning.

Only two hens fluttered out when she opened the door. Puzzled, she peered inside. She instantly stepped back, reeling from the ugly tangle of blood and gore and the savage scent of raw flesh and death. Some of the chickens were partially eaten, others simply slaughtered, as if the killer had done it for the pure pleasure of killing. And Topsy, sweet, funny Topsy, was mangled worst of all.

Rosalyn leaned against the old pickup and burst into tears. Tears of loss, tears of anger and resentment and frustration. The scarf blew from her head, and rain and wind whipped her hair and shoulders but she barely noticed.

Why? Why all of this? Why any of it?

She was so lost in her own private world of tears that she didn't even hear the truck rattle to a stop beside the pickup. Not until Shea's big hand touched her shoulder did she realize she wasn't alone.

"Rosalyn?"

She looked up, startled. He hadn't shaved and a rough red stubble covered his jaws. Oil stained his shirt and a rip in his pants exposed a knee. But Rosalyn had never been so glad to see anyone. Big and strong and competent, solid as a brick mountain. She whirled to him and pressed her cheek against the hard brawn of his chest. She wrapped her arms around him and savored the smell of damp wool and fresh-cut pine, pungent oil and hard work, good, honest male scents that were so wonderfully reassuring and comforting. And then she cried some more.

Shea held her close, his hand smoothing her hair as he used his body to protect her from the wind and rain. He didn't yet know what had happened here, but his heart ached for her tears. So briefly he had known her, and yet he'd missed her as if their lives were already entwined. Not so long ago he'd doubted he would ever love again; he doubted it no more. His feelings for her were growing like a tiny flame exploding into a wildfire. His work-roughened fingers snagged on her soft hair, but she didn't seem to mind.

"I'm crying over chickens, dead chickens." Her voice, muffled against his chest, came out a bewildered, tear-rasped croak. "We'd probably have stewed them someday."

Without releasing her from his arms he leaned over and peered at a bloody slaughter in the chicken coop in the back of the pickup. The work of a skunk or weasel, he recognized. A weasel could slither through almost any crack.

He pressed his lips against her hair. "It isn't just the chickens. It's everything."

He turned her face up, wanting to kiss the closed eyelids, so nearly translucent with tears, wanting to kiss away her pain, but he wiped her streaked cheek with a callused thumb instead, a gesture that accomplished little in the falling rain.

She opened her eyes and looked at him through the shimmer of tears and rain. "You're a very perceptive man, Shea Donahue. How did you know I needed you right now?"

I'm a man falling in love.

She hurried on before he could answer. "I bought the chickens and I was so pleased with them. I was already making these big plans to,…" she swallowed and managed a wobbly smile, "to make my fortune selling eggs, I suppose. And then…Oh, Shea, I'm so glad you're back! I didn't think you'd be home until tonight."

The words enveloped him in a warmth neither chill, rain, nor wind could penetrate. "The rain finally washed us out and we shut down early." He hadn't even been home yet. He was too eager to see her.

"Where's Jessie?"

He nodded toward the truck.

As if she had a sudden attack of self-consciousness, Rosalyn suddenly removed her arms and backed away. She wiped her face with both hands and looped a wet strand of hair behind her ear, pulling herself together with characteristic courage.

"You take Jessie and go on inside. I'll clean up here. And dry off," he scolded gently. "You're soaked."

He got a shovel from the truck and buried the mangled chickens. Afterward, when he went inside he discovered the blanket-draped, broken window they'd been coping with for several days.

"How did it get broken?" he asked curiously.

Rosalyn just sighed and shook her head. "Don't ask. I hate to ask you to do any more for us, but—?"

"I'll fix it."

Rosalyn Fallon, he thought as he headed back to the truck for a hammer, *you need a husband. And I plan to apply for the position just as soon as I think there's a chance you'll say yes.*

It took him only a few minutes to nail boards across the broken window. Not a pretty repair job but protection until he could replace the glass. He also reinforced the chicken coop so the two remaining chickens would be secure from danger at night.

Life brightened for Rosalyn during the week Shea was home from the logging camp. He stopped by every day, once bringing a half dozen traps to help control their burgeoning mouse population. He also, to Rosalyn's relief, took care of emptying the filled traps. He put new glass in the dining room window and built a movable wooden fence to protect Andy, who, even though he wasn't quite crawling yet, used a creative combination of squirming, rolling, and slithering to get around with astonishing speed. He repaired loose chinking between the logs and brought a load of firewood.

But once more church eluded them. The pickup refused to start. They couldn't all go in Shea's truck because the cab wasn't large enough, and by the time he got the pickup running, it was too late to go.

The following week, while Shea was back at work, nothing truly disastrous happened. The weather wasn't stormy, merely gray and depressing. Often fog blotted out everything beyond the woodshed.

Rosalyn had never thought of herself as one who craved good times, but the days did seem so drearily uneventful. Cook. Clean. Carry in wood. Carry out ashes. Haul water. Wash clothes. Worry about money. The property tax payment was something she hadn't anticipated. Sometimes, in spite of a determination not to, she found herself thinking yearningly of movies and stage plays, sunny picnics and swimming parties, dressing up for dinner in a fine restaurant, midnight giggles in the dorm at Wellesley. And the big college dances. She'd planned to invite Robbie to one this fall…

Nadine, in her better moods, liked to tease Rosalyn about Shea, mischievously remarking on his fine "courting squash" or "courting onions." Usually Rosalyn just scoffed or ignored the teasing, but sometimes it irritated her because she strongly suspected Nadine was right, that Shea's feelings for her did go beyond the simple helpfulness of a neighbor. And how was she going to deal with that?

She liked Shea; she liked him very much. He was honest and trustworthy, good-humored and generous, a wonderful father to Jessie. He was also ambitious and hard working and capable, a man who didn't confine his Christian values to Sunday; he lived them daily. And, though she didn't like to overrate outward physical appearance, his brawny masculine physique and pulse-raising grin and red-headed good looks could hardly go unnoticed.

If her heart wasn't still all tangled up with Robbie, if it didn't still feel slashed and torn by those twin strands of betrayal…

More often now Nadine wasn't in a teasing frame of mind. She moped around silently. She did her share of work and took conscientious care of Andy, but her disposition was often so blue…a contagious blue…that Rosalyn sometimes wanted to throw a chunk of firewood at her. She seldom mentioned her husband, but a frequent brooding, faraway look in her eyes made Rosalyn suspect she thought about him often.

Ellen had taken up mending, including a basket of Shea's things, and her embroidery skills translated nicely into efficient sock repair. Otherwise she remained uncomplaining and compliant but distant, as if a glass wall stood between her and real life. Her usual answer, whenever Rosalyn tried to include her in some decision-making process, was still a vague, "Whatever you think best, dear."

By Saturday evening Rosalyn was thoroughly tired of everyone's company, including her own. When Shea showed up at the door, grinning and cheerful, she was so glad to see him that it was all she could do to keep from throwing her arms around him and kissing him.

They finally went to church the following morning. The church lacked the grandeur of the impressive brick structure back in Gideon. There were no stained glass windows, no formal choir, no fragrant flowers. Both the pews and bare wooden floor were rough and worn, and when a harsh downpour started during the service a persistent drip in one corner accompanied the sermon. Despite the gloomy weather outside, though, Rosalyn felt the warmth of God's presence among the small family of believers inside.

There was a potluck dinner in the church basement after the service. Rosalyn wasn't inclined to stay. Not knowing about the meal, they hadn't brought anything to contribute. But a friendly invitation was repeated by so many people that she finally gave in, and it was sumptuous. Casseroles and salads and desserts of all kinds. Rosalyn had an airy wedge of lemon meringue pie, something she hadn't eaten since the happy days of Hattie's cooking back home—days that now felt as if they must have been lived on some other continent in some other century. Or dreamed.

The only puzzle of the day was the open curiosity of the organ player, a very pretty dark-haired woman named Rachel who played with a nice verve. Rachel asked her about everything from family background and education to her relationship with Nadine and the baby. She was so charming, however, that it was a while before Rosalyn realized she was being quizzed, but finally, as she found she was confiding in this near stranger about her leathery bread, she stopped short.

Unexpectedly the woman gave her a hug. "I think you'll do," she said with a smile before moving on.

Now what in the world was that all about? Rosalyn wondered, bewildered.

Shea came up, looking uncharacteristically uneasy. "What did she have to say?"

"She said that she thought I'd do."

Shea offered no explanation, just grinned. "She's right."

That evening Shea reminded Rosalyn of something she had forgotten in this place where calendar and time seemed nonexistent: Thanksgiving was only a week away. And he was cooking dinner. Rosalyn protested that he did too much for them already, but he was adamant. He'd traded firewood for a turkey, and he was cooking it.

The irrelevant thought—or was it so irrelevant?—occurred to her that this was about the last thing she could ever imagine Robbie doing.

They were sitting around the stove, the only space in their living quarters that was truly warm enough to be comfortable. Rosalyn looked to her mother and Nadine for their opinion on the Thanksgiving invitation. Nadine's nod was eager, Ellen indifferent.

"I guess we're coming to dinner, then," Rosalyn said.

She followed him to the door. He was carrying Jessie, as usual. She was cheerfully independent most of the time, indignantly refusing assistance, but she always insisted on this little departure routine. "Can we bring something to the dinner?" Rosalyn asked.

"A pie, if you'd like. And bread or rolls."

Rosalyn laughed. "Shea Donahue, you're a brave man." Nadine had facetiously suggested she might try patenting her bread as a marvelous new tire-repair material.

"I have confidence in you," he said as Jessie leaned over in his arms to give Rosalyn the usual affectionate goodbye kiss.

Rosalyn's gaze met Shea's over Jessie's plump cheek. Since that one time he had never repeated his half-teasing, half-serious "Me, too?"

Which was proper and best, of course.

So why did she have this vaguely let-down feeling?

On Thanksgiving Day they piled into the pickup for the mile drive up to Shea's house. Rosalyn found herself quite excited about the outing. It felt like fun, even though the day was decidedly miserable, with stinging rain driven by a gusting wind, and, at the last minute, she'd almost had to drag her mother along.

Shea's one-story log house was larger than Rosalyn had expected, because he usually referred to it as a cabin. He'd transplanted wild azaleas and rhododendrons to landscape the yard, and a small orchard stood beyond the inevitable woodshed.

They dashed to the house, loaded down with baby and assorted baby things, pies, bread, and jars of Hattie's apricot jam and bread-and-butter pickles.

"I'm glad you're all here," Shea said. His words were directed to everyone as he welcomed them into the homey kitchen, but the warmth in his blue eyes as his gaze lingered on Rosalyn left no doubt who he was most glad to see. He had a smudge of flour on his cheek, muscular forearms exposed by rolled-up sleeves, heavy boots, a pair of pliers in his back pocket, a wooden spoon in his hand, and a long white apron over everything, an unlikely combination that made him look appealingly rough and masculine and domestic all at once.

Rosalyn felt a rush of affection and tenderness toward him, a feeling momentarily so intense that she didn't know what to do with it. "Doesn't that turkey smell wonderful!" she gushed in an awkward effort to cover the surprise and confusion following in the wake of the wave of unexpected feelings.

"I'm making mashed 'taters," Jessie announced confidently from where she stood on a chair by the kitchen counter, and Rosalyn was grateful for the excuse to hurry over and admire the "'taters." While Shea took their coats to the bedroom, Rosalyn briefly glanced into the combination living/dining room. It had few feminine touches other than a braided rug on the floor and ruffled curtains at the windows. The sofa and one upholstered chair looked store bought, but an overflowing bookcase, a desk, a child-sized rocker, and a chest of drawers all showed Shea's hand-made touch that tended more toward rough sturdiness than polished detail. And the room was so wonderfully warm and cozy, not a cold draft anywhere!

Shea offered the prayer before dinner, a plain, simple thanks for the food, for being together, and all their other blessings. Jessie followed with a Bible verse Shea had helped her memorize for the occasion. Dinner itself was jovial and a bit noisy, with Andy deciding to make a lusty contribution of some newly discovered noises. The dishes were unmatched, even chipped in places, but the turkey was juicy and tender, the stuffing memorable, and Rosalyn's bread and pies quite acceptable. After dinner, they sang and shared memories of other Thanksgivings. Even Ellen joined in and told about holidays at her childhood home in the South.

Rosalyn reveled in a wonderful sense of warmth and belonging, of family, even if they were something of a patchwork family. They had so much to be thankful for!

Finally, after they'd all pitched in to clean up dishes and the kitchen, and then had another piece of pie, Rosalyn reluctantly said they should be going home. Shea insisted on packing up most of the turkey and other leftovers to take home with them.

"I'll probably be over to eat some of it," he added, grinning.

"You're welcome anytime," Rosalyn said, and she meant it sincerely.

Ellen had already gone out to the pickup, and Nadine was in the bathroom—a real bathroom—cleaning pie off Andy.

"Thanks so much for inviting us," Rosalyn added. "It's been a wonderful day."

"Thanks for coming."

"Thanks—"

He interrupted the thanks that were beginning to stretch to inane lengths by pulling her firmly into his arms. With equal firmness he kissed her, and after only a split second of hesitation Rosalyn surrendered to the sweet magic of the kiss.

She didn't hear the door open or Nadine trying to tiptoe by without being noticed. She was too engrossed in the feel of Shea's strong arms and tender lips and her own thundering heartbeat. But Andy's cheerful squeal would have startled a hibernating bear.

Rosalyn's eyes flew open and she started to jerk away, embarrassed. But Shea's arms didn't let her go.

Unperturbed he remarked affably to Nadine, "We were just saying goodnight."

"Then don't let me interrupt," Nadine said as she scooted toward the door.

Shea didn't. Nadine wasn't even out the door before he kissed Rosalyn again.

CHAPTER

Eighteen

Rosalyn contemplated those kisses frequently over the next few days. Too frequently, she finally decided, annoyed with herself.

The kisses did not appear to have changed their basic relationship, however, which relieved her. Shea did not seem to feel that they granted rights to more; he simply remained his usual friendly, helpful self.

On Monday, Rosalyn and Nadine carried water to the house and washed clothes, their hands red and raw by the time they finished. In the evening Nadine decided to write a letter to some friends back in St. Louis, a project that required considerable help from Rosalyn with the spelling. Nadine's handwriting, Rosalyn saw as Nadine copied the address from a small notebook to the envelope, was a childlike printing.

On Tuesday they took the letter to town and bought more supplies, including a few clothes for Andy, who was bursting out of everything Nadine had for him.

Money, money, Rosalyn thought distractedly as she purchased a money order at the post office to send payment of the property taxes. In former days she never gave it a thought; now it

188

was seldom out of her thoughts.

On Tuesday evening as she was spending a few calming minutes with her Bible, the sound of a vehicle engine startled her. It didn't stop in front of the house, but instead pulled right around to the back door. Smiley, who'd gone outside earlier, barked furiously and abruptly stopped.

Rosalyn's heart thudded. Shea was at the logging camp, so it couldn't be him. He had said they were reasonably safe out here, but he'd also warned not to be too trusting. So now she did what she'd never done before, picked up her father's rifle from the shelf by the back door and shakily shoved a bullet in the chamber. She had a family to protect.

She motioned her mother and Nadine to the shadows of the dining room. She stood back from the door to give herself room to use the gun if she had to. It felt cold and slick in her sweaty hands.

A heavy knock rattled the door. She made no sound.

"Rosalyn? You in there?"

Furiously she raised the bar and flung the door open. "Shea Donahue, you scared the wits out of us! What do you mean sneaking up on us like this? You're supposed to be at the logging camp."

Shea reared back, lamplight glinting on the crisp curls of his red hair, and blinked in astonishment at both her fiery accusation and the rifle in her hands. Then he grinned, an infuriating grin, Rosalyn thought, considering the circumstances and how shaken she was.

"And I was worried that you were helpless here alone. That in an emergency you'd forget which end of the gun to point." Cautiously he took the rifle from her hands and unloaded it before placing it back on the shelf. Contritely he added, "But it was dumb of me not to realize I'd scare you coming in like this."

Rosalyn closed the door to shut out the damp air. "So now that you've scared us half to death, why are you here?"

She was glad to see him, but she wasn't about to say so, given how annoyed she was. He was wearing the clothes in which she'd first seen him, dark work pants, ragged at the bottom, and what she now knew were called calk boots, the soles spiked with metal to keep them from slipping in the woods.

"I have a job for you!"

"A job?"

"As hasher at the logging camp. The cook's niece Lulu has been hasher, but they got in a big fight and Lulu just walked out right in the middle of dinner. I told Mrs. Dubuque you wanted a job and had experience in a soup kitchen, and she said the job is yours if you'll be there by breakfast tomorrow—"

"Shea, wait, slow down. Just what is a 'hasher'?"

"Waitress, basically. Plus helping in the kitchen."

Waitress. She hadn't really been a waitress at the soup kitchen, but surely she could do it. She would do it! Yes. And with just a little money coming in they could survive here. The Lord was indeed providing for them!

"Mrs. Dubuque is not noted for her serene disposition," Shea added, "but you'll get along okay if you just do things her way. You'll share a room with her—"

"You mean, I'd have to go off and leave my mother and Nadine and Andy all alone here?" Rosalyn interrupted in dismay, her brief excitement plunging.

But of course a job at the logging camp would require staying there during the week. Otherwise Shea would be home nights with Jessie. She looked doubtfully at her mother and Nadine who had returned from the shadows now that their intruder was identified.

"What do you think?"

190

Ellen looked mildly troubled, but all she did was murmur, "Whatever you think best, dear."

"I suppose we can manage," Nadine muttered.

"You can ride to and from camp in the truck with me, so the pickup will be here for Nadine and your mother to use in an emergency." Rosalyn considered the situation a few minutes longer. It was hardly ideal, leaving her mother and Nadine to fend for themselves. But she'd prayed often enough that the Lord would provide for them, and apparently this was it.

She nodded resolutely. "I'll do it."

She and Shea briefly discussed returning to the logging camp immediately but decided arriving late and disturbing the cantankerous Mrs. Dubuque's sleep wasn't a good idea. Shea said he'd pick her up at three-thirty the next morning.

After he was gone, Rosalyn carefully went through everything she thought Nadine needed to know about the stove and gun and pickup. She also reminded Nadine to keep an eye on Ellen, who occasionally wandered in the night, to make certain she didn't go upstairs and fall. Nadine nodded, but her attitude seemed oddly sullen.

When the lamp was blown out and they were in bed, Nadine sighed and said apologetically, "I'm sorry. You took me in and you've done so much for me and Andy. I'm grateful even when I don't show it."

"I know."

"I guess I just wish it was me going off to work somewhere. Sometimes I think God wasn't too smart giving me Andy so soon."

"Nadine, what a terrible thing to say!" Rosalyn said, shocked at those appalling words coming out of the darkness. Although she knew how overwhelmed she would feel in Nadine's circumstances. "A baby is a wonderful gift from God."

"Andrew must not have thought so," Nadine muttered, "or he wouldn't have run off and left us."

Rosalyn didn't know what to say to that. She always included Nadine in her prayers, but this night she put in an especially fervent plea that Nadine, too, would find the place of refuge—that only God could create—within herself.

Shea turned the truck so the headlights lit the back of the house. Rosalyn was out the door and hurrying through the gauzy fog before he had a chance to get out of the cab and help her. She thrust a valise onto the seat beside him and climbed in after it, bringing a faint, clean fragrance of soap and immediately filling the cab with the warmth of her feminine presence. In the faint light he could see a beading of drops gleaming like diamonds in her hair and eyelashes.

"I'm not sure I'm quite awake." She blinked, scattering diamonds, and fingered her hair as if wondering if she'd combed it.

He wheeled the truck into a reverse arc around the house. "Why don't you lean back and get some sleep? It takes a couple hours to drive to camp."

"I have to stay awake so I can see how to get there on my own. I'll be driving myself on the weeks you don't work."

Shea was so startled that his foot jerked on the gas pedal, and the truck gave a bronco leap. That was true. Of course it was true. Yet somehow in his eagerness to help her get the job, and the pleasing prospect of having her close to him at the logging camp, he had not even thought of that.

"I'm nervous," Rosalyn said. "I've never done any actual waitress work."

"You'll do fine—" He broke off. There was something else he hadn't thought about. A bit grimly he added, "Actually, the men

192

are going to be so happy to see someone pretty and cheerful around the cookhouse they won't even notice if you're a good hasher or not."

What had he done here? he wondered in dismay. Only a few days ago he'd heard one of the men muttering that if he had a choice between kissing the cook's niece, Lulu, and a mule, he'd take the mule any day. But no man on earth, let alone those woman-hungry sharks at the logging camp, would ever make such a statement about Rosalyn.

It would be bad enough during the weeks he was there to keep an eye on her. And during the weeks he wasn't there? He sighed, apparently not silently.

"Is something wrong?"

Yes, the something wrong was that he was an idiot. What sensible man would bring the woman he loved—

He paused. Yes, the woman he loved. He was no longer merely falling in love with her. He was there, all the way. Last night he'd slept very little. He'd kept seeing Rosalyn there at the door with the gun, scared and courageous, angry and beautiful.

The question returned. What sensible man brought the woman he loved within reach of some forty rough, ready, woman-hungry men?

Yet he knew how strained their finances were. He couldn't put his own discomfort with the situation ahead of her needs.

He looked across the cab at her. But if they were married... Did he dare bring up the subject of marriage yet? No. He was ready to love again, but he must remember that her heartbreak was still too fresh, that she was still working through the emotions of her father's troubling death and the radical changes in her life.

Patience, Shea Donahue, he told himself with gritted teeth. Patience.

Yet he couldn't help warning, "You and Mrs. Dubuque will be the only women at the camp."

"I assumed that." She sounded untroubled.

"The men can be kind of rough and rowdy at times. You may hear language that isn't fit for a lady's ears."

"Mrs. Dubuque allows that?"

"Mrs. Dubuque can be rather rough herself. She's been known to sling a frying pan with remarkably good aim if something displeases her."

"Then perhaps I shall have to learn to wield a frying pan, too."

No, if any of the men got out of line or tried to get fresh with Rosalyn, she wouldn't need a frying pan; they'd have him to answer to. But what about all those weeks he wouldn't be at camp?

He sighed deeply again, although this time he was careful to keep it to himself.

Daylight hadn't yet arrived when they reached the logging camp, but life was stirring. Shea pointed out the cookhouse, the long oblongs of the two bunkhouses, and various other ramshackle-looking buildings. At the cookhouse, Mrs. Dubuque was already frying what looked like a mountain of hash browns, aided by a couple of kitchen helpers that Shea introduced as her nephews, boys of about fifteen or sixteen. Mrs. Dubuque was a hefty, raw-boned woman whose sharp brown eyes inspected Rosalyn with a certain scorn, as if she were some delicate hothouse flower who might not survive the day. Without preliminaries she put Rosalyn to work setting out plates and silverware. Don't, Mrs. Dubuque warned, waste time fussin' to make 'em look pretty.

The first thing Rosalyn discovered at breakfast was that big and brawny was the norm for loggers. And all the men, even the few smaller, wiry ones, ate as if they hadn't had a full meal in months, although she would soon learn this was the way loggers always ate, like hungry lions falling on their prey. They kept her running refilling dishes and bringing fresh coffee.

Almost all the men wore ragged-bottom pants, like Shea's. She'd assumed his were that way because he had no wife to fix them, but a whispered question to kitchen-helper Jeff brought the information that the men shortened the pants on purpose, for safety reasons—cuffs or a heavy hem on pants could get hung up in the woods or on logging equipment. And getting hung up in a logging operation could cost a man his life.

The men were polite enough and Rosalyn heard no unfit language, but she realized she must be drawing unusual attention when Mrs. Dubuque grumbled, "Shea never said nothin' about you being a looker, or I mighta just told him I'd git my own hasher." She looked out over the tables where a man was waving to get Rosalyn's attention and muttered sourly, "Need a tub a ice water thrown over 'em, the whole bunch of 'em."

Rosalyn had a few minutes to get settled in her room after the bagged lunches, which Mrs. Dubuque referred to as nose bags, were handed out. The camp was mostly quiet then, although in the distance she could hear frequent shrill whistles and the crash of trees and sometimes see puffs of steam or smoke from beyond a hill. Mrs. Dubuque said that came from something called a steam donkey, a piece of equipment that was used to move the logs around.

The room Rosalyn shared with Mrs. Dubuque was rough and plain, but it was part of the cookhouse and received a nice overflow of warmth from the kitchen. The only place to store her belongings was in open boxes nailed to the wall; boxes with the word "dynamite" stenciled diagonally across the sides. At a different time in her life she'd have been appalled with the hard, narrow beds, but now, after sleeping on a homemade mattress on the floor, this bed felt like luxurious comfort.

She spent most of the afternoon helping Mrs. Dubuque prepare the big evening meal of meat, potatoes, biscuits, and gravy, with a hearty bread pudding for dessert. Her last task before serving the meal was to bang the big iron triangle to call the men to eat. She ate her own meal in the kitchen after finishing her duties.

Later that evening, several of the men, including Shea, returned to the cookhouse. Rosalyn assumed this was a standard part of the day's activities, until Mrs. Dubuque's grumblings let her know that the men usually hung around the bunkhouse playing cards or telling tall stories in the evening.

"Didn't have all this goin' on when Lulu was here," Mrs. Dubuque muttered darkly. But she did like the music from the Victrola the men brought up from the bunkhouse, even though there were only two records to play over and over.

When Rosalyn inquired why there were no more records, a dark-haired, good-looking guy named Johnny explained that a couple of men got in a fistfight at the bunkhouse, and in the general brawl that followed all the other records were broken.

"What in the world is there to fight about here?" Rosalyn asked.

"Cards. Insults. Boredom. Although in this case the fight was over a girl in town." With a flirty flash of smile and a bold stroll of dark eyes from Rosalyn's hair to toes, Johnny added, "And she wasn't half as pretty as you."

A dull crunching sound drew everyone's attention. In the light of the kerosene lanterns Shea's face was expressionless, but the tin cup from which he had been drinking coffee now had a midsection crushed to the size of a silver dollar.

"Accident," he muttered.

Rosalyn had vaguely assumed, before working at the camp, that a logger simply went out and sawed down trees every day. Now she had an inkling there were many different jobs. While she was kneading bread one morning, she asked Mrs. Dubuque, who for once seemed in a cheerful, talkative mood, about what the men did.

"Well, first off, there's the guys who work the misery whips—"

"Whips!" Rosalyn interrupted, shocked.

Mrs. Dubuque rolled her eyes at Rosalyn's Indiana ignorance, and explained that misery whips were the two-man crosscut saws with which the trees were cut down. The men working the saws were the fallers and buckers, who felled the trees and cut them into proper log lengths. There were also choker setters and hook tenders, and other tasks, everything from keeping the saws sharp to operating the steam donkey. A young beginner was usually assigned the lowly job of whistle punk, sending signals to the "donkey puncher" about moving the logs.

"And then, of course, there's the high rigger, like Shea, who cuts the spar pole and rigs the cables for the steam donkey."

Rosalyn's puzzled look apparently told Mrs. Dubuque that what Shea did was still a mystery to her.

With uncharacteristic generosity the cook suggested, "Take a look from out front and you can probably see him." Rosalyn wiped her hands on her apron and hurried to the front steps. Mrs. Dubuque came along and pointed across the canyon to where a figure that looked miniature against the soaring height of a tree was scaling the bare trunk by throwing a loop of rope upward, climbing to it and throwing it again. A flash of familiar red hair told Rosalyn the climber was indeed Shea. A metallic glint at his heels came from what Mrs. Dubuque said were climbing spurs. Mrs. Dubuque's generosity didn't extend to letting her just stand there and gawk, but she snatched a minute occasionally to run out and watch. She saw Shea progress from sawing off limbs when he reached them, working ever upward, until he started cutting through the trunk itself. He must be, she realized, close to two hundred feet off the ground.

She gasped when the upper section of the tree toppled, but it was the action of the section of tree remaining that made her hand fly to her throat. The bare trunk with Shea clinging to it whipped back and forth like an angry vertical snake—an over-sized flagpole gone berserk—twisting and arcing dizzily to one side and then the other. What if it snapped, flinging Shea into space? It seemed to Rosalyn that the whipping tree took forever to calm to a gentle sway.

"Now he'll start riggin' the cables up there," Mrs. Dubuque said as if this were some everyday occurrence. Which it probably was, Rosalyn realized, feeling dazed. Jessie had gotten the details a bit muddled, but she was right: Shea did climb trees that "reached the sky" to chop part of them down! The cook prodded her with a sharp elbow. "C'mon, time to git back to work."

Rosalyn had always respected Shea as a fine and godly man, a good father and caring neighbor; now she had a new respect for the dangerous work he did daily.

After that first week, life didn't turn rosy, but money coming in from Rosalyn's job eased some of the sharpest worries and they even splurged a bit to buy real mattresses, used but sturdy. Nadine and Ellen managed satisfactorily in her absence, although Ellen still showed little interest in life. Andy, now crawling, was a small whirlwind getting into everything. There were no more cougar tracks, apparently meaning the predator had moved on to less-populated territory. Robbie was less often in Rosalyn's thoughts.

The two families shared a wonderful Christmas of worship and togetherness, although the temporary shutdown of logging operations due to bad weather dimmed much of the hope that the new year might bring.

January was an uneasy month. The pickup broke down and required money-gobbling replacement parts. A windstorm temporarily blocked the road with downed trees, and a big madrone blew over behind the woodshed. Shea cut and stacked the wood, but he warned they shouldn't burn it until next winter because the sap in green madrone could cause a creosote-like buildup in a chimney and start a fire. The wood he cut to sell had been down and drying since the previous year.

For Rosalyn, with the worrisome task of juggling their precarious finances, the startup of logging in what Shea called an unseasonably dry February came none too soon.

Nineteen

During the weeks Shea was present at the logging camp many of the young men paid Rosalyn attention but his icy glares kept them cautious. Rosalyn was sometimes piqued by what she considered his unnecessary protectiveness, but usually she simply ignored it. On the days he wasn't there two men in particular openly vied for her favor: Johnny with the flirty smile and dashing mustache, and Corwin, who played guitar and sang more sweetly than anything that came out of the Victrola. Mrs. Dubuque was becoming increasingly hostile to these men who cluttered up her cookhouse in the evenings.

One evening, Corwin arrived first with his guitar. Next came the young whistle punk, who was saddled with the triple burdens of inexperience, a tendency to blush the color of a rose, and the name Theodore, which the other men teasingly liked to stretch out to all three syllables. Several others followed. All simply sat there quietly listening to the good music and occasionally giving Rosalyn surreptitious, moony glances. But when Johnny sauntered in he had a restless scowl on his good-looking face and listened for only a few minutes before unexpectedly suggesting he and Rosalyn dance. Without waiting for an answer he pulled her to her feet. Rosalyn protested, but he just laughed and whirled her between the long tables.

The guitar music abruptly stopped. Johnny, whose breath suggested a few swallows of the moonshine, said arrogantly, "C'mon, Corwin, let's have some more music."

"Really, I don't want to dance—" Rosalyn tried to pull away, but Johnny clamped a cable-hard arm around her waist.

"Something lively," Johnny commanded, ignoring Rosalyn's protests. "I'll bet Rosalyn would love to Charleston—"

"No! No, I would not!"

Unexpectedly, shy and lightweight Theodore stood, slender hands clenched into fists. "She said she don't want to dance. Let her go."

Johnny turned to him defiantly. "Yeah? You gonna make me, The-o-dore?" he sneered.

"Maybe he can't, but I can." Corwin slammed down the guitar, and in one streaked-lightning leap jumped to his feet and rocketed head first into Johnny's midsection.

Johnny oofed in surprise as he went down, but he took Corwin with him, and a moment later they were rolling on the floor like a couple of fighting tomcats. A bench went down, and then a table, already set for breakfast, rocked like a wave-tossed boat, and plates and silverware skittered and crashed. Someone tried to separate the men, got a fist in the jaw and joined the fray. A moment later everyone but Rosalyn was part of the thrashing, tumbling, crashing melee. She screamed at them to stop but no one paid any attention.

Then Mrs. Dubuque's intimidating voice boomed, "Hey, you addlebrained idiots, STOP! NOW!"

The brawl, which hadn't responded to Rosalyn's shrieks and pleas, instantly halted. The men froze in whatever position her voice had caught them. Like children in a game of statues.

She crossed her arms over her husky chest. "Any of you cheeseheads who ain't out of here by the time I count to five will never eat in my cookhouse again. One, two—"

Under this dire threat to their stomachs, the cookhouse emptied faster than an apple pie disappearing at dinner. Mrs. Dubuque stalked between the tables, surveying the damage and then turned her attention to Rosalyn.

"You, too," she said. "Out." She jerked a thumb toward the door.

"Out?" For a moment Rosalyn thought Mrs. Dubuque meant she should follow the men, but then she realized the larger, more devastating meaning. "You're firing me?" she gasped.

"Right. Git your stuff and go."

"But I didn't do anything!"

Mrs. Dubuque surveyed the damage again. "Didn't have no lovesick idiots hanging 'round my cookhouse when Lulu was here. No brawlin' neither. I'll just git her back."

"No! Please. I need this job. You can't fire me!"

Mrs. Dubuque crossed her arms again. "I just did. Now git."

Panicking, Rosalyn spied the dim light of a lantern still glowing in the small building that Milton Warrenton, the logging operation boss, used as both office and sleeping quarters. She dashed across the muddy yard and found him in the doorway, peering out to see what the commotion was.

"Please, you can't let Mrs. Dubuque fire me! I can't lose this job."

Apparently Mr. Warrenton had a good idea what had happened without asking for details. He was older than most of the men who worked for him, but no less brawny. The loggers ousted from the cookhouse had already disappeared into the bunkhouse, fight apparently abandoned or postponed.

"I'm sorry. If she tried to fire one of the men, I couldn't let that happen, of course. But if I try to tell her she has to keep you on, she might up and leave."

"Couldn't you just talk to her?"

"I'm sorry. She runs the cookhouse. I don't interfere."

Rosalyn made another try to soothe Mrs. Dubuque, asking if she couldn't please have another chance, but the woman wouldn't budge in her decision. She lay on her bed stubbornly reading a love story magazine and ignoring Rosalyn slowly gathering her things and carrying them out to the pickup.

What now? Rosalyn wondered wearily as she cautiously navigated the treacherous canyon road out of the logging camp. She had thought the Lord was providing for them with this job, and now it was gone.

Ellen was not feeling well the night Rosalyn got home and two days later she was down with stomach cramps and vomiting, throbbing headache, and a respiratory infection. She refused to consider going to a doctor, but a day later Rosalyn and Shea overruled her protests and took her. From the one busy doctor in Castle Beach they learned that it was an influenza going around, very contagious. Three days later, Andy became ill.

Every day Rosalyn's prayers were frantic pleas for their recovery, with the added plea that she and Nadine remain healthy and able to care for them.

Those prayers were answered, but by the time Ellen and Andy were on the mend two weeks later, Rosalyn felt depleted physically and emotionally—and financially. Doctor bills, medications, and special soft and nourishing foods, had rampaged like a hungry wolf through their meager funds.

It was, she decided grimly, time to play her "ace in the hole."

She still had a few days' pay coming, and when she went to

collect it from Milton Warrenton at the logging camp she approached the subject in as businesslike manner as possible.

"We've decided, for financial reasons, to log our property, eighty acres of fine timber. Perhaps you'd like to look at it and make an offer?" She spoke briskly, refusing to dwell on a vision of what the property would look like after cross-cut saws and steam donkey had done their work. It would take time, but the Lord would grow the forest back again. How much was the timber worth? Hopeful figures flitted through her head. Five hundred dollars? A thousand? Two? The last figure glowed like a tempting jewel.

"I'm sorry. In good times, we'd be running several logging camps instead of just this one, and we'd be interested. But the bottom has fallen out of the lumber market."

The jewel splintered. Rosalyn swallowed and stiffened her shoulders. "I'd be willing to take less than the going rate. We are in...rather desperate need of the money."

"I'm sorry. I really am. But we have more than enough timber on land we already own. We're just not buying at any price right now." As if he didn't want to leave her totally without hope, he added, "Of course that will likely change in a few years."

Rosalyn found no hope in the statement. The possibility of selling the timber in a few years was no help now. She steadied herself with a hand on Mr. Warrenton's desk. "Perhaps you could give me the name of another logging company that might be interested?"

He shook his head, his first words those with which he seemed to start every statement to her. "I'm sorry. We're the last logging company still working in the area. There just isn't a market for timber now."

Her "ace in the hole" proved worthless.

She silently accepted her paycheck, suspecting he kindly

stretched her time to the limit to give her a few extra dollars.

"Thank you."

"I'm sorry—"

Rosalyn lifted her chin. "We'll manage."

Rosalyn made no mention to her mother or Nadine about this latest setback, but she did tell Shea when he stopped by on his way to town with a load of firewood. He did not seem surprised, and she dispiritedly realized that if she'd asked him, he could probably have told her the prospects for selling the timber were nil.

The next day he suggested they take a hike down to the waterfall. Disregarding waiting work that needed doing, Rosalyn readily said yes. The day was lovely, scented with spring freshness, and she felt a restless need to get out of the house.

In spite of all the winter rain that had fallen since she first saw the waterfall, she was somehow expecting the same tranquil scene. But this! No longer did long ribbons of waterfall slide gracefully into a calm pool. Now a single avalanche of water thundered from wall to wall of the rocky canyon, and the serene pool was a surging cauldron of whitewater reaching to within inches of where their feet had once dangled. Wild spray spattered them and a branch shot up from the depths and whirled dizzily in the pool below.

"Shea, it's beautiful…and frightening…and spectacular…and breathtaking!"

It wasn't until he took her hand and led her to a quieter spot downstream that Rosalyn suspected Shea had something more on his mind than sharing this wild beauty with her.

Twenty

⟨❦⟩

Shea stroked Rosalyn's fingers lightly. They showed the ravages of hard work, but nothing could alter their slim elegance. He loved her so much! So many times he had ached to tell her, but he'd also wanted to give her the time to work through her painful past and especially time to put her old love far behind her.

Patience, he'd kept telling himself. And, although it had never been one of his stronger assets, like a well-exercised muscle it had strengthened enough with usage and prayer to keep him from storming too soon through Rosalyn's tangled emotions. Yet with the ever more difficult circumstances of her life he had decided he could wait no longer.

How could he tell her his feelings? Robbie in Indiana, he thought wryly, would no doubt know the perfect romantic words to say, complete with exquisite ring and flowers in hand. He probably also wouldn't have chosen a damp, hard rock as a setting, with a beady-eyed bluejay as an audience. But all Shea could do was say what was in his heart. "Rosalyn, I love you."

He paused, stopped by the faint change of expression in her brown eyes. Surprise? Dismay? Alarm?

He chose the first emotion as the easiest to deal with. "You can't really be too surprised. I think I started falling in love with you the first time I saw you. Maybe even the first time I heard your voice through the door."

"I was holding a chunk of firewood, ready to clobber you."

He smiled. Somehow that didn't surprise him. And the fact that she had that fiery, courageous heart under a sweetly gentle exterior was probably another of the reasons he loved her. "I've wanted to tell you for a long time," he added softly.

Her averted gaze told him his declaration of love wasn't a startling surprise to her, but it didn't tell him what feelings were in her heart. She didn't withdraw her hand and he took that as a hopeful sign. He carefully relaxed his grip so he wouldn't crush her delicate bones.

"I love you, Rosalyn," he repeated. "I want to marry you. Will you marry me?"

Still the downturned head, her soft, ginger-brown hair falling forward so that only a bit of her fine-skinned nose was visible.

"I see you struggling so hard here, and I want to take care of you and make things easier for you—"

Her head jerked up. "I don't want a man to marry me just because he feels sorry for me!" she flared indignantly. Shea groaned inwardly. There, he'd done it. Instantly said the wrong thing. He raked his fingers through his hair, feeling the unruly curls turn to corkscrews under the mauling.

"Rosalyn, I don't feel sorry for you. I just care. When you're hurting, I hurt, too. I admire your strength and courage in coming to a strange, wild place and starting out new as you've done. I respect the way you've taken on the responsibility for your mother and Nadine and Andy. And I suppose those are part of the reasons I love you." He hesitated briefly and then plowed on with his usual honesty. "I guess I'd probably help any woman struggling here alone as you are. But I'd never ask any woman to marry me if all I felt was sorry for her."

"Perhaps you want to marry me because you need a mother for Jessie." She spoke with head tilted in thoughtful speculation as she studied his face.

He met her scrutiny openly, not concerned that he might give away something he didn't want her to see, because there was nothing to conceal from her. He did not want to sound egotistical, but he could honestly say, "Rosalyn, if all I wanted was a mother for Jessie, there have been some capable and available candidates."

Her eyes registered sudden recognition. "Rachel Morgan, the organ player at church!"

He wasn't about to go into kiss-and-tell details, so all he did was rephrase his first statement. "If all I wanted was a mother for Jessie, I think I could have found someone."

Rosalyn studied his face for another minute. She nodded. "Yes, I'm sure you could have."

He grinned. "Okay, now that my motives are clarified, and we have that settled—"

"Don't my motives concern you? That if I decided to marry you now it might be because I'm desperate and panicky and don't know what else to do?"

"I'd rather you marry me because you are madly, passionately, and desperately in love with me." He smiled at this somewhat melodramatic listing, but he didn't hesitate to add, "As I am with you. But I want to marry you even if your feelings aren't quite that…intense."

"Oh, Shea—"

"And I'm realistic." He tucked a loose tendril of soft hair behind her ear. "I know that at this point your feelings for me aren't as strong as mine are for you. But there are feelings. I'm sure of it."

She nodded, not an impassioned enough agreement to raise his heartbeat to the muted thunder of the waterfall, but a definite nod. "Yes."

"I also know what it takes to get over heartbreak—"

"Yours was a far more tragic heartbreak than mine. You lost a wonderful wife." She grimaced. "I lost a man who sneaked around with my best friend. I should be over him. Most of the time I think I am. And then…" Her voice trailed off.

"I know I can't provide for you as handsomely as he could have. At least not yet," Shea added. Great wealth had never been his highest goal, but he had confidence that he could give her a comfortable life in coming years. A letter he'd received just a few days earlier opened the door for a new opportunity. "And he could never give you more love than I."

She touched his hand. "I believe that, Shea. I truly do. You're a good man. We couldn't have survived here without you. You're hardworking and trustworthy and honest and generous and kind—" For a moment her eyes unexpectedly sparkled with a small mischief. "As well as being the most handsome man in all of Castle Beach, a fantastic cook, and charming enough to dazzle any woman—"

"Do I hear a 'yes, I'll marry you' in there somewhere?"

She shook her head regretfully. "I'm sorry. I wish I could." She hesitated. "But, no."

"I'm not giving up, you know. I didn't make it the first time I tried to climb a two hundred foot tree, either. I got sick and nervous and dizzy. But I kept trying until I made it."

She smiled, a shimmer of mist in her eyes. "Would you mind if I just stayed here alone for a few minutes?"

He gave his answer by lifting her hand and touching his lips to the back of each finger. Then he gently bent them under, closing them into a small fist. "One favor?"

She tilted her head.

"Will you stop thinking of me as your friendly, red-haired neighbor, and start thinking of me as a possibility for a lifetime mate?" Then, not waiting for an answer, he leaned over and kissed her firmly on the mouth. And it was not a platonic, neighborly kiss.

Rosalyn watched him climb over the rocks, the flash of his hair the last thing to disappear in the green veil of forest. Briefly she thought of how many problems marrying Shea would solve. But she couldn't do that, of course. Shea deserved a woman who loved him wholeheartedly, not one whose emotions were still as tangled as the blackberry brambles in the underbrush.

She touched a fingertip to the warm tingle of her lips. She looked down at the fingers Shea had kissed as tenderly as if they were fragile crystal treasures. What would Robbie think if he could see those hands now? Thumb bruised from a chunk of firewood. Unpainted nails broken so often that she'd trimmed them almost to the quick. Skin roughened from dishwashing and laundry.

But Robbie really didn't occupy her thoughts much now. Time and distance had helped her recognize that he had been the wrong man for her, even without the final proof of his betrayal. Their values and goals were not the same; the Christian beliefs that were an intrinsic part of her life had never penetrated beyond the surface of his. Her efforts at forgiving both Robbie and Charlie were working; she no longer felt those twin strands of barbed wire cutting to the core. More often, she felt a twinge of concern for Charlie, a sadness and regret over the lost friendship. Unfortunately, none of that translated into a complete assurance that old ghosts of her feelings for Robbie weren't hiding somewhere in her heart, ready to leap out and haunt her.

But could she consider the possibility of Shea as a life mate? Oh, yes!

She was suddenly quite certain, in fact, that somewhere below her conscious level of awareness, her mind may have been tossing that possibility around already.

The end of February brought a week of glorious weather. Warm, springy days when the earth seemed bursting with vigor and hope. Moonlit evenings when new growth on the firs shimmered like silver lace and formerly inconspicuous wild brush filled the air with the sweet fragrance of its tiny blossoms.

Rosalyn felt energetic and industrious, although she had to nag a bit to get a restless Nadine to help her spade a garden space and plant peas and radishes and green onions and lettuce. Nadine, never a country girl, tried to find a job in town but with no success. Rosalyn hadn't confided to Nadine that Shea had asked her to marry him. Perhaps Nadine suspected—once she had muttered that maybe he wasn't such a great catch after all. Any woman who married him, she'd said, would be stuck out here in the sticks forever.

Actually, Rosalyn was giving Shea's proposal considerable thought, especially after the two of them had gone for a walk on the beach after Sunday evening services a few days earlier. In spite of the romance in the silver shimmer of moon on sea, and the love in his eyes, Shea didn't mention marriage again, and she was grateful for his ability to hold back and not push her.

Nadine, however, definitely pushed for what she wanted, and on this particular day it was to go to town. She was, she said, going to scream if she didn't see something besides trees and more trees. But Rosalyn, weeding around the wondrous sight of a pea plant in her garden, put her off with a "maybe tomorrow." In the distance she could hear an occasional crash as Shea felled another madrone for next year's firewood. Ellen was napping, something she did a lot of, even on these lovely sunny days.

Nadine, instead of putting Andy down for his usual afternoon nap, angrily snatched him up and said she was going for a walk up the hill.

Not for long, Rosalyn thought wryly to herself. The baby was getting heavier by the day. He was even taking a few wobbly steps now. But he certainly couldn't walk anywhere, and Nadine couldn't carry him up the steep, rocky hillside.

Rosalyn finished the weeding and then brought in the bedding she'd hung out earlier, sheets fragrant with fresh air and sunshine and a faint tang of pine. She'd just started making up the beds when a furious barking made her stop short. She'd never heard Smiley bark like that.

An intruder? No. She'd heard no car. A hunter on foot? Alarmed, she started for the door. Nadine and the baby were out there. If a hunter shot at something without knowing they were there...

But before she could get to the door, the barking changed. There were snarls, yowls, screeches, and yelps. Like a giant catfight.

Giant cat.

Cougar!

And a human scream.

Twenty-One

With trembling hands Rosalyn loaded the rifle, the terrifying noises numbing her fingers to stiff, awkward stumps. Fear stampeded her heartbeat and filled her mouth with an acid burn.

She jammed extra bullets into her pocket and raced outside. On the far side of the clearing an unidentifiable tangle of yelping, screeching fury rolled in the dirt, a blur of tan-colored bodies. Rosalyn clutched the gun with both hands, uncertain what to do, uncertain what was happening. She could hear Nadine's screams. Was she in that murderous tangle?

No! There she was, standing by a tree twenty feet from the savage battle, hands thrown up in horror, mouth open in an endless shrieking scream. But where was the baby?

Rosalyn ran toward Nadine, the long rifle bumping her body awkwardly. "Where's Andy?" Rosalyn cried. "Where is he?"

Only screams came from Nadine's terrified throat as she pointed. Just at that moment the battling animals split apart, crouching cougar and unsteady, bloodied dog. Rosalyn spotted the baby on the ground in the rough angle where two rocky ledges met behind Smiley. Andy was sitting up, neither crying nor moving, his eyes wide with terror.

Nadine finally got words out. "Do something! Do something!"

Smiley was between the cougar and the baby. But the cougar was between Rosalyn and the dog. There was no way to get to Andy without going through the cougar.

Rosalyn raised the gun with shaking hands. The animals faced each other, cougar with twitching tail, dog with bared teeth. A battle to the death, with no regard for humans nearby. Smiley swayed, gallantly holding her ground, but weakening. Rosalyn had shot the gun so few times. What if she missed, missed far enough to hit the baby! But if she didn't shoot—

Frantically she ran to the other side of the tree so she could aim at the cougar from a different angle and not risk hitting dog or baby.

Rosalyn prayed silently as she sighted down the barrel as Shea had taught her. Tears of fear and panic dimmed her vision, blurring the V at the end of the rifle. Furiously she blinked them away. She could do this. She had to do it. Carefully she brought the sight down on the big tan cat. The cougar raised a savage paw. Rosalyn pulled the trigger just as its powerful claws ripped into the side of Smiley's head.

The cougar screamed and went down. It clawed and spun in the dirt, and Rosalyn frantically reloaded and fired again. This time the tan body twitched and went motionless.

Nadine ran to the baby and snatched him up in her arms. She clutched him to her chest and buried her face in his hair.

"Is he all right?" Rosalyn asked.

"Yes, yes! Thank you, oh, thank you!"

Only then did Rosalyn realize that not one but two tan bodies lay on the ground. She ran to the fallen dog.

"Smiley. Oh, Smiley…no!"

The dog's tail moved in a weak twitch, a pathetic imitation of her usual enthusiastic wag. An automatic reaction rather than a conscious one, Rosalyn realized, as an up-close view revealed the lethal seriousness of the dog's wounds. Blood pooled beneath the gaping tear in her belly, and Rosalyn sickened at the sight of her internal organs spilling out. The side of her head and throat that the cougar's claws had slashed was hidden, but more blood darkened the ground beneath it. The dog's agony showed in the glazed eye that beseeched Rosalyn for help.

Help that was beyond Rosalyn's abilities to give. She stroked the dog's head helplessly and the tail, by some supreme effort, moved again. Only to be followed by a convulsion of pain that momentarily twisted the limp body. Smiley was dying. Rosalyn knew it and there was nothing she could do.

Yet how long would it take? Minutes? Hours? Hours of agony for a sweet and noble animal that never deserved this painful fate.

No, she couldn't let that happen.

She leaned over and touched her cheek to the dog's head in a gesture of love and caring—a final goodbye. Then she unsteadily rose to her feet and reloaded the rifle. She stood behind Smiley's gentle head so the dog couldn't see what was coming.

And fired.

They were still standing in numbed shock when Shea's truck roared into the yard only moments later. He spotted them at the edge of the clearing, a tableau of horror.

"I heard shots!" he yelled.

Rosalyn heard his breath catch harshly in his throat when he saw the scattered bits of tan hair and fur, the scuffed and bloodied ground, and the mangled bodies. The scent of death hung in the air.

"What happened?"

Rosalyn, dazed, handed him the gun she still clutched. He dropped it to the ground and wrapped his arms protectively around her. She couldn't speak, but Nadine couldn't seem to stop babbling now. She was holding Andy so tightly that he started crying.

"I—I just wanted to get out of the house, that's all! But Andy was sleepy and he was so heavy. So I put him down there by the rocks just for a while. The pine needles were thick there. He went right to sleep." Her words came in disjointed spurts, her eyes large and pleading. "I didn't mean to stay away so long. I found some wildflowers…"

The flowers were there on the ground where she had dropped them, a crushed bouquet of purple shooting stars mixed with ferns.

"Smiley stayed with Andy." She gulped and smoothed Andy's hair with her palm. "Then I heard Smiley barking, a terrible barking, and I came running…" Her voice trailed off with a small sob.

From within the security of Shea's encircling arms Rosalyn saw scratches on Nadine's face from crashing through the brush. At some point Ellen had also come from the house and joined them. She said nothing, just clutched her hands against her shoulders as if desperately trying to create a barrier between herself and all this.

"And Smiley was standing there in front of the baby growling and the cougar was a few feet away…and then they were fighting and screeching. Then Rosalyn came running with the gun."

Rosalyn shivered and started shaking uncontrollably. "I never wanted to kill anything, not even a cougar! And then I had to shoot Smiley, too, because she was suffering so much."

"It was the right thing to do. You did everything just right," Shea murmured soothingly into her hair.

A gentle breeze sighed in the treetops and Andy gave a muffled whimper. Rosalyn felt dizzy and lightheaded, not sure she could stand on her own. A dull, numbed horror at all that had just happened slowly filled her.

Finally Shea said, "You go to the house. I'll take care of this." He gave Rosalyn a reassuring brush of lips against her temple before she turned to leave.

She looked back at the scene from the corner of the house, while Shea went to the truck for a shovel. Tall, waving grass hid the fallen bodies, and the scene looked peaceful. Serene.

But Rosalyn knew she would never forget the agony in Smiley's eyes, or the feel of the rifle butt slamming against her shoulder, or the scent of blood and death.

Inside the house, none of them had much to say. Rosalyn automatically set about preparing dinner, although she doubted anyone had an appetite. Shea stayed to eat with them, not because he was hungry, she knew, but to reassure them with his presence. He had an inborn sensitivity to other's needs, and Rosalyn appreciated the gesture more than she could say. The danger was over, and yet she found herself shaking every few minutes. After the meal, Shea drew Rosalyn outside, into the evening that had an incongruously lilting fragrance of spring.

"I could stay the night, if it would help. I can sleep upstairs, or in the truck—"

"We'll be okay." Yes, for the night. But beyond that she was dizzily uncertain. She suddenly felt like a stranger here, a stranger in an alien, savage land.

He gathered her into his arms. "I love you so much, Rosalyn. When I see you hurting..." The warmth and strength of his embrace comforted her.

"Would the cougar have hurt Andy?"

"I don't know. Cougars are unpredictable. It might just have sniffed around him, or it might have—" He left the possibilities unspoken. "But Smiley was willing to give her life to see that nothing happened."

"Yes."

"Good night, Rosalyn." He held her by the shoulders and kissed her lightly on the lips. "I'll check on you tomorrow."

Rosalyn lay awake a long time that night, staring at the slim crescent of moon moving slowly across the oblong of the window, listening to the brush of branches against the upstairs wall. She missed the feel of Smiley's warm body curled against her feet, missed the security of knowing that the dog's alert ears and nose were always on guard. Once more, something precious had been snatched from her.

All the past losses that had brought them to this strange, wild land, all the fresh disappointments they had suffered here crowded into her mind. Her job, the possibility of logging the trees, and now even Smiley. All gone. What more would God take from her?

No! She must not start thinking like that, must not start blaming or accusing God. Almost frantically she jumped up and paced the dark room, occasionally stopping to stare out the window at the silver and shadows, praying and desperately trying to think of comforting verses of scripture.

She intended to use physical activity to keep her mind from dwelling on what had happened, but by morning a storm had swept in and rain poured down in endless gray sheets. Ellen sat by the stove crocheting, and Rosalyn was afraid she'd scream if her mother repeated what she'd done last week, crochet a while and then simply rip it all out and start over.

Nadine knelt by the window, elbows on the sill, chin resting in her hands as she stared out at the falling rain. Sometimes she'd turn and study Andy playing on the mattress with some wooden blocks Shea had made for him, a strange unreadable expression on her face. Rosalyn knew how guilty Nadine felt about leaving Andy alone the day before, how she agonized over what had happened to Smiley. Once she went over and looped her arms around Nadine.

"Everything's all right. Don't keep thinking about it." When that got no response, Rosalyn added, "Or maybe it would help to talk about it. Don't just keep hammering away at yourself."

Nadine reached up and patted Rosalyn's hand absent-mindedly, as if she were buried too deeply in misery to speak.

At midmorning Rosalyn made an impulsive decision.

"Let's go to town. It will do us good to get away from everything."

For one who was always eager to go to town, Nadine's response this time was oddly restrained, as if it were some momentous decision. But finally she nodded and said, "I'll be ready in a few minutes."

"Mother?" Rosalyn inquired tentatively.

"Oh, I don't think so, dear. I'll just stay here and—" Ellen looked around vaguely. "Keep the fire going."

Rosalyn hesitated uneasily. Her mother might not keep the fire going and end up sitting here in the damp cold. Or she might decide to go up and sort through her precious box and tumble down the stairs.

"You come with us," Rosalyn said firmly. "We'll buy more crochet thread and perhaps we can find a pattern for you to work on."

Ellen didn't argue. "Whatever you think best, dear."

Nadine said she had a letter to write first, but this time she did it alone, her head close to the page as she struggled with the spelling. While Rosalyn was filling the stove and setting the damper so the fire would burn as slowly as possible while they were gone, Nadine went through her meager belongings and dressed in her best things. Rosalyn didn't bother to change. Driving to town on the rutted, rain-slick road was not a time for dressing up.

By the time they were squeezed into the cab of the pickup, her mother's silence and Nadine's lack of enthusiasm had Rosalyn halfway regretting she'd ever suggested this trip. Yet at the same time, she found herself wishing they would never have to come back. Wouldn't it be wonderful if this were only a rustic country house, some place where they'd been roughing it for a weekend, and now they were heading back to lights and warmth and city comforts?

In town, she asked if Nadine wanted to take her letter to the post office first, but Nadine said she'd do it later. They went to the general store, where Andy wanted to touch and feel everything. Nadine bought him two pieces of candy for a penny, and his eyes grew large at the unaccustomed sweetness. While Rosalyn was trying to interest her mother in crochet thread, Nadine suddenly said she was going to run down to the post office and mail her letter now after all.

She handed Andy to Ellen. "Will you take care of him for a few minutes? I'll meet you back at the pickup." She cupped her hands around Andy's face for a long moment, looked into his eyes, and said with a strange fierceness, "Mommy loves you." Then she kissed him and streaked out the door.

Nadine clearly was still upset and shaken by what had happened yesterday. Rosalyn was too.

They spent a good half hour at the store. Ellen couldn't make up her mind about crochet thread, probably, Rosalyn realized with a sigh, because she didn't really care about any of it. They ran into a friendly woman from the church who chattered at length about an upcoming potluck dinner and her husband's neuralgia.

The rain was pouring down as relentlessly as ever when Rosalyn and her mother finally returned to the pickup with their few purchases. Nadine hadn't returned to the pickup yet, which seemed odd, because it was parked only two blocks from the post office.

Then, as Rosalyn was getting her mother and Andy settled, she spotted the folded paper propped on the steering wheel. She recognized it instantly as a page of her own stationery. With an ominous sense of apprehension she unfolded the paper and scanned the blocky printing.

Dear Rosalyn
I no your going to hate me for this but I cant give litle Andy no kind of life. I almost got him kild. So Im leeving him with you. Pleas love him and tak car of him. Your god people.
Love from Nadine

Twenty-Two

❧

"What is it?" Ellen's voice registered uncharacteristic alarm as she looked at Rosalyn's stunned expression.

"Nadine is gone. She's walked out."

"She's deserted Andy?"

"Yes." She handed the note to her mother and they both looked at the small, innocent boy sleepily snuggled in Ellen's lap.

"But why would she do this? Where will she go?" Ellen asked in bewilderment. She smoothed a rebellious cowlick of blond hair on Andy's head.

Rosalyn hastily started the engine, both angry and frightened. Nadine couldn't have gotten far in such a short time, she assured herself. Rain still poured down as if a bucket had been overturned on the world. They'd find her and talk sense into her. Twice she drove slowly up and down the street, peering into doorways, stopping to search the post office and cafe. On the south edge of town she spotted an older woman plodding along under a black umbrella.

Rosalyn opened the window. "Have you seen a young woman, blond, wearing a dark blue jacket?" After a moment's consideration she added, "She may have been carrying something, a satchel or suitcase." Nadine could have sneaked her belongings into the back of the pickup while Rosalyn was in the outhouse.

"Girl looked like that was standing over there when I walked up town." The woman pointed to a sheltered spot under a shed next to the road. "Appeared she was trying to get a ride."

The spot was empty now.

Rosalyn raced down the road as fast as the old pickup would go, peering at the surprised-looking occupants of vehicles as she flew by. If she could just catch up with the car that had given Nadine a ride!

Within a few miles, she knew the chase was useless. Nadine had too much of a head start. She was gone.

Rosalyn didn't know what else to do but go home, her anger at Nadine numbing to a weary desperation. What now? And what would become of Nadine all alone out there?

Shea had left a note on the door that he was delivering a load of wood and would see her the next day. Inside, a quick inspection revealed that Nadine had indeed taken most of her pitifully few belongings with her. In a sudden rush of suspicion, Rosalyn checked the soup can in the cupboard where she kept their money. She knew the amount to the penny. Two one-dollar bills were missing.

Rosalyn's first burst of anger at the theft dissolved into pity. Two dollars to take her...where? She tried to pray for Nadine, but words wouldn't come and she abandoned the task until later.

The fire had gone out, and the house was already cold and damp. They needed a real heating stove, not just the kitchen range that wouldn't hold enough wood to keep a fire going long. Getting up in the night to add wood was automatic with Rosalyn now, but suddenly, as she struck a match to re-start the fire, she hated it. She also hated the outhouse, the stove, the lack of electricity...everything. And now she had a baby to care for, too!

It was too much.

She didn't want to upset her mother, but she couldn't hold back the tears any longer. She retreated to the woodshed and let them flow freely. She felt so helpless. Angry, resentful...betrayed!

Betrayed by all the people she'd loved and trusted. Her best friend. The man she loved. Her father, who had abandoned them when they needed him most. And now, betrayed by Nadine, too.

Yet those human betrayals were not what hurt the most, she realized, not what made her feel most alone and desperate. All along she'd depended on the Lord. He would see them through, she'd kept telling herself.

But he hadn't! He'd betrayed her, too. Home, college, loved ones, he'd taken all and left her with a strange, distant mother and someone else's baby to care for! And no means of survival.

Now she knew why the words of prayer for Nadine wouldn't come earlier. Because she felt too alone, too abandoned. Too betrayed by a Lord who didn't care. Unless those people who didn't even believe in God's existence were right and there was not even a Lord to care.

During another sleepless night, she wrestled with harsh facts. Andy was sweet, a small, precious treasure, but she didn't know how she and her mother were going to survive, and adding a baby was impossible. In the morning she told her mother what they must do.

Ellen looked up from the table, where she was helping Andy drink from a cup, which was how he insisted on having his milk now. "Put him in an orphanage?" she gasped.

Orphanage. The word sent a chill through Rosalyn. She'd been thinking more along the lines of a good, caring family. But even an orphanage wasn't permanent, she assured herself; orphanages found good homes for abandoned children. "We'll go to town and talk to the proper authorities—"

"Rosalyn, you can't mean this!"

"Nadine has no right to expect us to raise her son just because she didn't want to do it."

"I don't think she didn't want to do it," Ellen said, her face troubled. "I think I know how alone she's felt, without her husband, so lost and overwhelmed by everything."

Rosalyn had never thought about that similarity between her mother and Nadine. But it didn't change anything. "I feel overwhelmed, too. I can't take on the sole care and responsibility for a baby on top of everything else."

"He wouldn't be your sole care," Ellen pointed out. "I'm here."

Rosalyn didn't want to be unkind or accusing, so she carefully said, "I just don't think you're up to that responsibility."

Ellen looked at Andy who was trying to capture the cup in his small hands. "We can't just give him away as if he were a worn-out shoe or an unwanted puppy!"

"I think it's best for everyone concerned."

"No!" Ellen lifted the baby protectively to her hip, as though Rosalyn might snatch him and march out the door. "If you'll let him stay, I'll take care of him. I'll do everything. Feed him, bathe him, wash his clothes, get up with him at night. I've been helping Nadine with him, you know."

"That's not the same as having complete responsibility."

"I did it for you when you were a baby!" Ellen countered with unexpected spirit. "I never let the servants care for you."

Rosalyn shook her head, not wanting to say what she was thinking. *That was long ago. Back when you were capable of caring for a lively baby.*

Ellen shifted the baby to her other hip. "I know what you're thinking, that I can't possibly do it. I can't blame you for thinking that. I know how...strange I've been. I could see myself behaving strangely, though sometimes it seems as if I'm watching someone else. But I just didn't care. Nothing mattered. I know how unfair that has been to you, how you've had to take on all the responsibilities. But it never meant I didn't love you, that I didn't care about you—"

"I know." Rosalyn reached out and squeezed her mother's arm. "I never thought that."

"Please, Rosalyn? Just try it for a while? And if I can't do it, then we'll...think about something else."

"Mother, it isn't just Andy's daily care." Rosalyn felt trapped and helpless again, as if she were a cruel ogre forcing her mother to give up one more treasure. "I don't know how you and I are going to survive. How am I going to provide for us, let alone a baby?"

"The Lord will provide."

The serene, confident words unexpectedly angered Rosalyn. "Will he?" she retorted cynically. She shook her head and resolutely started across the room to the boxes where Nadine kept Andy's clothes and toys. They'd take his things to town with them.

But Ellen, in a startling contrast to her usual lethargy, and in spite of the impediment of the sturdy baby in her arms, dashed around the table with astonishing speed. She set Andy on the mattress and stood between him and Rosalyn, her chin up and fragile body braced, as if she expected physical assault and was prepared to counterattack. "No. I won't let you do this."

Rosalyn stared at this strangely ferocious woman blocking her way. "Mother, we can't take care of him. There is no way—"

"I can take care of him. I *will* take care of him." With soft fierceness Ellen added, "I won't let you abandon him to strangers in an orphanage."

Rosalyn hesitated. For the first time in months her mother looked alert and alive. Her hazel eyes sparked with fierce determination and she was definitely not wandering in some vague world outside reality now. Yet none of that could alter the facts.

"Mother, I have no job. We have only a few dollars left in the can. We can't sell the timber—"

"The Lord will provide."

The Lord will provide. Bitterly Rosalyn heard the echo of the words with which she had so long sustained herself. And which she no longer believed.

Carefully, not committing herself, she said, "Well, we'll think about it for a few days and see how things go."

Shea came over that afternoon. In the woodshed, outside her mother's presence, Rosalyn told him all that had happened. She showed him Nadine's letter as they sat side by side on the big chopping block. He read it slowly and, with the gesture that seemed instinctive after reading something so puzzling, turned the paper over as if looking for more explanation on the other side.

"She's really gone?"

"I looked everywhere for her. I think she hitchhiked out of town."

"She was so upset about what happened with Smiley and the cougar and Andy. And she's never liked it here," Shea said with the gentle insight that always surprised Rosalyn in one so big and rough.

"Mother wants to keep Andy with us. But I don't see how we can do that. I told her we'll have to take him to some place that takes in abandoned children." The words came out sounding harsh and unfeeling even to her own ears, and she tipped her head down, unwilling to meet his eyes.

He didn't chastise or accuse her of being hard and uncaring. He simply took her small hand in both his big ones.

"Rosalyn, Nadine no doubt meant to say in her letter that you are 'good people.' She just got the spelling wrong. But what she wound up saying was right anyway. You and your mother are 'god people.' You're God's people."

They sat in silence. Rainwater dripped off the roof, plopping softly on the sawdust-covered ground. The air smelled rain-washed and fresh. A bright-eyed ground squirrel popped its head out of a tunnel dug under the woodshed, eyed them for a moment and disappeared again. Shea's hands felt warm and rough and reassuring around hers.

"What you're saying is that people of God can't just give away a baby as if it were an old shoe or a puppy," Rosalyn said reluctantly, quoting her mother's words. "That as God's people our consciences won't let us do it."

Again Shea offered neither advice or rebuke. "Is that what *you* are saying?" he asked.

"I suppose." She sat there in silence again for a long moment, and then the fiery, anguished words burst out of her. She turned her face up to his. "But I don't feel like one of God's people! All along I've trusted and prayed and believed he'd see us through, that we could always depend on him. But how can I believe that when he's abandoned us, when he doesn't answer prayers, when he steals one precious thing after another from me, when he lays one burden after another on me, when he hasn't seen us through? I feel betrayed, Shea, betrayed by God, just as everyone else has betrayed me!"

"Oh, Rosalyn." Shea put his arms around her and rocked her gently, his chin against the top of her head.

After a while, with sudden intuition, she said, "Now I suppose you'll ask me to marry you again."

"Would that be so terrible?" When she didn't immediately answer, he tilted her chin up so her eyes met his again. "Rosalyn, I know how things look to you at the moment. I know how it feels when it seems the Lord doesn't care and doesn't answer prayer, or maybe isn't even there. I've felt that way, too. But he is there and he does care and he doesn't abandon us. He will see us through." He paused thoughtfully. "Although sometimes his way of doing that is simply giving us the strength and courage to get through the bad times."

"I'm afraid my strength and courage have worn out. The bad times are far from over."

"Many times he answers prayer or provides for us in some way far different than what we expect or would like him to do. I lost a job not long before you came here. I was discouraged. Even when I found another job, it was only a part-time one. But not long after I lost that other job, the company went broke and the men didn't even get their last two weeks' pay. He doesn't necessarily do things our way. He does them his way. His Word tells us that 'all things work together for good to them that love God.' Maybe that's what's happening here."

"What do you mean?"

Shea simply raised an eyebrow and smiled.

Rosalyn knew what he was thinking: He was God's answer in the midst of her dilemma. This big, rough, red-headed bear of a man a gift from God? In spite of her despair Rosalyn couldn't help chuckling.

Shea seemed to sense her reaction and laughed with her, his big laugh that could chase away chills like a roaring fire.

After a few minutes he spoke again, his expression serious, his voice humble. "Maybe I am how the Lord is seeing you through.

229

Maybe you are how the Lord is seeing me through."

Could that be? Rosalyn thought, suddenly embracing the wonder of the thought.

"You need my help as a father for Andy," Shea pointed out. "I need your help as a mother for Jessie. It isn't the only reason I need you. I love you. But Eunice can't take care of Jessie much longer, and I'll have to find someone new. I don't like shuffling her from one family to another."

"It all sounds so...practical," Rosalyn murmured.

"It is practical," he agreed. "And yes, I'm asking you to marry me again." Rosalyn sat there, fingers absent-mindedly stroking Shea's weathered hands.

"Many a happy and lasting marriage has been based on need as well as love. And many an unhappy and short-lived marriage has been based on wild infatuation and romantic notions and urges of passion. Not," he said with a faint reddening of skin beneath curly red hair, "that I don't feel those urges toward you."

"Where would we live?"

"My house would be best, I think. Your mother and Jessie and Andy can share one bedroom. You and I will have the other. This summer we'll add a couple more rooms."

Rosalyn smiled at the quick answer. "You've been thinking about this, haven't you?"

He nodded and smiled, his honest eyes the blue of a stained glass window in the church back home. "I have the new addition all measured out."

But was her need and this warmth of affection she felt for him enough to build a marriage that would last a lifetime?

Twenty-Three

S hea returned the following day. Dark shadows lingered around Rosalyn's eyes as if she hadn't slept well, but Ellen looked bright-eyed and alert. She bustled around getting Andy ready to go out for some fresh air, cheerfully inviting Jessie along, her step more energetic than he'd seen before.

He commented on this new, spirited Ellen while watching the trio from the dining room window. Ellen bent down to show Andy something on the ground. Jessie picked up a squirmy worm. Ellen shrieked then laughed playfully.

Shea glanced down at Rosalyn, standing close but not touching him.

The drawn lines on her face softened into a smile. "It's so good to see her more like she used to be. I think she really can take care of Andy. She fixed his breakfast this morning and gave him a bath."

"But he needs a man around, too. Every little boy does."

"You wouldn't mind taking on that responsibility?"

He grinned. "We'll have these two, Jessie and Andy, and then a couple more."

"Don't rush me, Shea Donahue," Rosalyn warned. If her scowl was meant to be ferocious, it fell somewhat short. "I'm still thinking."

"Would it help if I got down on one knee and proposed properly? I didn't do it very romantically, did I?" Once on a damp rock. Once in a woodshed. He suddenly wished that he'd done something memorable.

"The proposals were fine," she assured him. "It's just that I'm still thinking."

Trying to figure out if she had any better choices? he wondered wryly. "Rosalyn, if none of this had happened, if you weren't financially strapped, with an abandoned baby and all your other problems, and I'd asked you to marry me, would you even consider the proposal seriously?"

She paused, eyes momentarily unfocused, as if she were peering inward, and she sounded almost surprised when her gaze returned to him. "Yes, yes, I would."

So perhaps that gave her something new to think about!

Two days later they were at the spring, filling buckets with water for Ellen to wash the diapers, when Rosalyn asked Shea to pick up more laundry soap for her the next time he went to town. Almost off-handedly she added, "And if that offer is still open, I've decided to marry you."

For a moment he thought he'd imagined those most-wanted words. He set his bucket down and stared at her.

"Of course I suppose I could have chosen a more romantic way to accept. A nice curtsy, perhaps?" she added teasingly, with a graceful dip of knee and a pretend spreading of skirts.

"Anywhere, any way you want to say you'll marry me is fine with me." He put his arms around her tentatively, and even though they'd kissed before, she shyly lifted her face to his. His voice went husky with emotion when he said, "I love you,

Rosalyn. I'll do my best to take care of you and make you happy."

He then claimed her lips with the joyous knowledge that this was his future wife he was kissing, and the added joy of having her kiss him back with greater fervency than he expected.

He released her and picked up the full bucket of water. He fully intended to walk calmly to the house and tell her mother the news and start making sensible plans. He did take a few decorous steps, but suddenly the joy was too much. It burst through the calm surface in an exuberant yell.

"Whoo-eeee! Wow-eeee! Yow-eee!" Several more uninhibited noises whooped out of him and boomed across the mountains and valleys.

With equal exuberance he tossed the full bucket high into the sky, where it spun a lazy half circle and rained water on him as if his own private cloud had stopped overhead. The bucket crashed to earth and there he stood, wet from head to toe, curly red hair plastered to his head, water dripping across his face and down his shirt.

Rosalyn stared at him in complete astonishment, as if she couldn't quite believe she'd just agreed to marry this strange man. Well, he'd gone this far…too late to hold in his exuberance now! Recklessly he picked Rosalyn up and swung her around until green treetops and blue sky melted into a spinning circle overhead. Her hair came out of the restraining ribbon and whirled like a short, wild mane behind her.

"We're getting married…married…married!" he shouted.

His triumphant words followed them like some record spinning on a Victrola, until dizziness overcame him and they collapsed together in a heap on the ground. He kissed her again.

Rosalyn shook her head dizzily when he finally let her sit up. She was wet by now, too, her dress plastered to her body. "I'm marrying a wild man," she said.

He traced the curve of her sweet mouth with a loving finger-tip. "Yes. Wild about you. Crazy with love. When are we getting married? Where? How soon?"

"I don't think we should be in too big a hurry—"

"I've scared you, haven't I?" he asked remorsefully. He stood up and helped her to her feet. "By acting like a crazy man. Flinging buckets around…flinging you around!"

"No." She paused, smiling up at him. "I'm happy to see you're so…enthusiastic about our marriage. But I do think we shouldn't be too impulsive."

"How long is not too impulsive?"

She hesitated and firmly said, "A month."

"A month?" he repeated in dismay. "It wouldn't take more than a few days to get the license and arrange things with the minister."

"A month," she repeated firmly. "I need time to, oh…decide what I'm going to wear and everything."

He started to object but then closed his mouth. Eager and anxious as he might be, he mustn't chance ruining everything by trying to rush her. "One month," he agreed. *And not a minute longer.*

The question of what to wear was answered immediately when they returned to the house and announced the news to Ellen. She went upstairs and came back with something carefully folded in sheets of tissue paper.

"Your wedding gown!" Rosalyn exclaimed as Ellen opened the tissue.

"It was one of the things I just couldn't leave behind." Ellen stroked the soft satin, her eyes misty. "I saved it for you."

234

"Oh, Mother—" Rosalyn hugged her mother as they hadn't hugged in much too long. "What a wonderful surprise!"

"I hope it will be the start of as happy a marriage for the two of you as it was for Oliver and me."

They shook out the folds and admired the lace-trimmed bodice and full skirt. Shea's big finger hovered over the satin and lace, as if he wanted to touch the fabric but was afraid it might break if he did. Rosalyn lifted the shimmering skirt, mellow as candlelight, and brushed it against his cheek. He grinned.

Ellen took the dress back to the box for safe keeping. The only place they had to hang clothing was on a wire strung across a corner of the dining room, and it might get smoky there because the metal stovepipe occasionally let out a grumpy puff. Or Andy might pull it down.

While Ellen was upstairs, Shea draped his arms around Rosalyn. His blue eyes shone with the happy glint of a man with a newly discovered treasure. It was a nice feeling to know that she was his treasure. He reached around to nibble on her earlobe. "I have to wait a whole month to see you in the dress?"

"Yes! I'm sure the dress will probably require some remodeling to fit properly. I also have to think about my hair. And shoes."

All that was true, but Rosalyn knew those surface concerns weren't the total truth. She had decided to marry Shea. She had looked inside herself and found love hiding there. But she needed time to…what? Back home she had known engagements that lasted a year or more, weddings that had taken months to plan, accompanied by a social whirl of showers and parties. Yet none of that, she knew, had anything to do with this marriage.

In all honesty, she had to admit she wasn't certain why she needed time. Shea obviously didn't! But she did.

Over the next two weeks, everything seemed to slip neatly into place. Rosalyn and Shea worked together making changes at his house to accommodate the new occupants. They talked of having children and moving to town when it was time for Jessie to start school. They discussed money and how they would manage until full-time work in the woods opened up again; they talked of the possibility of Shea starting his own logging company, or going back to college for both of them, or politics.

But it wasn't all serious talk. They laughed together, teased, once got in a messy play-battle slinging seaweed he'd brought from the beach to fertilize their new garden. Often they simply paused for an impulsive hug and kiss. And gradually Rosalyn felt the small flame of love she'd discovered hiding inside her expanding to something larger and more exciting.

Yes, the Lord was providing for them, she thought gratefully. He was seeing them through, just as he had always promised. As Shea had said, the Lord doesn't necessarily answer prayers in the way his people might like or prefer, doesn't always answer them in neat, convenient ways, but he answers them. And God knows what is best. Rosalyn asked his forgiveness for the lapse in her faith and the rebellious thoughts and words that had come out of her during that dark period. She didn't, perhaps, feel the bubbly giddiness she'd seen in some brides-to-be back home, but she felt a serenity with her decision.

A serenity that shattered with the arrival of a snappy Studebaker roadster one sunny afternoon.

Twenty-Four

osalyn blinked, hardly able to believe what she was seeing as Robbie Grenwich uncoiled his lean body from the muddy automobile.

Shea was working at the logging camp that week. Rosalyn had spent the morning scraping a sticky black substance off the stovepipe. Now, smudged and dirty herself, she was carrying water from the spring so that she could clean up and do the laundry. She set the bucket down and stared as Robbie walked toward her as casually as if he were strolling to the door of the big house in Indiana.

"Rosalyn." He smiled and said her name with satisfaction, as if it were some hard-earned reward.

Rosalyn's first reaction was pure astonishment. Then she was flustered as she saw herself through his eyes. Hair untidy, loose strands spilling from a carelessly tied ribbon. Shirt sleeves rolled up, sticky black soot on her bare arm, old trousers stained at the knees. Certainly not the well-groomed Rosalyn he'd known back home! Yet if he was shocked by what he saw, he didn't let on.

He looked the same as always. Tan pants with a neat cuff, jaunty sports jacket, thin-soled leather shoes. His white shirt, without a tie, was open at the throat, his windblown brown hair rakish and carefree. He didn't exude an ostentatious display of wealth, but the car, clothes, and general demeanor bore little resemblance to the average citizen of Castle Beach.

Rosalyn suddenly was angry at herself for noticing any of this and especially for caring even a smidgen about how she looked to him. He lifted his arms as if he expected her to tumble into them, but she warily set the water bucket between them. "What are you doing here?"

"You are not an easy woman to find, you know that?" He grinned as if she'd been playing some teasing game of hide-and-seek with him.

"So how did you find me? And why?"

He laughed, that easy chuckle that for months had sent sweet tingles dancing up and down her spine. "I tried Lassiter, the lawyer for Fallon-Richards Pharmaceuticals, but he wouldn't tell me a thing. Then, after diligent investigation among the servants in the area of your old home, I learned where your handyman Geoffrey had gone to work and contacted him. He was a bit surly, too, but when I explained things to him he finally gave me the name of this town in Oregon. So here I am." He spread his arms wide again.

"How did you find your way out here from town?"

"The postmistress gave me directions. I only got lost twice." He grinned again. "See how much effort I put into finding you? And you're scowling at me as if I'm the sheriff with an arrest warrant."

Reluctantly, Rosalyn had to admit he had indeed gone to considerable effort to find her.

"Is there somewhere we can talk?" He looked around at towering trees and knee-high grass as if they were unwelcome intruders.

"I'm busy. I really haven't the time. Or anything to say."

"I think we have a lot to discuss. Let's sit here on the porch," he coaxed.

Just at that moment Rosalyn's mother, carrying Andy, came around the corner of the house. She stopped short, obviously as startled as Rosalyn was by Robbie's presence.

"I'll be in to start the laundry in a few minutes," Rosalyn called. "Just keep the pans on the stove."

"Maybe there's even more to talk about than I thought," Robbie murmured with a hint of speculation as Ellen retreated without acknowledging his presence.

Rosalyn could see him counting back over the months and felt herself coloring at what he was apparently thinking, that after she left Gideon she'd entered into an intimate relationship with someone. Yet after a few seconds he looked puzzled. The months didn't add up, of course; the baby couldn't be hers. Rosalyn said nothing. She owed him no explanations!

"You aren't married, are you?" he finally asked tentatively.

"No. But you are!" she flashed back. "And I will be in less than two weeks."

Neither statement appeared to faze him. "Then I've arrived just in time," he said with a return of jaunty self-confidence.

Robbie brushed pine needles from a spot on the porch. Rosalyn sat down, although she carefully left a wide space between herself and Robbie. Even from a distance she caught the faint masculine scent of the expensive aftershave lotion he always wore.

"First, I'd like to say how sorry I am about your father. He was a fine man."

"Thank you for the flowers you and Charlie sent."

There was nothing accusing in the words, but he shifted uncomfortably on the rough boards as if he felt accused. "You say you're getting married?"

"Yes."

"May I ask to whom?"

"I don't think that's any of your concern." Bluntly she asked, "Why are you here, Robbie?"

"Because I made a mistake. The biggest mistake of my life. And I want to correct it."

"And this mistake was?"

"Leaving you and marrying Charlie." He turned to face Rosalyn, one foot on the ground and the other resting on the weathered porch. "But I'd like to explain how it happened—"

"I'm really not interested. The fact is, it did happen. I was... extremely upset for a while, but I'm over that now."

"Then perhaps the first thing I should tell you is that I'm in the process of correcting the mistake."

Rosalyn's gaze flew to his. "A divorce?"

"No. An annulment." He scooted closer and reached for Rosalyn's hand, his long, aristocratic fingers curling coolly and firmly around hers. "I know you disapprove of divorce. But an annulment is different; it doesn't end a marriage as divorce does. An annulment makes it as if there had never even been a marriage. An annulment just wipes it out and leaves both parties with a clean slate."

"A clean slate?" Rosalyn repeated, the hurt she'd suffered revealed in the catch in her voice.

"I know." Robbie sighed and slapped his palm against his thigh in a gesture of frustration. "There's no clean slate on the unforgivable way I treated you. Nothing can wipe that out. I look back and I'm both bewildered and appalled by my actions. But I would like to offer as much explanation as possible. Please?"

Rosalyn withdrew her hand from his and tucked both hands between her locked-together knees. When she didn't tell him specifically not to go on, he took the silence as assent.

"I'd never really noticed Charlie—"

"It's very difficult not to notice someone as beautiful as Charlie!"

He shrugged. "Oh, sure, I knew she was attractive, but I always thought of her simply as your friend. Then I ran into her alone a couple of times downtown, and a little later she called me at the radio station and said she'd like to talk to me about something. She sounded mysterious, and I was...intrigued."

"And what did she want to talk about?"

"Not much. She didn't try to hide the fact that it was just a ploy to see me because she was attracted to me. I was shocked that as your best friend she'd go after the man you were seeing—"

The man I was in love with, Rosalyn corrected silently.

"But at the same time I was flattered," he admitted. "Foolishly flattered. And Charlie can be, as you no doubt know, devastatingly charming. Full of fun and adventure, and alluring and exciting and challenging—"

"Everything I wasn't," Rosalyn suggested wryly.

"She's also, as I soon found out, self-centered, greedy, and jealous. Her only interests are having a good time and acquiring possessions. She lacks your dependability, level-headedness, sweet temper, and conscience. I should have realized instantly that a woman who will deliberately go after her best friend's guy isn't exactly of sterling character. She also throws things."

"Throws things?"

"A poached egg at breakfast. An ashtray at a party. A golf ball out on the links."

"All totally without reason? You were a fine husband and her anger was completely unjustified?" Rosalyn felt an unexpected bristle of defensiveness about these criticisms of her old friend. Charlie had her faults, some big faults, but Rosalyn doubted

Charlie was totally to blame for whatever was wrong in the marriage.

His blue eyes gleamed with sudden amusement. "Do I detect a bit of facetiousness in that question?"

"Perhaps."

"No, her anger wasn't unjustified," he admitted. "I stayed out all night playing cards. I looked at other women. I threw things, too. But all because I realized very soon that our marriage was a disastrous mistake and I felt like a tiger trapped in a birdcage. I should have been thrown into a dungeon for the way I treated you. I can't explain it and I certainly can't justify it. All I can say is that an infatuated man is not a man of good judgment or exemplary behavior. And Charlie can be so…" He shook his head with uncharacteristic helplessness, as if explaining Charlie's appeal was not easy to put into words.

Yes, Rosalyn thought reluctantly, she knew how Charlie could be. She well remembered Charlie's blithe, confident statement that she could get any man to propose to her. She knew how Charlie enjoyed using her beauty and charm and flirty tease to captivate men. She didn't doubt but that when Charlie made up her mind to marry Robbie, he had little more chance of escape than a goldfish in a bowl.

"But you couldn't be bothered with the decency of a phone call or visit to let me know it was over between us. You left me dangling and let me hear the news of your marriage from someone else."

"I'm sorry, Rosalyn. Sorry about everything."

"Did she love you?"

"In the middle of a screaming argument, she admitted she married me because she was panic-stricken at the idea of living in poverty."

"And what about Charlie now, when you're, as you put it, in

242

the process of 'correcting the mistake'?"

"Do you really care?"

"Yes," Rosalyn answered honestly. "I do."

He laughed bitterly. "She won't be living in poverty. She's getting the house and a very generous chunk of cash in return for her cooperation with the annulment. It seemed a cheap enough price to pay for my freedom."

Rosalyn silently rubbed at the stains on the knees of her trousers. Absent-mindedly she asked, "What became of our old house?"

"It's for sale, but getting rid of a big, expensive house isn't easy these days." His eyes lit up. "Why didn't I think of this before? We can buy it!"

"We?"

"We—you and me." He laughed. "Except I'm getting ahead of myself. First things first." He didn't waste time with preliminaries. "Will you marry me, Rosalyn?"

In the back of her mind she'd known this was why he had come. He hadn't driven all the way to Oregon to apologize for bad behavior. Yet hearing the actual words of a proposal shocked her.

"Just say yes and—"

"You seem to be forgetting that you're still in the process of getting the annulment."

He dismissed her statement with an airy wave of his hand. "It's just a formality. You can come back to Indiana and stay with my parents until it's final."

Her surprise and shock at his arrival jumped to sudden anger at this presumption she'd leap at the chance to marry him. "I've told you, I'm planning to marry someone else."

"But much can change in two weeks." His long look of appraisal felt as if it weighed and measured all the doubts she'd wrestled with before making her decision. "Do you love him?"

"Yes! Shea is a wonderful man. I love him very much. And I'm eager to marry him."

"What's that old saying? Methinks she doth protest too much." Robbie tilted his head skeptically. "Is it me you're trying to convince of how much you love him, or yourself?" She had no doubts about Shea being a wonderful man, and she'd come to know and respect him even more during these last two weeks. But sometimes, when she compared how she felt about him to how she had once felt about Robbie, she did have shivery moments of uncertainty. And now here was Robbie, sitting beside her, saying the words she'd once yearned to hear.

"But it appears you're not going to give me a big 'yes, I'll marry you' right off the bat, are you?" he asked ruefully.

"No, I certainly am not!" But she felt a quick surge of relief that he didn't ask if he had any chance with her, because she was suddenly as unsure about an answer as a beginning tightrope walker.

"I know I did you wrong, and I can't blame you for being hurt and angry and not wanting to rush into anything with me. I know I have to earn your respect and love again." He grinned engagingly. "I'm probably lucky you didn't throw that bucket of water on me the minute I got out of my car."

The mention of the bucket of water made Rosalyn remember Shea's exuberant reaction when she agreed to marry him. How would he take it if she changed her mind?

Oh, but she wasn't seriously considering changing her mind...was she? No. Definitely not. Robbie couldn't just jump back into her life and expect her to swoon with happiness. And technically he wasn't yet back to that never-married status he claimed annulment created.

Robbie laughed. "Fortunately for me, you're not a throwing-things kind of woman. Which is one of the many reasons I love you."

I love you. The words made Rosalyn feel oddly dizzy, as if the old porch were slowly rotating around her. "I've learned a hard lesson, Rosalyn. I'm a changed man." He moved his leg and his trousers snagged on the rough wood of the old porch. He raised his leg and picked a long sliver out of the expensive fabric. Almost plaintively he asked, "Rosalyn, what are you doing in this terrible place anyway?"

Rosalyn felt a flash of indignation at the implication in both tone and words that living here was somehow a blemish on her respectability. Briefly she explained about this having been her father's hunting lodge and the only home they had available after his death. She did not mention that Robbie and Charlie's marriage had also played a part in her desire to get as far away from Gideon as possible. Suddenly, as he listened with tenderness and concern in his eyes, she jumped up and put a porch post between them. She had a panicky feeling that she must get away from Robbie before the spell of his old magnetic appeal trapped her. She had her plans made; she must not let him disrupt them.

"You'll have to excuse me now," she said abruptly. "I have work to do."

Robbie glanced at the alligator-banded watch on his left wrist. "I suppose I should run back to town and see if there's a decent place to stay." He paused and lifted his eyebrows as if waiting for her to fill in with some good-hostess invitation. When she didn't he smiled. "You wouldn't happen to have an extra room? I know inviting oneself isn't exactly proper etiquette, but I've been told that I do make a very entertaining houseguest. And it's a long, rough drive back to town."

"You'd like to stay here?" The thought almost made Rosalyn laugh.

Sophisticated, comfort-loving Robbie coping with the frontier amenities they had to offer? Apparently he did not yet realize exactly how "terrible" this place was. On sudden impulse she said, "Yes, do come in and look around and say hello to Mother. And would you carry that bucket for me, please?"

She led the way, Robbie stiffly holding the bucket away from his body so the water wouldn't slop on his pants or polished shoes.

She motioned as she went. "That's the woodshed and beside it the cooler, which takes the place of a refrigerator because we have no electricity to run a refrigerator, of course. There's our outhouse and inside—" she opened the door with a grand flourish, although Robbie was still looking in astonished shock at the outhouse, "—is our combination kitchen, dining room, and bedroom. And these are the washtubs for our laundry and bathing."

She could see his expression growing more dismayed by the moment and found she was rather enjoying shocking him with this display of their primitive living conditions.

"You remember my mother, of course." She motioned to Ellen, who was sorting the laundry into piles. "And that's Andy."

Robbie nodded to Rosalyn's mother, but if he was still curious about the baby, he was too dazed to ask questions.

"Just set the bucket by the stove," Rosalyn instructed, "I'm heating water to do the laundry."

Robbie was looking around with the horrified air of one who has stumbled into a den of uncivilized savages. "Rosalyn, you're really living like this? Without beds or plumbing or water or electricity?" He eyed the steaming pans on the stove as if they contained hot poison. He shook his head. "I can't believe this."

Rosalyn had intended to tell him archly that he could sleep in the "guest room" upstairs, if he didn't mind the companionship of a few mice, but suddenly she simply felt weary and foolish.

246

"If you don't mind, I really do have to get started on the laundry." She opened a cabinet and took out her metal washboard.

Robbie stared at it in disbelief. He then stalked to the piles of laundry and began bundling them up in a sheet.

"What are you doing?"

"We're taking this stuff to town and hiring someone to wash it. You are not doing it."

"We can't afford—"

"I can."

"No, I won't let you—"

"The laundry is going to town, Rosalyn," he stated with authority. "If you want to make certain I don't just toss it out somewhere, I suggest you come along."

Rosalyn, after a small hesitation, went.

In town, Robbie efficiently located a woman who took in washing. She said she'd have it ready by Saturday. He took out his wallet and set a bill on the table.

"Tomorrow?" he suggested.

"Oh, yes. Tomorrow. Yes, indeed!" She beamed and pocketed the bill before it could get away from her.

Outside, Robbie brushed his hands together as if he were wiping away something distasteful. "There. Now what we need is food. Is there a decent restaurant in this town?"

"I don't know," Rosalyn admitted. "I've never eaten in a restaurant here."

"You mean this guy you're planning to marry doesn't even take you out to dinner?"

Rosalyn resented the implication that Shea was remiss in some social duty, but any explanation would only emphasize the financial canyon between the two men and she did not want to do that. "I'll show you what's here, and you can choose," she said.

The choice was not large. There was Emma's Cafe and The Logger's Den. Robbie wrinkled his nose, laughed, and finally chose Emma's.

Inside Emma's, checked oilcloth covered the tables. The only other diners were three men in rough work clothes sitting on stools at the counter. Robbie opened the stained menu with one finger and chose the salmon dinner. Rosalyn nodded agreement. As soon as the single waitress took their order, Robbie reached across the table for Rosalyn's hand.

She ducked her hands under the table and planted them in her lap. Brightly she said, "How are your parents? And the radio station?"

"Parents are fine. Radio station is fine. Movie theaters are fine. Everything's fine." His tone was amused, yet he obviously was not going to let her get away with the attempt to detour the conversation. "Does that take care of everything?"

"I suppose so."

"Then let's get down to more important matters. I want to marry you. I know you're engaged to this other guy, but I can't help but think it's more a marriage of convenience or desperation—"

"I am not desperate to get married," Rosalyn said indignantly.

He smiled. "Okay. Bad choice of words. But I can see how you live, Rosalyn. You deserve better, and perhaps he can improve your situation somewhat. But can he give you the kind of life I can?"

"Things are different now," Rosalyn said carefully. "I haven't just myself to consider. There's Mother—"

"There's plenty of room in that big house in Gideon for her to live with us. And don't you think she'd be happier in her old home than stuck out here in this barbaric wilderness?"

"It isn't barbaric," Rosalyn protested. "People don't have

248

much, but they're good people."

"You're dodging my question. Can you really believe your mother would prefer staying here to living in the beautiful house that was her home for years? Seeing her old friends? Enjoying the comforts of electricity and running water—" He paused and smiled. "And by running, I don't mean you running it by bucket to the house."

Rosalyn smiled too, but also shook her head. "It isn't just Mother. There's Andy, too."

"Yes, I noticed an unfamiliar addition to the family," Robbie said dryly. "Just who is Andy?"

Their meals arrived, huge slabs of salmon flanked by fried potatoes and canned green beans, enough food to satisfy a logger's appetite. Rosalyn, whose hard work precluded any lagging appetite these days, ate as she told how Nadine had joined and then left them.

"You mean she just walked off and abandoned the baby? How could she do that to you? He isn't your responsibility."

Briefly Rosalyn noted that Robbie did not express any concern for Andy's welfare, only for the inconvenience in their lives. "Actually, having Andy to care for has been good for Mother. She's had a very difficult time since Father's death."

"To say nothing of the difficulty of living in that wretched log house," Robbie muttered. He had pushed the limp green beans and greasy potatoes aside but apparently found the salmon acceptable. "Rosalyn, you can't be expected to raise someone else's child. There are institutions for that sort of thing."

"But I am going to raise him," Rosalyn said quietly. By now she knew she never could have dumped him with strangers, even if her mother hadn't intervened.

"I see." Robbie took a sip of the strong coffee that had come with the meal. "Perhaps we could provide the two of them, the baby and your mother, a nice house somewhere."

"There'd be plenty of room in the big house. And Andy needs a father."

"Rosalyn, that's asking a bit much, don't you think?" Robbie protested. "We'll soon be wanting to start our own family."

Yes, it probably was asking a lot, Rosalyn agreed silently. But Shea hadn't balked at the prospect.

By the time they left the cafe, darkness had fallen. As the car's headlights cut a narrow tunnel through the forest on the long drive home, Robbie started a new series of questions.

"Is this guy—you might at least tell me his name so I won't have to keep thinking of him as 'this guy.'"

"Shea Donahue."

"Where did you meet him?"

"He lives nearby."

"Ah, propinquity," Robbie stated as if he had just discovered some basic truth.

"Pardon?"

"Propinquity. It's a word that means nearness in place or time—"

"I know what it means. What I don't know is what it has to do with anything."

"It has to do with you and Shea Donahue. Whatever is between you is because of propinquity, the fact that you're neighbors and handy for each other."

"That is ridiculous!" Rosalyn protested. Yet she felt a certain jolt of unpleasant possibility in Robbie's words. Her relationship with Shea had developed primarily because they were neighbors. They'd probably never even have met otherwise.

"Tell me about him. Let me see what I'm up against."

Reluctantly Rosalyn offered a few facts. "He's twenty-eight. A logger. Originally from Michigan. He has a little girl named Jessie. His wife was killed in a fishing boat accident on the ocean."

"So you'll be an instant mother to two. That's quite a responsibility."

"I'm not the carefree college girl I was when you knew me."

"No, you're not," he agreed with a sideways glance in the dimness of the Studebaker's interior. "Maturity becomes you. You're more attractive than ever."

"How can you say that?" Rosalyn flared, unexpectedly feeling a quick gathering of tears. "I dress like an old farmer. I haven't had my hair done in months. My hands are red and rough and my nails ragged and ugly. Surely you noticed all that!"

"Yes, I noticed. But nothing about you is ugly. Especially the you that's deep down inside. I can appreciate that kind of beauty now more than I could a while back." Lightly he added, "Although I might point out that married to me you'll have all the money you need to visit the hairdresser and manicurist and dressmaker."

Rosalyn remained silent. She didn't want to admit even to herself how wonderful it would feel to be pampered in a beauty shop, to spend a luxurious hour in a hot bubble bath, and then to dress in something frivolous and frilly. Not to have to wash anything ever again on that knuckle-skinning old scrubboard, or to carry water or dash to that ugly outhouse.

Then she resolutely shoved such thoughts out of her mind. Those were not the important things in life and she must not covet them and give them greater importance than they deserved.

"You're an intelligent, educated woman, Rosalyn. Somehow I can't see you married to a backwoods logger."

"Shea attended college as long as you did—or longer!"

Rosalyn defended hotly. Although she knew the Oregon college could not match the prestige of Princeton.

"Christian?"

"Yes. A fine Christian."

"Ah, I see. Did God tell you to marry him?"

"Now you're mocking me," Rosalyn said angrily. "Making fun of me."

Robbie sighed. "I'm sorry. Charlie and I became rather adept at exchanging barbs. But perhaps you should consider the possibility that God sent me here to rescue you from all this."

Rosalyn tilted her head, frowning.

Robbie hurried on as if sensing her skepticism. "Unfortunately, Charlie and I did not bring out the best in each other in that area. After a night of partying, we tended to sleep until noon on Sundays. But that was also part of what was wrong in the marriage—it had no spiritual roots. I think you will bring out the best in me, Rosalyn. I want to get on the right track with both you and God."

The kerosene lamp sent only a dim glow through the windows when Robbie walked Rosalyn from the Studebaker to the house. At the back door he cupped his hands lightly around her elbows.

"You could stay upstairs," Rosalyn said reluctantly, not eager for him to share their rough accommodations but feeling guilty about sending him on the long drive back to town.

"Thanks, no. I'm afraid I need the comforts of civilization, such as a hot bath and a mattress with a bed under it. But I appreciate the offer. I think you're feeling perhaps a bit less...hostile toward me than you were earlier?"

"Perhaps."

If he thought about trying to kiss her, he thought better of it. She'd have stopped him, of course. But that couldn't keep her from feeling an unwanted quickening of heartbeat at the prospect.

"I'll see you tomorrow then. I'll be out right after breakfast."

Rosalyn hesitated and then said, "Come for breakfast, if you like."

"I'll do that. In fact, you can expect to find me right here on your doorstep more or less indefinitely."

"Oh?"

"I'm not going back to Indiana without you," he warned.

"You can't just stuff me in your Studebaker and carry me off!"

"Oh, can't I?" he challenged.

He came for breakfast and in the afternoon they drove back to town to pick up the laundry, all clean and neatly folded. Instead of taking the road home, however, Robbie zipped right on by it.

"You'll have to turn around. We missed the turnoff—"

"We didn't miss it. I'm kidnapping you. We're driving up to the next town, which the hotel clerk tells me has a movie theater and a larger selection of restaurants."

"I can't do that—"

"Why not?"

She had work to do at home, of course. Weed the early peas and radishes coming up in the garden, fix the latch on the chicken coop so nothing could get her last two chickens. She also knew Shea would hardly approve of such a jaunt.

But it had been so long since she'd seen a movie or done anything simply for the frivolous fun of it. Life was always work and worry, scrimp and struggle, make do and do without. Surely Shea wouldn't begrudge her one carefree evening of fun.

And fun they had. Robbie kept her laughing with stories about incidents at the radio station and what was going on in a world that had faded from her life. In the movies, a new dance duo, Fred Astaire and Ginger Rogers, was the rage, and big crowds had flocked to the theaters to see a silly cartoon movie called *The Three Little Pigs.* Experts were saying that someday a medium called television that sent images across the airwaves would be as common as radio now was, and even as Robbie was confidently saying he intended to get in on the ground floor with it, Rosalyn was thinking wistfully that she didn't even have a radio.

They saw an old Marx Brothers comedy, slapstick and silly, but a lighthearted vacation from the problems that daily confronted Rosalyn. Afterward they ate ice cream flooded with chocolate sauce, a taste extravagance Rosalyn hadn't enjoyed in months. When she paused at a rack of magazines, Robbie instantly scooped up a handful and bought them for her.

Rosalyn had the uneasy feeling that she shouldn't be enjoying this nearly as much as she was, and yet she also had to ask herself a troubling question: If she was really in love with Shea, would she be enjoying herself so much with Robbie? Was there some meaningful significance in the fact that she'd never gotten rid of that amethyst bracelet he had given her?

Was it possible that she'd never truly fallen out of love with Robbie?

Twenty-Five

The next morning Robbie suggested that they spend the day at the beach. Rosalyn was pleased that he included her mother and Andy in the invitation. So far Ellen hadn't had much to say about Robbie. She had simply frowned and kept on crocheting when Rosalyn explained the difference between divorce and annulment. A fine-line difference that Rosalyn was none too comfortable with herself.

Still, when Robbie approached Ellen directly about going to the beach, she looked tempted. A day of play was rare in her life, too.

"Come on, Mother, let's do it. It's a beautiful day and Andy will love the sand," Rosalyn urged impulsively, although she had to offer a warning to Robbie. "But the beach here is no Atlantic City. It's just sand and rocks and seaweed."

His response was charmingly gallant. "I know. But Atlantic City doesn't have you as an attraction."

Neither pickup cab nor Studebaker would hold all of them, so Rosalyn made herself a nest of blankets in the back of the pickup. It was an uncomfortable ride, but Andy's squeals of delight when they arrived was worth the discomfort. Rosalyn and Robbie walked barefoot in the cold surf, Robbie occasionally kicking at seafoam or popping a seaweed bulb, and Rosalyn enjoyed his boyish playfulness. They built a driftwood fire and ate a picnic lunch Robbie had persuaded Emma at the cafe to pack.

They stayed on the beach most of the day, until a formidable bank of clouds charged in. Robbie suggested he rent an extra room at the hotel for Rosalyn and her mother and Andy to spend the night. Rosalyn was tempted. If rain started, she'd get soaked riding home in the back of the pickup. Again she was reminded of the quick comforts money could provide. But letting Robbie pay for the room didn't feel right, and they certainly couldn't afford such a luxury themselves. So they raced home barely ahead of the moving clouds and dashed for the house as the first fat raindrops started to fall.

Inside, the house was cold and, as she struggled to get a fire going, Rosalyn wistfully remembered the easy warmth of the big house back in Gideon. The big house Robbie wanted to provide for her.

After a meal of picnic leftovers, Ellen rocked Andy in a chair by the stove. While Rosalyn mended a sheet, Robbie read a magazine story aloud, his powerful voice as expressive as ever. She knew this pleasant interlude must end soon. Shea would return from the logging camp Saturday evening, and she must get her feelings organized by then. Where only a few days ago she had been certain she was doing the right thing marrying Shea, now her thoughts and emotions wobbled like unsteady wings.

She was so absorbed in the story that she didn't hear the first knocks on the door at all. It was only when Robbie stopped reading and looked at her questioningly that the sound penetrated.

Shea!

She hadn't meant for him to encounter Robbie like this. Not that she intended to conceal anything, of course. But she'd planned to tell him Robbie was here, not have him crash headlong into the fact without warning.

She opened the door and Shea immediately swallowed her in a big bear hug. He grinned at her. "Do you know how much I've missed you?"

Conflicting feelings skittered within her. She was glad to see him, happy to feel the familiar warmth of his arms around her. Yet she was also aware of the rough stubble of whiskers scratching her cheek and the scents of forest and grease clinging to him. "Shea—"

"I have some great news!"

"Shea, we have company. Didn't you see the car in the yard?"

"Perhaps not." Robbie stood up, as tall as Shea although not as formidably brawny. "It's parked under the trees on the far side of the house."

She knew each man instantly realized who the other was, but she stumbled through an awkward formal introduction. The two men eyed each other like a pair of circling wolves. They shook hands, but the possibility of confrontation hung raw as fresh meat in the air.

Through Shea's eyes she saw Robbie, with his smooth hands and fashionable slacks and sweater: city slicker, with money to burn, attitude superior and condescending.

She saw Shea through Robbie's eyes. Backwoods logger. Shea hadn't shaved all week, and a red stubble forested his jaws. His hair stuck out in wiry red curls from under a shapeless khaki rain hat, and his usual grease-stained work pants hung ragged at his ankles.

Shea saw Rosalyn's glance dart uncomfortably between himself and Robbie Grenwich. He was shocked to see the man here, and yet, in some small corner of his mind, he wasn't totally surprised. He'd never been able to understand how any man could walk away from Rosalyn's love. But Robbie was married!

257

Robbie's appearance was not exactly what Shea had imagined. Good-looking and well dressed; yes, he'd known that. A full measure of that invisible aura of money common to rich men, along with the easy self-confidence that said "I have wealth and power and I know how to use it"; that also was expected. But Robbie also had a lanky height, a long-muscled build, and the alert stance of an athlete.

Which was not enough, however, to make him a match for a roughneck logger who had no intention of letting some slick easterner make off with his bride-to-be, Shea thought with a certain grimness.

Rosalyn thrust words into the awkward silence. "Robbie drove out from Indiana for a few days." Her voice held a false brightness, and she laced her fingers together nervously. "I wasn't expecting you back from the logging camp until tomorrow night."

For a moment the word "obviously!" hung in the air, but he discarded it. Rosalyn would never try to deceive him; she was simply in a most awkward situation here. And yet, he realized with a wrench of heart, she wasn't standing with him, the two of them united as a couple to face the man who had betrayed her.

He'd purposely gotten away from camp in midweek because he was eager to share his good news with Rosalyn, but now was not the time, so all he said was, "Yes, I'm early."

Rosalyn threw a frantic glance at Ellen, as if looking for help, but her mother simply kept on crocheting.

"May I speak to you in private for a minute?" Shea managed to ask the question of Rosalyn politely, but his hands clenched into fists at his sides. Robbie had such a cool, insolent smile on his face, as if he were confident Shea's interruption was just a minor inconvenience. He strolled back to the chair he'd apparently been occupying before Shea arrived, and with an air of proprietorship, propped his feet on the stack of wood by the stove.

Rosalyn glanced around as if uncertain what to do with Shea's request. Slanting rain hammered the door, so they could hardly step outside for a private conversation.

"Upstairs?" he suggested.

She grabbed an extra kerosene lamp out of the cupboard and tried to light it, but her hands were so unsteady that he had to do it for her. She led the way around the table to the stairs, and Shea was aware of the noisy clump of his boots on the wooden steps.

There was nothing in the cold upstairs except Ellen's wooden box, carefully resealed with candle wax to keep out mice, and the discarded, homemade mattresses. Rosalyn set the lamp on a shelf beside the door that led outside, a door useless because only a couple of dangling steps remained of the stairway to the ground. Branches brushed the side of the house in an erratic whisper and scrape.

"What's going on, Rosalyn?" Shea asked bluntly. Rosalyn explained how Robbie had appeared totally without warning. "Where's his wife?"

"Robbie and Charlie's marriage is being annulled."

No surprise at the demise of that marriage, Shea thought. But doing it as annulment rather than divorce…Had Robbie deliberately chosen that route in the hope annulment would be more acceptable to Rosalyn? "And he wants you back."

"Yes."

"Rosalyn, I love you. I want to marry you." His fists instinctively clenched again. "If you want me to prove that by picking a fight or running him off, I can."

Rosalyn's eyes widened in alarm, as if she had a vision of the two of them brawling in the muddy yard. Shea had a brief, appealing vision of his own, after he'd won the battle, of ramming his big truck right in the middle of whatever expensive car Robbie had parked out there under the trees.

"No! Of course not," Rosalyn said.

Shea took a deep breath, ashamed of his unchristian thoughts of doing physical damage to both man and vehicle. That wasn't the way. "I'm sorry. But I don't think he has any right trying to win you back with fancy promises. Which is what he's doing, isn't it?"

"He says he's changed. That he's learned a hard lesson."

Shea's throat constricted. "You've already decided you want what he has to offer?"

"No, I haven't! Right now I just feel...confused."

"I know he could give you an easier life, a nicer home and servants and other advantages I can't offer now. But he can't give you more love."

Rosalyn smiled through a brilliant shimmer of tears. "I know."

"So what matters here is who you love, what you want."

He wanted to kiss her. He wanted to snatch her up in his arms and carry her far away from the man waiting downstairs. He still felt a rumble of fight lurking deep inside him. But he forced himself merely to touch Rosalyn's hand briefly, say, "I love you," and give a tight, civil nod to Robbie as he strode to the door.

Immediately after the door closed behind Shea, Ellen said she was ready for bed. Robbie took the hint and said good night also. Rosalyn thought her mother would have some comment about the situation after both men were gone. She suspected that during the drive to the beach and back that Robbie had used all his persuasive charm to try to make her his ally. But the only advice she offered was, "Pray about it, Rosalyn. Ask the Lord what his will is for you."

Rosalyn followed that advice when she knelt by the window, chin on her crossed arms resting on the rough windowsill. Yet if the Lord had advice to give, it wasn't getting through to her. All she felt was churning confusion. Her feelings for Shea were strong, but with Robbie around she felt a tremulous resurgence of old feelings, too. Shea had said the decision was hers to make, based on whom she loved, but she couldn't make a decision without considering her mother and Andy. Ellen would surely be more comfortable back in Indiana than she could ever be here. Shea's house was not as primitive as this one. It had running water and wasn't cold and drafty, but it still lacked most of the comforts of the home in Indiana.

And Andy. There, too, nothing was black and white. Back in Indiana Andy would have access to education and advantages he could never have here. But here Shea would give him love and be a real father to him, which Robbie had made it clear he could not.

It all jumbled together in haphazard confusion, the balance of her mental scales swinging first in one direction and then another, and she felt angry with herself. A woman should know who she loved; there should be no question of it. How could she not know?

Show me the way, Lord, she pleaded silently.

It wasn't until she had given up and was drifting on the edge of sleep that she remembered Shea saying something about "great news." She felt remorseful that she hadn't pursued this, had instead let it get brushed aside in her own muddy situation. Tomorrow she must ask him about that news.

Morning arrived fresh-washed and sunny, with the faint tang of sea that sometimes drifted far inland. In decided contrast were Rosalyn's storm-tossed emotions. She was nervously wondering how to cope when both Robbie and Shea arrived to assert their claims to her, but to her surprise neither man made an appearance.

261

Well, wouldn't that be something, Rosalyn thought wryly, if both men had decided the other one was welcome to her. A good lesson to remind her that she was not some devastating femme fatale who could quirk a finger and watch men dance to her bidding.

She spent the morning working in the garden. Ellen came out of the house to get an armload of firewood from the woodshed. She had taken over some of the cooking and was trying her hand at bread today.

"I'll carry it for you," Rosalyn called. She disliked carrying wood, leery of lurking spiders and ants, but even more she hated seeing her mother struggle with it.

She gathered an armload of dry madrone, noting that the stack of green, undried wood had shrunk considerably. She reminded her mother that they weren't supposed to burn the green wood. Ellen smiled and shook her head ruefully. "I'm afraid wood all looks alike to me."

And she didn't, Rosalyn knew, care much for any of it.

She had just deposited the wood in the box beside the stove when she heard the sound of an automobile engine in the yard. Shea? No, the noise wasn't loud enough for his truck. Robbie, then, and she wavered between apprehension and anticipation at seeing him. But it was neither Shea nor Robbie who dashed through the open door and raced across the room to scoop up Andy. The flying blond figure was followed by one of the biggest men Rosalyn had ever seen. He wrapped his arms around both woman and baby, and the three huddled there laughing and crying together. When the trio finally separated, all Rosalyn could say was an astonished, "Nadine!"

Nadine braced Andy on her hip with one hand and with the other grabbed the hand of the big man beside her. She brought their joined hands up to rub away the tears running into her smile. "This is my husband, Andrew. Honey, this is Rosalyn

Fallon and her mother Ellen, the people who rescued me."

Andrew, the size of his shyness apparently as big as his astonishing physique, just grinned and nodded.

Nadine put the baby in her husband's arms and crossed the room to Rosalyn. She took both Rosalyn's hands in hers. "You must have thought I was crazy, running off like that, deserting Andy—"

"We hardly knew what to think."

"I think I was a little crazy. I felt so guilty and awful about almost letting something terrible happen to him with the cougar. As if I didn't deserve him. And getting Smiley killed..." She blinked, tears starting again.

"Raising a baby can be an almost overwhelming responsibility." Rosalyn knew, having contemplated the prospect herself.

"What would you have done if I'd never come back?"

"Mother and I had already decided to raise him as our own."

Nadine nodded. "I knew you would. You're good people, the Lord's people. But it was a terrible thing I did."

"People make mistakes when they're troubled." She glanced at Andrew, remembering how he had walked out on both Nadine and his little son. She wasn't as willing as Nadine apparently was to ignore that. Nadine saw the glance and read its meaning. "I was wrong. Andrew didn't abandon us. He got to California and went to work, but then he got his knee hurt, hurt bad. You should see the scar! He didn't want to worry me about him being in the hospital, but by the time he got out and tried to get in touch with me, I was already gone. He about went crazy, too, wondering what became of us."

Nadine smiled at Andrew, the love glowing in her eyes, and Rosalyn felt a sharp regret that she wasn't radiating that glow. That was how a woman should feel about the man she married. Andy, who couldn't have any memory of his father, was looking at this big blond giant of a man with an amazed curiosity.

"So how did you find each other?"

"It was the Lord working, because it sure couldn't have happened any other way. I called the Lord not too smart once, didn't I? And that just shows how dumb I am! You remember those friends I wrote to back in St. Louis?"

Rosalyn nodded.

"They didn't get the letter. I had the address wrong on the envelope. So that meant when Andrew telephoned them trying to locate me, they didn't know where I was."

"Didn't that just complicate the problem?"

"Maybe." Nadine tilted her head thoughtfully. "But God knew what he was doing."

"He always does."

"Anyway, it took me a while to hitchhike back to St. Louis, but when I got there I went to my friends' place. They knew exactly where Andrew was! They loaned me money for a bus ticket, and a few days later I just strolled up to the rooming house where Andrew was staying."

The reunited couple exchanged another happy glance, and Rosalyn impulsively hugged Nadine. "I'm so happy for you. All of you."

"I know I've never been a person who deserved the Lord's help, but he did it anyway, first sending you and your mother to me that day in Colorado and then bringing Andrew and me back together."

"That's what Jesus did for all of us. He died on the cross to save us, even though we didn't deserve it."

Nadine nodded. "Sometimes the Lord has to kind of hit you over the head with something before it gets through."

Was that what she needed, Rosalyn wondered wryly, a hit on the head? "Can you stay a while?" she asked.

"No, we have to get right back to California. Andrew's running a gas station in Sacramento," Nadine said proudly. "The owner's going to let us live in a house right behind the station, and there's a backyard and swing for Andy."

After that, the day took on a holiday air. Shea showed up, and the happy reunion story had to be repeated for his benefit. Andy chose this day to toddle alone farther than he ever had before, with everyone cheering him on. Andrew, who'd hardly said three words so far, apparently recognized a kindred spirit in Shea and asked if he knew anything about Ford engines. "Some," Shea answered, and the two men immediately headed outside together, like a couple of schoolboys with a new ball. "Men stuff," Nadine said, managing to sound both scornful and proud. "You bring in those sacks first, before you start messing with engines," she called after Andrew.

Nadine, familiar with the needs of this household, had brought two big sacks of groceries and supplies. "We're going to have a big reunion dinner! Although I guess it will be a farewell dinner, too, won't it? But it doesn't have to be," she added with sudden inspiration. "You and Ellen can come back to California with us!"

When Rosalyn hesitated, Nadine's blue eyes widened and she nodded knowingly. "You've decided to marry Shea, haven't you?"

Rosalyn paused with a can of peaches in her hand. "I did decide to marry him, but then Robbie Grenwich showed up—"

"That man who married your best friend? Of all the nerve! Ill bet you had plenty to say to him!"

"Well, yes," Rosalyn agreed awkwardly. "But then he told me the marriage is being annulled and how sorry he is about everything. Now he wants to take us back to our old home in Indiana and marry me."

Nadine looked dumbfounded. "What are you going to do?"

"I don't know. I just don't know."

Robbie arrived as the women were putting the meal on the table. Rosalyn knew he felt out of place and uncomfortable, but he also wasn't about to turn tail and run. In a whispered aside, he explained to Rosalyn that he hadn't arrived earlier because he was trying to put a phone call through to Indiana. "I was checking to make sure the house is still available. It is," he added significantly.

At the start of the meal, when Shea usually said the blessing, Nadine touched his shoulder lightly. "May I?"

And then Nadine, who'd always been silent and skeptical during both church and prayers, offered a heartfelt prayer of thanks and blessing that touched Rosalyn's heart and brought a shimmer of tears to her eyes.

Nadine, however, grinned at Rosalyn when she looked up. "And that's why the Lord separated Andrew and me for a while, so I'd be here with you and come to know him. It finally got through to me." After the meal the three women packed Andy's things and the few possessions Nadine had left behind. Rosalyn tried to talk them into staying the night rather than starting out so late in the day, but they planned to take turns driving so that Andrew could get back to work as soon as possible.

The Lord did indeed answer prayer in unexpected ways, Rosalyn thought as they all hugged and waved goodbye in the front yard. Shea, although he looked uneasy about it, drove out behind Nadine and Andrew. He had to go into town for Jessie because the family that cared for her, not expecting him on a week night, had not been home the previous evening when he went by the house.

But as soon as everyone was out of sight, a fresh and disturbing thought struck Rosalyn. Her mother's recovery had come about because Andy's needs had reawakened her interest in life. What now? Would she sink back into her old lethargy and depression? When Ellen turned to go back to the house Rosalyn started to follow, but Robbie detained her with a light touch on her arm.

"Well, this changes everything, doesn't it?"

"What do you mean?" Rosalyn asked.

"Before I came, you hadn't much choice but to marry Shea. You needed him financially, you needed him because of your mother and Andy. All of you needed him to survive."

Not a flattering image, her desperation, but more-or-less true, Rosalyn conceded.

"But all that is changed now! Andy is reunited with his parents. And I'm here. Now you don't have to try to convince yourself that you're in love with Shea Donahue."

Twenty-Six

❧

Rosalyn started to protest and then caught her lower lip between her teeth.

"Rosalyn, he's a decent guy. I'm not arguing that. And I'm sure he loves you. In this particular world—" Robbie's sweeping gesture included not only the dark walls of forest and decaying house but also the primitive hardness of her life here, the laundry and gardening, the wood-burning stove and outhouse, the scrimping and doing without. "Here he can probably take better care of you than I ever could. But Rosalyn, you don't have to stay in this harsh world! You don't belong here. I can give you a good life in the kind of world where you do belong."

Rosalyn turned to look at the house, where the trees that crowded close on one side stood like dark warriors patiently waiting for victory over this man-made intruder. It was true that a woman never need fear the wilds with Shea around. He could offer protection and experience and knowledge of everything from finding a spring for water to repairing a house to squeezing a living out of this wild land. He'd taught her to shoot, a skill that could make the difference between life and death here.

But with Robbie she wouldn't have to live in a place where

such survival skills and knowledge even mattered. "Rosalyn, I love you," Robbie said softly. "I know I said I wouldn't go home without you. But I can't wait indefinitely. I have duties and responsibilities."

"I know."

"I don't mean to be rude or impertinent, but I honestly can't see what makes the decision so difficult." He smiled and touched her chin with a fingertip to tilt her face to his. "Just follow your heart, and you'll find me right there waiting."

"My heart," she said unhappily, "is all tied up in knots. I was all ready to marry Shea, and then you came and turned everything upside down."

"Good for me."

"But I really care for Shea. He's been so good to us. Generous and kind and caring and helpful—"

"You can't marry a man just because you're grateful to him!"

"I also can't marry a man simply because he can provide an easy, luxurious life for me," she flared.

"There's more than that between us. Our love went astray because of my terrible mistake. But I'm very sure of my love for you now, and I think if you look deep in your heart you'll find you love me, too."

"I look in my heart and all I see is a whirlwind of confusion!"

"Look, I have an idea. Give me a day. One complete day just for the two of us to enjoy alone. If your true feelings don't become plain as the nose on your face—" he touched that nose lightly with his fingertip, "then I'll just turn around and head back to Indiana. Fair enough?"

She hesitated. Robbie did indeed seem different in some ways; he had learned, as he said, a "hard lesson." But she was uneasy with the way he had come here with the annulment merely started, not final; neither was she totally comfortable with his easy acceptance of the idea that annulment erased, not merely ended, a marriage. She appreciated the statement he'd made earlier about wanting to get on the right track with God. But he'd said similar things in the past. Were there still large differences in their basic beliefs and values?

At this point, as confused as her feelings were, perhaps she had no right to be considering marrying either man.

"One day?" he repeated.

Another hesitation. Perhaps she owed him that much. "One day," she finally agreed.

The weather did not cooperate. Rain wasn't falling, but when Rosalyn slipped out of bed the next morning foggy clouds drifted at treetop level, dismal and dreary. Robbie arrived while she was just getting the fire going, looking more cheerful and energetic than a man had a right to be on such a gloomy morning. With a flourish he produced a covered pan from behind his back.

"If we were married, this would be breakfast in bed, served by your personal maid, but for now this will have to do." With another flourish he whipped off the cloth covering the pan and revealed a dozen cinnamon rolls, fragrant with a sweet aroma that took Rosalyn back to the days of Hattie's wonderful cooking.

She touched the pan. "They're still warm!"

In a whisper, as if it were a secret, he confided that he'd dropped in on Emma of Emma's Cafe the previous evening and bribed her into having the rolls ready for his early-morning drive out here "She also had this for me to give you," he added, producing a newspaper-wrapped bouquet of daffodils from his back pocket. "I think she's really a romantic at heart."

Rosalyn had to laugh at the idea that Emma, who looked big and tough enough to be a fisherman or logger herself, had any thoughts of romance, but maybe it was true. Suddenly the day, with Robbie grinning at her, and the warm, fragrant rolls tempting her, didn't seem nearly so dreary.

After breakfast, on the way to town, Robbie made a confession. "I asked for a day, and here it is, just the two of us, but I really don't have any marvelous ideas about how to spend it. If we had time to drive up to Portland, we could find movies and plays and museums and stores. We could go to a jewelry store and pick out engagement and wedding rings! I'd love to shower you with gifts—"

Teasingly she said, "I could use a new scrub board—"

"Never," he vowed. "Never. But tell me, really, how would you like to spend this day?"

Rosalyn leaned back in the roadster's luxurious seat. "I'd like to spend it doing nothing," she said dreamily. "Every day I have chores and more chores to do. I'd like a day just to do nothing."

"Nothing it shall be," he vowed.

So they drove and talked and laughed, occasionally stopping to view some spectacular bit of coast scenery. They lunched and strolled around a little town miles north of Castle Beach. When they passed a tiny beauty shop, Robbie had a suggestion.

"I'm not sure what kind of treatment you're apt to get in a two-bit burg like this, but how about a manicure on your do-nothing day?"

Rosalyn looked down at her reddened hands with rough cuticles and stubby nails. A manicure. Leave it to Robbie to think of something so frivolously useless—and wonderful!

So she had a manicure, a soothing lotion massaged into her hands, a pampered treatment to her rough cuticles, a lovely shimmer of pale pink polish on her nails, and all the while Robbie waited patiently, reading a magazine and occasionally looking up to grin at her.

271

"I feel like a princess," she said when they walked out. She fluttered her hands to admire them. "A pampered princess."

"There is nothing I'd like better than to pamper you for the rest of your life."

The day drifted on. They had dinner, saw a movie, and the stars shone brilliantly in a night sky when they finally drove back through the dark canyon of trees to home. All day Robbie hadn't pressed her for a decision, but she knew the time was coming.

They were a couple of miles from the house when Rosalyn noted a peculiar glow in the sky. "What's that?" she asked uneasily.

"Probably just the moon coming up behind the mountains. Perhaps we should park and watch it rise."

"No! That's no moon. Robbie, hurry, something's wrong!"

Twenty-Seven

Robbie screeched the roadster to a stop at the edge of the clearing across from the house. A torch of flames roared out of the chimney, red-gold tongues shooting skyward, above the flames a boil of black smoke and a fireworks explosion of glowing sparks. Already smaller flames licked at the roof on one side of the chimney, and everywhere falling sparks nibbled hungrily at the old shingles.

"Mother!" Rosalyn screamed. "Where is my mother?" She leaped from the automobile and screamed again. "Mother! Mother!"

No answer but the evil crackle and roar of flames. Hot ash was falling everywhere, and she slapped at a piece that floated into her hair.

"She must be around back!" Robbie raced toward the rear of the house, Rosalyn right behind him.

"Mother, Mother, where are you?" Frantically Rosalyn peered in the woodshed. She flung the door of the cooler open, the scent of a box of apples someone at church had given them incongruously sweet.

Robbie yelled too. "Ellen! Ellen! Answer us, where are you?"

The only answer was the rumble and crash of something falling inside the house. The windows, usually lit only by the dim glow of the kerosene lamps, now blazed with a fierce fury of light. Flickering shadows danced on Robbie's face as they stared at each other.

Rosalyn swallowed with a feeling like blackberry thorns caught in her throat. "She must be in there."

"We can still get in the front door—"

"It won't do any good. There are boards nailed across the door between the front of the house and this back part where we live."

"We can't get in this way—"

"We have to." She hesitated only a moment before saying determinedly, "I'm going in."

"No! I'll do it."

Swiftly Robbie dipped a handkerchief in a puddle of rainwater beside the woodshed and tied it across his face. His gesture motioned Rosalyn back, but she followed him and they crept to the door like burglars in the night. Surprisingly little heat came through the thick log walls, but when Robbie touched the metal latch on the door he yanked his hand back with a grunt of pain.

Determinedly he tried again, taking off his jacket and wrapping it around his hand for protection. They both fell back as flames shot out the open door. Robbie took the brunt of the flash, and Rosalyn smelled singed hair.

"Robbie, are you all right?"

He got to his knees, coughing and shaking his head. "I'll be okay. Just let me catch my breath a minute and I'll try a window."

But a moment later the tall window over the sink exploded in a spray of flying glass. On the ground the pieces glittered like fallen eyes in the reflection of the flames. Smoke surged out both window and door now, and flames licked hungrily around the openings. With a fresh supply of air, the fire roared with energized fury.

Robbie grabbed a chunk of wood and headed for the dining room windows, courageously ignoring the danger of another explosion of glass. But even before he could break the glass, Rosalyn knew it was no use.

"Robbie! Come back!"

Already flames encircled the inside of the window like a deadly curtain. Robbie retreated, and they looked at each other wordlessly for a moment. He was no longer the elegant sophisticate now. His eyes, frustrated with the helplessness of their situation, stared out of a smoke-smudged face, eyebrows almost gone, dark hair singed.

"Maybe I can go in the front way and knock the boards loose."

They raced around to the front of the house. Here the knob wasn't hot when he touched it, but the moment he shouldered the door open smoke billowed out in choking clouds.

"I don't know what to do!" he cried in helpless fury.

They both turned as headlights flashed into the clearing. Shea leaped out of the truck. He's seen the glow of fire from his place and come!

"Are you all here? Is everyone okay?"

"We can't find Mother. She must be in there. But we can't get in! The whole back side of the house is on fire!"

Shea stood as motionless as one of the trees standing at the edge of the clearing. Only his eyes moved, taking in the situation, flicking from smoke billowing out the open door to blazing chimney and lacy frills of flame licking at the shingles. He wasted no time in frantic, futile motion; he assessed and measured and judged on some level beyond Rosalyn's comprehension.

Then he ran to his truck, that treasure-trove of equipment for coping with emergencies in the wilds, rummaged in the back and came up with a coil of rope. He slung it over his shoulder and ran to the clump of fir trees beside the house, the trees whose branches Rosalyn often heard brushing against the wall. He had none of the tree-climbing equipment he used when topping a tall tree in the woods, but with powerful legs and strong arms he shimmied up the rough bark. He passed the bottom branches and disappeared into the dark foliage.

"What's he doing?" Robbie asked, puzzled.

"I don't know!"

Rosalyn followed his progress by movement of the branches. He was almost to rooftop level now. He climbed out a branch, and she could see it droop with his weight. Then it snapped up. Rosalyn gasped and felt her heart thunder. Had he fallen? No, there he was. He'd purposely slipped down to a lower branch. It dipped lower and lower with his weight, until his upright figure showed between the branches, light from the flames shining on his red hair.

Now it was Rosalyn's turn to ask frantically, "What is he doing?"

"He's going to use the rope to swing over to that door on the second floor. I never thought of that!" Robbie paused. "I couldn't have done it if I had thought of it."

Rosalyn could see the slender thread of rope now. He'd tied it on a higher branch and then dropped below it to make his swing. "But it won't work! That flimsy landing will break when he hits it." The fire hadn't yet broken through that windowless side of the house, and it was in featureless shadow, but she could picture the broken, dangling steps that led to nowhere. "There's nothing holding it up!"

"There he goes!"

She could see only the first half of the arc as he took a powerful leap and swung toward the house. Then he disappeared in the midnight shadow. A moment later she heard the crash as he hit something...or was it the steps crashing to the ground?

No, he'd smashed into the door! She knew because smoke surged out the new opening as if greedy to claim the open space. As it boiled upward, a faint outline of the opening became visible, like the doorway to a furnace below.

"Where is he?" Rosalyn cried. "Where is Shea? Did he fall?"

"No. He's inside."

They waited. They could do nothing else. Rosalyn laced her fingers together and pressed them to her lips, her gaze never leaving the doorway, her mind and mouth moving in silent prayer. Her mother was in there. Shea was in there.

The two people she loved most in all the world.

She looked at Robbie. He'd done his best to get inside. He hadn't lacked courage. She'd have been wild with worry and concern if he were inside that inferno trying to save her mother.

But it was Shea she loved. The sure knowledge came like a calm sea chasing away the storm waves that had churned in her mind. A peace that lasted no more than a fragile moment, because with panic in her heart she knew it might be too late. Shea might never come out of that inferno of flames.

Robbie tore his gaze away from the mesmerizing scene before them, and as their eyes met she knew instinctively that in that brief moment he also knew her true feelings.

He squeezed her hand. "He'll make it."

Would he? The moments stretched out endlessly, Rosalyn's emotions blazing as fiercely as the flames that now engulfed the entire half of the roof beyond the chimney. *I love you! I love you! I love you!* The silent words mixed with her heartbeat and thundered in her ears along with the roar of fire. *Please, Lord. Save them. Save my mother and Shea. I love them. Please, Lord, please!*

"There he is! He's got her!"

Shea's dark silhouette filled the doorway, the figure in his arms pitifully limp.

"Grab her as I let her down with the rope!" Shea yelled hoarsely.

Both Robbie and Rosalyn ran to the spot below the dangling stairs. Above them she could hear Shea's harsh breathing and grunts as he struggled with the rope. Then Rosalyn's mother was above them, rope tied in a rough sling under her arms, swaying like a ghostly wraith as Shea lowered her to their waiting arms.

Robbie's longer reach got her first. He lowered her gently to the ground and slipped her out of the makeshift sling. Then he snatched her up and carried her away from the house.

Rosalyn expected Shea to follow down the rope immediately, but when she backed away so she could see the doorway he wasn't there.

"Shea! Shea, where are you?" she cried frantically.

A moment later he reappeared, something heavy and bulky in his arms. "Watch out! I'm going to drop this!"

It landed a few feet from Rosalyn with a crashing thud. The box! Her mother's precious box. Was that what had trapped her inside, her determination to save her box? And Shea, knowing what it meant to her, had saved the box, too.

He leaped from the flimsy landing, swinging on the rope, and Rosalyn heard the snap of the branch breaking as he was halfway to the ground. But that didn't matter because he was safe, safe!

She ran to him, and he enveloped her in his arms.

"Oh, Shea! Shea!" The sweet embrace was painfully brief. But long enough for Rosalyn to say fiercely, "I love you!"

Then he snatched up the box, now lopsided and broken from its crash, and they both ran to where Robbie had set Ellen on the ground. A scent of burned hair and clothing came from her, but her eyes flickered open. She started coughing and Robbie helped her to a sitting position.

"She probably inhaled a lot of smoke," Shea said. "She had collapsed about halfway down the stairs when I found her. She'd dragged the box that far trying to get it out."

Behind them the fire raged on. Flames shot out the upstairs doorway now. With an explosive crash the entire roof suddenly collapsed, momentarily snuffing the interior fire, and the standing walls stood like blazing skeletons with the fireplace chimneys dark sentinels rising above the fiery walls. After a few moments the fire burst through the fallen roof and reached out to engulf the rest of the house.

Rosalyn turned her back on the scene of destruction. What did it matter? Everything important was right here, safe.

Ellen lay back again, shaking but steadily breathing the fresh air now.

"Oh, Mother, Mother," Rosalyn chided softly. "Why did you try to rescue that old box? You might have been killed in there!"

"I was crocheting and must have fallen asleep in the chair," Ellen said. "When I woke the stovepipe was glowing red hot and…and roaring…and flames were shooting out at the ceiling and the wall was on fire, too. And all I could think was I didn't want your wedding dress to burn. I tried to get the box, and then everything started burning…I'm so sorry, Rozzie." Ellen struggled to sit up again, but Rosalyn gently pressed her down. "If I hadn't built the fire up so much…or hadn't fallen asleep…"

"It doesn't matter. Everything's okay." Rosalyn remembered the grumpy puffs the stovepipe occasionally emitted and the sticky black ooze she'd scraped off a while back. She should have realized then that residue from the woodsap was probably building up inside the chimney and could catch on fire. It had happened to others; two houses in town had been lost due to chimney fires during the winter. "Shea even saved your box."

Shea put the shattered box in the back of the truck, carefully tucking the loose contents inside, and then carried Ellen to the cab. Rosalyn slipped in to hold her mother gently in her arms, and with Robbie following, they drove slowly to Shea's house.

Once there, Rosalyn washed her mother's face and checked for injuries. Ellen had a few minor burns on her arms, and she was still coughing occasionally, but there were no serious injuries. Finally Rosalyn helped her to the bed she and Shea had prepared for her when they were readying the house for all of them to live in. Rosalyn would sleep in Jessie's bed.

Shea had already set the broken box and its spilled contents in the room, and for the first time Rosalyn saw the items it contained in addition to the wedding dress: photo albums and loose photos; the family Bible, with birth and death dates of long-gone family members Rosalyn had never known; several leather-covered books that looked like diaries; baby clothes and Rosalyn's favorite childhood doll. And the broken pieces of some fragile old dishes that hadn't survived the fall.

She stayed until Ellen fell asleep before closing the door softly behind her as she went out to the kitchen. Robbie was sitting at the table drinking a cup of coffee, Shea standing beside the sink with his cup. Both were smoke-smudged, red-eyed, bedraggled, and weary looking. Robbie drained his cup and stood up.

"I'd better be going…but may I talk to you for a moment, please, Rosalyn?" Unexpectedly he turned to Shea and the two men shook hands wordlessly as if some silent understanding passed between them.

Rosalyn followed Robbie outside. In the distance a faint reddish glow still lingered in the direction of the burned house and a scent of smoke hung heavily in the night air.

Robbie smiled lightly. "You don't have to tell me. I could see it tonight. You love him, not me."

"I do. It took me a while to figure it out, but I love him. Very much." What was it Nadine had said? Sometimes the Lord had to hit us over the head with something before it got through to us? He had shown her the way tonight, although definitely not by any means she might have expected. Or, she thought wryly, would have preferred. But the Lord knew best.

"I should give you back that amethyst bracelet. But now it's gone—"

He dismissed the bracelet with a shrug. "I'll be leaving in the morning. And I want you to know I do wish you and Shea the very best."

"Thank you. And Robbie—"

"Yes?"

"Don't give up too soon on Charlie. I'll be praying for both of you. When you see her would you tell her that I care about her and miss her?" She paused for a moment then went on, her voice soft. "And tell her that I'll always love her as my almost-sister."

She suspected some snappy retort came to mind, but whatever it was he managed to smile again and say only, "Goodbye, Rosalyn. And best wishes." He touched her hand lightly and was gone.

She watched until the red taillights disappeared in the dark trees. Today, she realized slowly, she had lost almost every material possession she owned. But nothing that really mattered.

She then turned and walked into the log house, into the arms of the man she loved. And at long last she finally had the chance to ask him about the "great news" he had once started to tell her but which had kept getting pushed aside.

He smiled, a welcoming flash in his smoke-darkened face. "The government is going to build one of those new Civilian Conservation Corps camps, the CCC they call it, just outside Castle Beach. I'd talked to one of the supervisors when I was working on a big forest fire last summer, and, starting next month, I'll have a job helping construct it."

"Shea, that's wonderful!"

"That isn't the best part. The best part is that after it's built I'm going to be supervising the men working on forestry projects out in the woods. We'll be cleaning up some of the worst areas damaged by logging, thinning others and reforesting both logged and burned-over areas. It's a foot in the door toward what I've long wanted to do."

"I'm so glad."

"The only thing is…a few weeks ago we set a wedding date—"

"I'll be there." With a teasing smile she added, "Will you?"

He nodded, very serious and dignified, but a moment later that irrepressible boyish side of him broke through. He picked Rosalyn up and whirled her around, unmindful of danger to dishes and furniture, and she knew only concern for her sleeping mother kept him from punctuating the whirl with another series of exuberant whoops and hollers.

At the church, her mother helped Rosalyn dress in the white satin gown she and her mother before her had worn at their weddings. It had one tiny mended place near the hem, a small reminder of the drop from the burning building and a faint, although oddly not unpleasant, fragrance of smoke.

"Will you be all right, Mother?" Rosalyn asked anxiously as Ellen arranged the white veil around her face.

"Jessie and I will be just fine," Ellen assured her. Rosalyn and Shea were taking a two-night honeymoon up the coast. Ellen and Jessie would be alone at the cabin.

"I don't mean just while we're gone," Rosalyn said hesitantly. "I mean…"

"I know. You want to know if I will go back to being like I was before?" Ellen shook her head. "No. I'll always mourn the loss of your father, but I know now that life still has purpose and meaning. The Lord has shown me that."

Rosalyn held out her arms and hugged her mother. From the sanctuary she could hear the strains of the old organ and the shuffle of feet as people arrived. They had invited everyone from the church, and it sounded as if many were here to celebrate the ceremony with them.

"Rozzie, I don't have a real wedding present for you—"

"Knowing you're going to be okay is the best gift you could give me."

"But I am crocheting a bedspread for you, and I do have this." From her purse Ellen took one of the leather-covered books Rosalyn had seen in the box. "For years Oliver wrote in his journal several times a week just before bedtime. I couldn't throw the journals away, but neither could I bring myself to read them until just a few days ago. I'd like you to read the last entry."

Wonderingly Rosalyn took the journal and opened it to the page marked with a narrow strip of blue ribbon. It was dated the day before her father died. He wrote of his shock over the news about losing the house and his concerns about Rosalyn and the situation with Robbie. He wrote, too, of his job interview scheduled for the following day. The final line read: *I don't believe I'll get this job, but I have several more prospects in mind and something will turn up. The Lord loves us and knows our needs. He is my rock and my fortress and my deliverer.*

Not words of portentous importance or earth-shaking significance, no deep spiritual revelations or great truths from the grave. Simply the ordinary, everyday words of a man with a deep faith in the Lord, a man hurt and discouraged and saddened by all that had happened, but a man with hope and courage, a man who expected to fill all those blank pages remaining in the journal.

And in their very ordinariness was the simple truth: These were not the despairing words of a man planning to abandon his wife and daughter and step in front of a car.

"I know you've always suspected he killed himself, that he lost his faith and stepped in front of that car deliberately," Ellen said softly.

"Did you ever think that?"

Ellen nodded regretfully. "I wish I'd read this earlier and both our minds could have been set at rest. He was a good man, Rozzie. A wonderful man." She smiled. "And I think you're marrying a man who is also good and wonderful."

Rosalyn put her arms around her mother again. "Thank you," she said simply. "Thank you for the two most special wedding gifts a woman could ever receive." Ellen tucked into her daughter's hand the small, white New Testament she was carrying for the ceremony, plus the bouquet of delicate wildflowers Shea had picked for her corsage.

A moment later Rosalyn stepped into the aisle at the rear of the church. She breathed deeply of the sweet scents of wild rhododendrons and azaleas filling the baskets, and then the beautiful old strains of the wedding march began. Nearby, little Jessie, as ringbearer, held the simple golden rings on a satin pillow, the dance in her eyes belying her solemn expression. Shea stood at the altar, his strength and dignity only emphasized by a few unruly red curls defying all efforts to tame them for this occasion. And on his face a look of love and happiness that lit up the whole church.

With joy and peace in her heart, Rosalyn took the first steps toward the beginning of a lifetime with him, this man she loved.

Dear Reader:

I have had a number of romance novels published, but *Betrayed* is only my second inspirational Christian romance. It is also the book that has been the most meaningful and rewarding for me. I consider it a real privilege to be able to serve the Lord through my writing, and I'm pleased to have this book published in the Palisades line in the company of so many other fine Christian writers. I plan to read them all!

I hope you find Rosalyn and Shea's story interesting, exciting and enjoyable. But I also hope, if you already know the peace and joy of full faith in the Lord, that the basic truths underlying *Betrayed* will reaffirm those beliefs for you. If you do not yet know the Lord, I hope the characters and their problems and conflicts, though fictional, may help you find the way.

Betrayed is set in the hardship years of the Great Depression. Looking back across time, I think it sometimes appears that even in those hard times that faith—and happy relationships between men and women—perhaps came more easily in that simpler, less frantic era. We see the past through those well known "rose-colored glasses." But both relationships and spiritual issues have always been complicated and difficult, and we shouldn't think that just because we're living in the nineties that our problems are somehow more insurmountable than those of earlier times. Our God is just as vital and alive, just as all-powerful and all-caring, as he was in all the generations before this one, and we can always put our trust in him to see us through whatever problems we encounter.

Readers are some of my favorite people, and I'm always delighted to hear from you. I'll try to answer all letters—

Blessings to you and yours,

Lorena Mc Courtney

Lorena McCourtney
c/o Palisades
P.O. Box 1720
Sisters, Oregon 97759

PALISADES...PURE ROMANCE

THE PALISADES LINE

Refuge, Lisa Tawn Bergren
ISBN 0-88070-621-X
Part One: A Montana rancher and a San Francisco marketing exec—only one incredible summer and God could bring such diverse lives together. *Part Two:* Lost and alone, Emily Walker needs and wants a new home, a sense of family. Can one man lead her to the greatest Father she could ever want and a life full of love?

Torchlight, Lisa Tawn Bergren
ISBN 0-88070-806-9
When beautiful heiress Julia Rierdon returns to Maine to remodel her family's estate, she finds herself torn between the man she plans to marry and unexpected feelings for a mysterious wanderer who threatens to steal her heart.

Treasure, Lisa Tawn Bergren
ISBN 0-88070-725-9
She arrived on the Caribbean island of Robert's Foe armed with a lifelong dream—to find her ancestor's sunken ship—and yet the only man who can help her stands stubbornly in her way. Can Christina and Mitch find their way to the ship *and* to each other?

Cherish, Constance Colson
ISBN 0-88070-802-6
Recovering from the heartbreak of a failed engagement, Rose Anson seeks refuge at a resort on Singing Pines Island, where she plans to spend a peaceful summer studying and painting the spectacular scenery of international Lake of the Woods. But when a flamboyant Canadian and a big-hearted American compete for her love, the young artist must face her past—and her future. What follows is a search for the source and meaning of true love: a journey that begins in the heart and concludes in the soul.

Angel Valley, Peggy Darty
ISBN 0-88070-778-X
When teacher Laurel Hollingsworth accepts a summer tutoring position for a wealthy socialite family, she faces an enormous challenge in her young student, Anna Lee Wentworth. However, the real challenge is ahead of her: hanging on to her heart when older brother Matthew Wentworth comes to visit. Soon Laurel and Matthew find that they share a faith in God...and powerful feelings for one another. Can Laurel and Matthew find time to explore their relationship while she helps the emotionally troubled Anna Lee and fights to defend her love for the beautiful *Angel Valley?*

Love Song, Sharon Gillenwater
ISBN 0-88070-747-X

When famous country singer Andrea Carson returns to her hometown to recuperate from a life-threatening illness, she seeks nothing more than a respite from the demands of stardom that have sapped her creativity and ability to perform. It's Andi's old high school friend Wade Jamison who helps her to realize that she needs inner healing as well. As Andi's strength grows, so do her feelings for the rancher who has captured her heart. But can their relationship withstand the demands of her career? Or will their romance be as fleeting as a beautiful *Love Song?*

Antiques, Sharon Gillenwater
ISBN 0-88070-801-8

Deeply wounded by the infidelity of his wife, widower Grant Adams swore off all women—until meeting charming antiques dealer Dawn Carson. Although he is drawn to her, Grant struggles to trust again. Dawn finds herself overwhelmingly attracted to the darkly brooding cowboy, but won't marry a non-believer. As Grant learns more about her faith, he is touched by its impact on her life and slowly begins to trust.

Secrets, Robin Jones Gunn
ISBN 0-88070-721-6

Seeking a new life as an English teacher in a peaceful Oregon town, Jessica tries desperately to hide the details of her identity from the community...until she falls in love. Will the past keep Jessica and Kyle apart forever?

Whispers, Robin Jones Gunn
ISBN 0-88070-755-0

Teri Moreno went to Maui eager to rekindle a romance. But when circumstances turn out to be quite different than she expects, she finds herself spending a great deal of time with a handsome, old high school crush who now works at a local resort. But the situation becomes more complicated when Teri meets Gordon, a clumsy, endearing Australian with a wild past, and both men begin to pursue her. Will Teri respond to God's gentle urgings toward true love? The answer lies in her response to the gentle *Whispers* in her heart.

Glory, Marilyn Kok
ISBN 0-88070-754-2

To Mariel Forrest, the teaching position in Taiwan provided more than a simple escape from grief; it also offered an opportunity to deal with her feelings toward the God she once loved, but ultimately blamed for the deaths of her family. Once there, Mariel dares to ask the timeless question: "If God is good, why do we suffer?" What follows is an inspiring story of love, healing, and renewed confidence in God's goodness.

Sierra, Shari MacDonald
ISBN 0-88070-726-7
When spirited photographer Celia Randall travels to eastern California for a short-term assignment, she quickly is drawn to—and locks horns with—editor Marcus Stratton. Will lingering heartaches destroy Celia's chance at true love? Or can she find hope and healing high in the *Sierra?*

Westward, Amanda MacLean
ISBN 0-88070-751-8
Running from a desperate fate in the South toward an unknown future in the West, plantation-born artist Juliana St. Clair finds herself torn between two men, one an undercover agent with a heart of gold, the other a man with evil intentions and a smooth facade. Witness Juliana's dangerous travels toward faith and love as she follows God's lead in this powerful historical novel.

Stonehaven, Amanda MacLean
ISBN 0-88070-757-7
Picking up in the years following *Westward, Stonehaven* follows Callie St. Clair back to the South where she has returned to reclaim her ancestral home. As she works to win back the plantation, the beautiful and dauntless Callie turns it into a station on the Underground Railroad. Covering her actions by playing the role of a Southern belle, Callie risks losing Hawk, the only man she has ever loved. Readers will find themselves quickly drawn into this fast-paced novel of treachery, intrigue, spiritual discovery, and unexpected love.

A Christmas Joy, MacLean, Darty, Gillenwater
ISBN 0-88070-780-1 (same length as other Palisades books)
Snow falls, hearts change, and love prevails! In this compilation, three experienced Palisades authors spin three separate novelettes centering around the Christmas season and message:
By Amanda MacLean: A Christmas pageant coordinator in a remote mountain village of Northern California is reunited with an old friend and discovers the greatest gift of all.
By Peggy Darty: A college skiclub reunion brings together model Heather Grant and an old flame. Will they gain a new understanding?
By Sharon Gillenwater: A chance meeting in an airport that neither of them could forget...and a Christmas reunion.